ADVANCES IN CONTENT ANALYSIS

SAGE ANNUAL REVIEWS OF COMMUNICATION RESEARCH

Other Books in this Series:

Volume 1: *Current Perspectives in Mass Communication Research*
F. Gerald Kline and Phillip J. Tichenor, Editors

Volume 2: *New Models for Communication Research*
Peter Clarke, Editor

Volume 3: *The Uses of Mass Communications:*
Current Perspectives on Gratification Research
Jay G. Blumler and Elihu Katz, Editors

Volume 4: *Political Communication: Issues and Strategies for Research*
Steven H. Chaffee, Editor

Volume 5: *Explorations in Interpersonal Communication*
Gerald R. Miller, Editor

Volume 6: *Strategies for Communication Research*
Paul M. Hirsch, Peter V. Miller, and F. Gerald Kline, Editors

Volume 7: *Children Communicating:*
Media and Development of Thought, Speech, Understanding
Ellen Wartella, Editor

Volume 8: *Persuasion: New Directions in Theory and Research*
Michael E. Roloff and Gerald R. Miller, Editors

Volume 9
SAGE ANNUAL REVIEWS OF COMMUNICATION RESEARCH

Advances in Content Analysis

KARL ERIK ROSENGREN

Editor

SAGE PUBLICATIONS   Beverly Hills   London

For information address:

SAGE Publications, Inc.
275 South Beverly Drive
Beverly Hills, California 90212

SAGE Publications Ltd
28 Banner Street
London EC1Y 8QE, England

Printed in the United States of America

Library of Congress Cataloging in Publication Data
Main entry under title:

Advances in content analysis.

   (Sage annual reviews of communication research ; v. 9)
   Includes bibliographies and index.
   1. Content analysis (Communication)--Addresses, essays, lectures. 2. Content analysis (Communication)--Research--Scandinavia--Addresses, essays, lectures. I. Rosengren, Karl Erik.
P93.A3   001.51   80-24142
ISBN 0-8039-1555-1
ISBN 0-8039-1556-X (pbk.)

FIRST PRINTING

CONTENTS

PREFACE

THIS VOLUME is one of the outcomes of the first Scandinavian Conference on Content Analysis, arranged in Rättvik, Sweden, March 13-17, 1979, with the support of the Nordic Cultural Foundation within the Nordic Council.

At the conference some twenty papers from Denmark, Finland, Norway, and Sweden were presented and discussed. The committee arranging the conference agreed that about a dozen of these would be of some interest to an international public. Most of these can be found in this volume; in some cases, however, the authors could not find the time and opportunity to make the adjustments and amendments always necessary in such cases. One paper not presented at the conference has also been included.

I would like to thank my fellow members of the committee arranging the conference—Dag Anckar, Lowe Hedman, Karen Siune, Per Torsvik, and Lennart Weibull—who also offered their kind advice in part of the editing process. Special thanks go to Lowe Hedman, the secretary of the group.

—*Karl Erik Rosengren*

ADVANCES IN SCANDINAVIAN CONTENT ANALYSIS
An Introduction

Karl Erik Rosengren

BACKGROUND

In Scandinavia, quantitative content analysis has a long history. In the eighteenth century, words in religious hymns and sermons were counted by Swedish authorities and dissidents to prove and disprove heresy—an early case of quantitative content analysis used to resolve a serious societal problem (Dovring, 1973). Heresy, of course, could be a matter of life or death for the accused; certainly a matter of freedom or imprisonment. Later Scandinavian content analyses have had less dramatic settings. However, a recent content analytical study of ads in Danish weeklies kindled a fierce, widespread, and drawn-out debate with clear political implications (see Sepstrup's chapter in this volume). And quantitative studies of news media content have often been used officially to prove or disprove bias in news and current affairs broadcast by the Swedish Broadcasting Corporation (Westerståhl, 1970, 1972, 1977; see Rosengren, 1979). While it is too early to sum up the effects of the Sepstrup debate in Denmark, it could be maintained that the analyses undertaken by Westerståhl and his group have probably contributed to keep the Swedish news media in the middle of the road. At the same time, accusations of left-wing bias have, as a rule, been rejected by experts and authorities, thereby offering some leeway for innovation. Thus, the Scandinavian content analysts of the twentieth century may have affected their society as much as their pious and learned colleagues from the eighteenth century. There are other reasons, however, why Scandinavian content analysis should have some interest to an international public. In its way, it offers an interesting picture of important developments within Scandinavian studies in the social sciences and the humanities.

European social science is often portrayed as philosophical, not to say speculative, while American social science is seen as matter-of-fact or empiricist. Europeans are said to be interested in macro phenomena; Americans in micro phenomena. European research is seen as critical or radical; American as apolitical and therefore, indirectly, conservative. In reality, matters are much more complicated, and the complications are well known. Many leading American social scientists of the 1940s and 1950s had either studied at European universities or otherwise had been deeply influenced by European social science from around the turn of the century: Homans, Lasswell, Merton, and Parsons are just a few examples of this trend. A leading representative of allegedly conservative American "empiricism" was an Austrian social-democrat emigré who many years ago had written a still readable essay on critical versus administrative communication research (Lazarsfeld, 1972)—one of many examples of the rich and many-faceted influence on American social science exerted by European intellectual emigrés in the thirties, forties, and fifties (Fleming and Bailyn, 1969). In spite of such complications, however, the conventional stereotype about American and European social science probably does capture some essential differences between the two research traditions.

Scandinavian social science has drawn upon both traditions. Waves of continental and American impulses have succeeded each other, sometimes under conditions of vehement competition. While the precise development has been different in different disciplines and also in the different Scandinavian countries, an overall pattern is clearly discernible, offering a parallel case—with some individual traits—to the developments in the rest of Europe and in the United States. The decades between the two world wars were characterized primarily by continental dominance, while the first two decades after World War II were characterized by American dominance. Toward the middle and end of the 1960s, a new wave of continental influence made itself felt, characterized by a revival of interest in Marx and other nineteenth-century classics of the social sciences, various short-lived fads and fashions, and more or less specialized schools of thought such as semiotics, structuralism, and interactionism.

In a small system, an influx of such magnitude and variety could result only in conflict; especially as the rapid expansion of the universities during the fifties and early sixties gradually came to a standstill, the dividing lines of thought ran at least partly parallel with age differentials, and a large proportion of the tenured positions already had been filled with young or middle-aged scholars who could be expected to block the career avenues for decades to come.

Surprisingly, it can be said that, on the whole, the outcome of the conflicts has been a positive one. The possibility exists for a happy synthesis of the European and American traditions, an unexpected marriage between hard-nosed empiricism and high-flown theorizing, which may well result in a period of creativity and productivity for social science in Scandinavia. It is obvious that the development sketched here has its parallels in other parts of Western Europe, as well as—with other complications—in America. More relevant in this connection is the importance of this overall development for communication research in general and content analysis in particular.

The two roots of Scandinavian social science—continental social philosophy and Anglo-American empiricism—have their counterparts in the two main types of content analysis, usually distinguished between qualitative and quantitative analysis (George, 1959). The latter distinction, of course, could be strictly defined, but in practice it is often used in a rather vague manner. On the one hand, the term "qualitative analysis" covers a wide range of content analyses, from more or less impressionistic, intuitive, and interpretive essays to systematic and strict content analyses carried out at the nominal scale level. On the other hand, what is termed quantitative content analysis is often based on data at the nominal scale level, aggregated cases of which are then analyzed at higher levels of precision: ordinal, interval, ratio (see Miller, 1977:125). Granted this vagueness, it could be maintained that the continental, social-philosophic tradition has tended to produce various instances of qualitative content analysis, while the Anglo-American tradition has resulted in mainly quantitative content analysis.

Broadly conceived here, qualitative content analysis blends into many interpretive activities applied to verbal and nonverbal, written and oral, mass mediated or individual messages (see the chapter by Lindkvist)—often brilliantly carried out, in a large number of disciplines within the humanities and the social sciences, with no awareness of the tradition of content analysis. It is therefore difficult even to sketch the history of the various activities which could be subsumed under the umbrella term "qualitative content analysis" in Scandinavia.

In spite of its early forerunners, Scandinavian quantitative content analysis has been less widely spread over the disciplines; but even so, it would be a quite respectable task to write its history. One reason is that its main ideas—to proceed systematically and, wherever possible, quantitatively—are central to the Anglo-American empirical-deductive tradition prevailing in Scandinavia for at least the first 20 years after World War II. This is probably part of the explanation for why isolated cases of full-blown quantitative "content analyses" have continually been produced in various disciplines by scholars with no or only passing acquaintance with quantitative content analysis in the Lasswell-Lazarsfeld-Berelson tradition.

This is an international phenomenon, and often examples may be found in the borderland between the history of literature and philology or linguistics. Swedish examples of such independent forerunners or reinventors of quantitative content analysis may be found, for example, in anglistics (Ellegård, 1958) and stylistics (Hallberg, 1951); these examples could no doubt be multiplied in the other Scandinavian countries—as in most other western countries.

While such cases are most often found in the humanities, content analysis proper (*sit venia verbo*) has tended to concentrate primarily in political science and sociology among the social sciences, and in history (mainly modern history) and the history of literature among the humanities. Typical examples are Anckar (1971), Rosengren (1968), Thomsen (1972) and Westerståhl (1972). Despite their publication dates, as a rule these studies were prepared and carried out in the late fifties and early sixties, the heyday of the wave of Anglo-American empiricism dominating the Scandinavian scene after World War II.

During the wave of influence from classical continental social philosophers that swept Scandinavia in the late sixties and early seventies, Berelsonian content analysis was under heavy attack as an example of naive positivism, characterized by fetishism of quantitative techniques and lack of theory. The attacks were rather general and tended to evade concrete examples. The single work of Scandinavian content analysis most discussed in these terms is probably Westerståhl (1972), the result of a sustained and impressive effort of "measuring objectivity" (Westerståhl, 1970; for short summaries of the criticism, see Hemánus, 1976, Rosengren, 1979; also Westerståhl, 1977). Another example of criticism directed against a concrete case of Scandinavian content analysis is Aspelin's (1975) criticism of Rosengren (1968), a criticism repeated some years later on a European scale by Zima (1977). Such common traits in criticism are the same as those in the more general debates: accusations for lack of theory (often combined with attacks on the theoretical base of the work under criticism) and sterile methodology (as a rule without offering concrete alternatives to the methodology used).

During the last few years, however, encouraging signs are multiplying that a new phase in the relationship between the continental and the Anglo-American tradition may be on its way. Adherents of the two research traditions meet and find that they can talk with each other in a meaningful way. As a result of such meetings, sterile antagonism is gradually being replaced by fruitful (if heated) discussions. Combined with this happy development, an increased interest in content analysis may be traced among humanists and social scientists, "Marxists" and "positivists" alike.

As long as it is still emerging, such a development can only be described subjectively, for there is no vantage point of overview available. What follows, therefore, must of necessity be personal impressions of an ongoing process.

In 1975, a group of Swedish humanists and social scientists agreed to join forces in a long-term, multidisciplinary research program called "Cultural Indicators: The Swedish Symbol System, 1945-1975" (CISSS). The program is funded by the Bank of Sweden Tercentenary Foundation. Its aim is to develop and apply so-called cultural indicators (Gerbner, 1970; Gerbner et al., 1979), much-needed complements to existing economic and social indicators. The method is mainly quantitative content analysis; the material, representative samples of the Swedish daily and weekly press during the postwar period. The program has two phases. During the first phase, cultural indicators are developed for, and applied to, selected areas of the Swedish symbol system: domestic and foreign policy, religion, literature, and advertising, each of the five subprojects of the program taking care of one such area. This phase is now drawing toward its end, and the first results from the different subprojects have been published or will be published soon (Goldmann, 1979; see also the chapters by Block and Andrén in this volume; Rosengren, forthcoming). During the second phase, the results from the different subprojects will be drawn together and compared with each other and with other Swedish time series data from the postwar period. It is hoped that this will promote increased understanding of the complex interplay among economic, social, and cultural factors in the development of an advanced industrial society.

While CISSS may have an interest of its own, it is referred to here for two reasons. It is a large research program building on content analysis, and in it, representatives of the humanities and the social sciences with both "Marxist" and "positivistic" outlooks cooperate closely to productive ends. It is thus a good example of the increased interest in content analysis and the beginning confluence of the continental and the Anglo-American research traditions, both phenomena being traceable in the humanities and the social sciences at large and more specifically within Scandinavian communication research.

Instrumental to this confluence have been the Scandinavian conferences of communication research arranged every second year since 1973. There is widespread agreement that these conferences have changed from functioning as forums for seemingly antagonistic conflicts between two enemy camps into forums for fruitful discussions between colleagues with different outlooks but common basic goals. The conferences have thus both mirrored and reinforced the general developments sketched above.

As a result partly of the common Scandinavian conferences and partly of other factors, national associations for communication research have been established in the five Scandinavian (more properly, Nordic)[1] countries, with the aim of furthering communication research in those countries. (Finland actually has two communication associations, an indication that for personal, institutional, historical and geopolitical reasons the gap between the two research traditions is deeper and more difficult to bridge in that country.)

Within the Swedish Association for Communication Research, a working group for content analysis was established in 1977. Its main purpose was to arrange an interdisciplinary conference on content analysis. The conference was held in 1977, with support from the Swedish Council for Research in the Humanities and the Social Sciences. It was considered a success, and a decision was made to repeat it on a Nordic basis. The Nordic conference on content analysis was held in March 1979, with the support of the Nordic Cultural Foundation within the Nordic Council. Like its Swedish predecessor, it was deemed a success, illustrating the two general tendencies discussed above: an increased interest in content analysis and an increased confluence between the two research traditions dominating the humanities and the social sciences in Scandinavia. This volume is based mainly on material from that conference; it therefore mirrors and elaborates the general traits which together have formed the basic theme of this presentation.

THE VOLUME

Over the years, the discussions between adherents of the two main research traditions in Scandinavian social science, the continental and the Anglo-American, have covered a wide range of subjects and topics. In connection with content analysis, however, they have often centered on the vague but controversial distinction between qualitative and quantitative content analysis. For a long time the discussions were rather sterile, reiterating the well-known arguments *pro et contra*. During the last few years, however, a clearly discernible trend has developed on both sides to listen to and sometimes even to take the arguments of the other side. It is as if, gradually, insight has dawned upon the discussants that it is futile to argue the overall superiority of a given approach or methodology. Approaches and methodologies are never good per se; they are good *for something*. A discussion of that "something" can be instructive.

A precondition for such an insight is an increased mutual knowledge of approaches and techniques at hand, a knowledge which probably has increased recently in Scandinavia. Kent Lindkvist's chapter in this volume regarding different approaches to textual analysis is a good example of such knowledge. The various approaches to the study of message shortly reviewed by Lindkvist are all important in their own right, and each offers its own special contribution to the understanding and explanation of textual features, their possible causes and effects. However, it is also clear that each approach has its limitations set by its presuppositions about the nature, origins, and consequences of the texts under study. Only by questioning such presuppositions and exposing themselves to influences from other research traditions can the adherents of the several approaches overcome these limitations.

Ultimately, this means that the scholars and researchers of the different traditions must be willing to work with techniques originally alien to their own tradition. That is precisely what happens in Scandinavian content analysis today. In his chapter on methodological developments in content analysis, Preben Sepstrup tries to reconcile a "Marxist" theoretical perspective with the methodological demands usually raised within "positivistic" content analysis. Similarly, Olle Findahl and Birgitta Höijer try to combine the insight and understanding of a qualitative, structuralist approach with the rigor usually associated with quantitative analysis, drawing upon ideas from cognitive psychology. Bo Fibiger also tries to add "a qualitative dimension to a quantitative analysis" (Berelson, quoted by Fibiger), thereby taking care of the problem with variability of meaning within the fixed categories of content analysis and at the same time opening up an increased possibility for validity checks. The line of thought followed by Tom Bryder runs parallel to that of Fibiger. Bryder maintains that the systematic use of empathetic understanding in combination with traditional content analysis techniques such as contingency analysis may enhance the validity of our inferences.

It is obvious, however, that such combinations of approaches otherwise regarded as irreconcilable have their own problems. Venturing into foreign territory always entails some risks. It is tempting, for example, to underestimate the difficulties of a technique new to its user—and also to underestimate what its old practitioners have already achieved. On the other hand, the contributions of one's own approach—future and past— may easily be overestimated. It is true that a combination of different approaches may be used to check and increase the validity of both, but at the same time it no doubt raises new problems of reliability and validity. The relations between these concepts, and more specifically the notion of reliability as used in various types of content analysis, form the subject of the chapter by Gunnar Andrén, who takes a new look at these time-honored problems of social science.

The beginning confluence of the two research traditions, then, seems to lead to a reconsideration of established ways of thought, which may ultimately result in a possibly fruitful reconceptualization. The necessity of always carefully analyzing one's basic concepts is driven home in the chapters by Anckar and Ramstedt-Silén and Hedman. In the former, the basic problem of the possibility of comparison between content analyses of different types of material is discussed with reference to policy research; in the latter, a classic question in the analysis of news, the distinction between "report" and "comment," is reformulated and applied to international news in Swedish newspapers.

A second strand in recent Scandinavian content analysis is its increased interest in the concept of time. Content analysis of data stretched over shorter or longer time periods can be found scattered all through the history of content analysis (see for example, Inglis, 1938; Davis, 1952; Shaw, 1967; Funkhouser, 1973; Beniger, 1978). It is also true that cries for an increased interest in time on the part of the social sciences have been heard from time to time during the last decades. The readers of the series in which this volume appears will remember that a substantial part of Volume 6 was dedicated to time in communication research (Hirsch et al., 1977). It is therefore reasonable to assume that the increased interest in temporal studies following in the wake of the emerging confluence between the continental and the Anglo-American research traditions in Scandinavian social science is the expression of a latent tendency which has now found an environment and circumstances favorable enough to make it manifest. Indeed, quantitative content analysis offers splendid instruments to those interested in historical studies and in the role of the past for the present. Verbal descriptions may be complemented with, and sometimes substituted by, precise measurements. Areas out of reach of survey research and institutional research may be covered (see Janowitz, 1976).

No less than six of the thirteen chapters in this volume use data from more than one point in time. It is interesting to note that all, directly or indirectly, raise the problem of the relationship between short-term and long-term change. Although dealing so far "only" with the analysis of political material from three or four Danish elections, the articles by Fibiger and Siune are outcomes of an avid interest of the Danish Social Science Research Council in time series data with a view to the study of long-term change. Gösta Carlsson and his co-authors, too, are limited by their data in their case, to an eight-year period. However, in the beginning of their study they stress that the relationships they are interested in— those between mass media content, political opinions in the public, and social change—must be different if the perspective is focused on short-term or long-term change.

It is obvious that in order to gain knowledge about such differential relationships it is mandatory to have access to time series data covering long periods of time, at comparatively short intervals (see Arundale, 1977). At present, few, if any, projects satisfy that double demand. In such a situation, the limitations of the data at hand present a challenge to be met by the researcher.

Gunnel Rikardsson's data cover some 25 years, but the nature of her data—opinion polls and content analyses of press material—forces her to operate imaginatively with uneven intervals. Johansson and Wiklund cover 60 years in their study, but the enormous amount of data implied by periods of such length has necessitated the intervals to be stretched to no less than 12 years. Consequently, the interest of the authors turns to long trends in the development of newspaper content presumably caused by the ever-increasing competition in capitalist society. Eva Block, with her yearly data covering 30 years, is closest to the ideal of long time series of data at relatively short intervals. Her project is part of the Cultural Indicators program (CISSS) mentioned earlier, and in its way that may be significant. It would seem that only by means of cooperation (and clever sampling techniques) will we ever be able to satisfy the double demand for long time series and short intervals. It is hoped that future research programs such as CISSS and the "View of the World Program"—of which Johansson's and Wiklund's chapter is an outcome—will gradually help satisfy that demand.

A third strand in recent Scandinavian content analysis is represented by efforts to combine content analysis data with other types of data. The necessity of such combinations was strongly stressed at the first Swedish conference on content analysis, and similar opinions were voiced also at the following Scandinavian conference on content analysis. This trend has been discernible for some time in Berelsonian content analysis, and it is reasonable to assume that it has been strengthened by the interest of Marxist or Marxisant communication researchers in media content as shaping and being shaped by society and its media institutions.

Methodologically, such combinations necessitate two sets of data: those on media content (intramedia data) and those on relevant conditions outside the media (extramedia data). Ideally, intramedia data and extramedia data should be independent of each other, in the sense that they should not stem from the same source (Rosengren, 1970, 1979). If they satisfy this condition, extramedia data can be used as a standard by means of which it is possible to evaluate the performance of the media. They can also be used in arguments about possible causes and effects of various types of media content.

In this volume, explicit or implicit comparisons between intra- and extramedia data may be found in several chapters. A formal analysis of the relationship between one type of intramedia data (political sympathies in newspaper editorials) and two types of extramedia data (political polls and economic trends) is undertaken by Carlsson and his co-authors. The emerging confluence of the continental and the Anglo-American tradition will probably bring along an increase in the study of the relationship between intra- and extramedia data. An increased interest in the relationship between mass media and society, in combination with a demand for increased sophistication in the analysis of that relationship, calls for the combined use of intra- and extramedia data.

Such a development may be regarded as typical for the situation in present-day Scandinavian social science in general and communication research in particular. The continental tradition has revived the interest in some vital and basic problems of social science; the Anglo-American tradition has gradually come to accept the relevance of these problems and provided some tools for their analysis. That is a happy situation—if the description is correct. If it is not correct, it would be worthwhile to try to make it so.

NOTE

1. Scandinavia proper consists of Denmark, Norway, and Sweden, while the Nordic countries also include Finland and Iceland.

REFERENCES

ANCKAR, D. (1971) Partiopinioner och utrikespolitik. Åbo: Åbo akademi.

ASPELIN, K. (1975) Textens dimensioner. Stockholm: P A Norstedt.

ARUNDALE, R. B. (1977) "Sampling across time for communication research: A simulation." Pp. 257-286 in P. M. Hirsch, P. V. Miller, and F. G. Kline (eds.), Strategies for communication research. Sage Annual Reviews of Communication Research, Volume 6. Beverly Hills, CA: Sage.

BENIGER, J. R. (1978) "Media content as social indicators. The Greenfield Index of agenda-setting." Communication Research, 5:437-453.

DAVIS, F. J. (1952) "Crime news in Colorado newspapers." American Journal of Sociology, 57: 325-330.

DOVRING, K. (1973) "Communication, dissenters and popular culture in eighteenth-century Europe." Journal of Popular Culture, 7: 559-568.

ELLEGÅRD, A. (1958) Darwin and the general reader. Stockholm: Almqvist & Wiksell.

FLEMING, D. and BAILYN, B. [eds.] (1969) The intellectual migration. Europe and America, 1930-1960. Cambridge: Harvard University Press.

FUNKHOUSER, G. R. (1973) "The issues of the sixties: An exploratory study in the dynamics of public opinion." Public Opinion Quarterly, 37: 62-75.

GEORGE, A. L. (1959) "Quantitative and qualitative content analysis." In I. De Sola Pool (ed.), Trends in content analysis. Urbana: University of Illinois Press.

GERBNER, G. (1970) "Cultural indicators." Annals of the American Academy of Political and Social Science, 388: 69-81.

GERBNER, G., GROSS, L., SIGNORIELLI, N., MORGAN, M., and JACKSON-BEECK, M. (1979) "The demonstration of power: Violence Profile No. 10." Journal of Communication, 29: 177-196.

GOLDMANN, K. (1979) Is my enemy's enemy my friend's friend? Cultural indicators: The Swedish Symbol System, 1945-1975. Report No. 1. Lund: Studentlitteratur.

HALLBERG, P. (1951) Natursymboler i svensk lyrik, I-III. Göteborg; Elanders.

HEMANUS, P. (1976) "What is news? Objectivity in news transmission." Journal of Communication, 26: 102-107.

HIRSCH, P. M., MILLER, P. V., and KLINE, F. G. (1977) Strategies for communication research. Sage Annual Reviews of Communication Research, Volume 6. Beverly Hills, CA: Sage.

JANOWITZ, M. (1976) "Content analysis and the study of sociopolitical change." Journal of Communication, 26: 10-26.

LAZARSFELD, P. F. (1972) "Administrative and critical communication research." In P. F. Lazarsfeld, Qualitative analysis. Boston: Allyn & Bacon.

MILLER, P. V. (1977) "Themes of measurement in communication research." Pp. 113-126 in P. M. Hirsch, P. V. Miller, and F. G. Kline (eds.), Strategies for communication research. Sage Annual Reviews of Communication Research, Volume 6. Beverly Hills, CA: Sage.

ROSENGREN, K. E. (1968) Sociological aspects of the literary system. Stockholm: Natur och Kultur.

ROSENGREN, K. E. (1970) "International news: Intra and extra media data." Acta Sociologica, 13: 96-109.

ROSENGREN, K. E. (1979) "Bias in news: Methods and concepts." Studies of Broadcasting, 15: 31-45.

ROSENGREN, K. E. (forthcoming) "Mass media and social change: Some current approaches." In E. Katz and T. Szesckö (eds.), Mass media and social change. London: Sage.

SHAW, D. L. (1967) "News bias and the telegraph: A study of historical change." Journalism Quarterly, 44: 3-12, 31.

THOMSEN, N. (1972) Dagbladskonkurrencen 1870-1970. Copenhagen: Gads Forlag.

WESTERSTÅHL, J. (1977) "Objektiv nyhetsförmedling." Statsvetenskaplig tidskrift, 80: 195-202.

——— (1972) Objektiv Nyhetsförmedling. Stockholm: Scandinavian University Books.

——— (1970) "Objectivity is measurable." EBU Review, 121B: 13-17.

ZIMA, P. V. (1977) "Le texte comme objet: une critique de la sociologie empirique de la littérature." Homme et la societé, 12: 151-170.

PART I

ANALYTICAL PERSPECTIVES

Chapter 1

APPROACHES TO TEXTUAL ANALYSIS

Kent Lindkvist

INTRODUCTION

The aim of this chapter is to compare different approaches with textual analysis: content analysis, analytical semantics, structuralism and hermeneutics. I regard textual analysis and interpretation as a form of model-building. What is regarded as a problem with a text? Which ideologies, theories, and methods are used by different approaches? Which texts are analyzed? Which role is ascribed to the researcher?

I will also briefly discuss "nontextual" ideas of interpretation and analysis, especially intentional interpretation. Finally, I will discuss the possibility of syntheses between the approaches.

APPROACHES TO TEXTUAL ANALYSIS

PRODUCER, CONSUMER, AND INTERPRETER MEANING

The meaning of a text can be identified with the producer, the consumer, and the interpreter of the text or with the text itself:

$$\text{Producer} \longrightarrow \text{Text} \longrightarrow \text{Consumer}$$
$$\uparrow$$
$$\text{Interpreter}$$

Producer Meaning

One way to identify the meaning of a text is to ask the author what he meant. If the author is not available to answer, it is sometimes possible to reconstruct an answer. It is often said that no one can express the intended thoughts better and more precisely than the author. However, the relationship between the text and the intentions of an author is not without problems. In different ways the claims of intentional analysis have been criticized by those who put the text in focus.

In *Validity and Interpretation,* Hirsch defends the intentional analysis and criticizes what he calls the doctrine of semantic autonomy. His criticism touches all approaches of textual analysis (I will discuss this later). According to Hirsch, the only valid norm of an objective analysis is to establish the intentions of the text producer. A text says nothing beyond the intentions of the text producer. The correct interpretation of a text is the same as the intentional interpretation of the author; the author has a monopoly on interpretation.

Such a theory of interpretation presupposes that intentions are unitary. Furthermore, Hirsch assumes that intentions can be established at certain points of time, and that the first intention of the author is the correct one. Putting the text in focus will give rise to an anarchy of interpretation. The objectivity will disappear: "If the meaning of a text is not the author's, then no interpretation can possibly correspond to *the* meaning of the text, since the text can have no determinate or determinable meaning" (Hirsch, 1967: 5-6).

According to Hirsch, the only alternative to intentional interpretation is the idea of semantic autonomy: a metaphysical idea which posits that linguistic signs express their own meaning. A sender can have different intentions with a text at different times. For example, a sender may have one intention when he first develops the idea, a second when the idea is worked out, a third when it is ready, and a fourth in his autobiography. But Hirsch maintains that a sender has only an original intention. In his later interpretations the sender is just a receiver of his own text. Which is the original intention—the first, the second, or the third? They are all related to the process of text production. Intentions are not phenomena that appear as distinct units at certain points in time. Instead, there is, I believe, a parallel between the process of text production and the intentional process. These problems are complicated when the sender consists of more than one person. It is possible to say that an organization, for instance, has intentions, in the sense that several persons within it have certain intentions in common. But how does one identify the intentions, especially the original intentions, when members have different opinions about them? It is difficult (or even impossible) to verify that an intentional interpretation is correct. Does the sender remember correctly? Is he cheating? How can one test propositions about the intentions of a dead author, or if the sender is a collective one? Hirsch maintains that the problem of verification is difficult but that one must work with degrees of probability when giving an intentional interpretation. In certain cases intentions cannot be established; in other cases this can be done with certainty. In the case of a collective sender, the problem of verification will be more difficult than in the case of an individual sender. Who had the original intention? How does one verify intentions in cases of contradictions?

One could argue that the sender may not know what he means; he may have had no distinct intention, or was not conscious of having formed one. However, Hirsch claims that one who so argues does not understand what an intention is. An intention, by Hirsch's definition, is conscious, and all texts must be written with conscious aims or they would be impossible to understand. For Hirsch the intention is there; it can be discovered or reconstructed with different degrees of probability.

The ideology of intentional interpretation can be regarded as invalid. It accepts the conditions settled by the text producer, and presupposes that the sender has a monopoly on the interpretation of what he says.

The adherents of an intentional interpretation assume that intentions are unitary and that these are necessary characteristics of intentions. However, we can regard intentions as ambiguous, as a process; and if they are uniform and unitary, then these attributes are occasional. It is possible that senders remember incorrectly, lie, delude, have no certain intentions, rationalize, and that their intentions can be a process in which no original intention can be found. On the other hand, language is used to convey messages. Language that does not further communication has a will of its own, with an internal meaning outside human communication; *die Sprache spricht,* as Heidegger says. However, language is limited by societal rules of context and meaning. A word cannot have infinite ambiguity; otherwise communication would be impossible.

If we deny the claims of intentional interpretation and regard the sender's intention as a comment on his own text, then it will be just a part of the relationship between sender and receiver.

Consumer and Interpreter Meaning

In the case of consumer meaning, the meaning is identified with the consumer's (reader's, receiver's) experience of the text. Different groups of consumers understand a text in different ways. In this case the role of the interpreter is sociologically directed: to identify the different consumers and how they understand a text.

Textual analysis has also been seen as completely dependent on the individuality of the qualified interpreter. The meaning of a text is the meaning ascribed to its interpreter.[1]

TEXTUAL MEANING

My main interest in this article is focused on four approaches of textual analysis, which identify the meaning of a text with the text itself: analytical semantics, structuralism, hermeneutics, and content analysis.

Analytical semantists such as Arne Naess and others within the Scandinavian tradition of analytical philosophy have elaborated a systematic qualitative textual analysis. At the beginning, semantists analyzed philosophical texts, but later semantics has been used to analyze arguments in many contexts: scientifical, ethical, political, ideological, among others.

Structuralists like Lévi-Strauss, Barthes, Kristeva, Derrida, and others have analyzed highly different kinds of texts, as well as other forms of communication or signs such as music, architecture, film, and art. Here we may distinguish between those who try to achieve general textual models which can be applied to all kinds of texts, and those who have less far-reaching ambitions but instead are building some kind of "middle-range" textual models.

In hermeneutics we can distinguish between an intentional approach (Hirsch and others) and a textual, antiintentional approach (Gadamer, Ricoeur, and others). The traditional textual focus has been literary, but also philosophical, legal, and political.

Content analysis as created in the tradition of Lasswell, Berelson, George, de Sola Pool, Holsti, and others is principally a technique for quantitative analysis of extensive texts within the framework of a communication model. Different content analysts emphasize different elements of the communication model.

Representatives of the different approaches criticize each other and sometimes accuse each other of being nonscientific or irrelevant. Therefore, an effort to compare these approaches in terms of questions along a number of dimensions seems to be warranted. Which are the contradictions between the approaches? Which are the similarities and differences? Are they studying the same object? Are they emphasizing different things? In what respect are they complementary? Is synthesis possible? Is it possible to benefit from different approaches when studying a concrete text? I am not capable of giving systematic answers to all these questions. This would presuppose a systematic—perhaps quantitative—analysis of the work done within different approaches. But my intention is to indicate where the answers can be found.

Different textual approaches usually have different concepts of "text." Three definitions of "text" are of interest in this connection:

(1) every *semiotic* structure of meaning (This is a broad definition of the text concept, common in structuralism and hermeneutics. Such

a concept includes not only language but music, architecture, picture, events, and social actions.);

(2) every *linguistic* means of expression (thus, music, for example, is excluded for the text concept);

(3) *written* language (which would exclude, for example, audiovisual language).

In content analysis and semantics the text concept usually is limited to the two latter definitions. When content analysts speak about "output" in the communication process, they generally use the first definition of the text concept.

To count and classify all possible context factors surrounding a text is an almost impossible task. A context is to be seen open: the contextual factors are infinite. Thus, one is forced to determine the contextual limits in the pursuit of a textual analysis.

Everyday talk, a commercial, or a political program are surrounded by an infinite number of external contextual characteristics. Contexts surrounding a political program can include the sender, the different intentions of the sender, the decisional situation, the interpretations of the receivers, the receivers' level of knowledge, their relationship to the sender, the receivers' educational level, their class position, inside information of the text, occasional mood of sender and receiver, layout, typography, extension, point of time for textual production and consumption, and political and historical connection.

We can distinguish between three types of internal contexts: (1) linguistic contexts, (2) structural contexts, (3) content contexts.

Content analysis and semantics emphasize internal textual contexts, while hermeneutics and structuralism emphasize the relation between external and internal textual contexts. Within the frame of the text, structuralists are most interested in the linguistic context and external factors referred to or derived from the text. Content analysts are interested in the linguistic context, especially the quantitative aspect. Semantists seldom leave the text, but limit themselves to contexts of the content in their ambition to show the internal connection of meaning in the text. Hermeneutists do not seem to give priority to any internal feature of the text.

The concept of interpretation is intimately related to different perspectives of textual analysis. Semantics usually regard interpretation as a form for eliminating ambiguity. Most content analysts distinguish between analysis and interpretation. The analysis consists of different forms of treatment of the manifest content in a text or an output of communication. Interpretation is usually seen as related to the latent content of a text. In the hermeneutic tradition the concept of interpretation is closely related to the concept of Verstehen. Structuralists are not directly using the concept of interpretation, because they regard their activity as a realization of objective structures. In all these cases, however, the researcher is assigned an active role in his analytical activity.

The four approaches have at least two ideas in common: the idea that texts "hide" something and the idea that the analysis must be systematic in one way or another. The idea of being systematic makes it possible to distinguish between legitimate interpretations and interpretations which are either wrong or just modifications. No textual elements must be excluded, unexplained, or vague. The analysis must explain the text both in part and in whole; both the elements and the structure.

Content analysis has in common a fundamental assumption about the interest of the text producer and the quantitative profile of the text. The text "hides" the interest of the text producer, but it can be revealed by quantitatively measuring the text. The manifest text is coded, but when relating the measured result to a general communication model, the character of different textual elements can be explained. Semantics presupposes that there is a basic ambiguity and vagueness in language. The grammar of a text "hides" linguistic functions, which can be revealed by means of precizations. Structuralists often assume that the diachrony of the text "hides" its synchrony or vice versa. In the synchrony/diachrony of the text basic structures are "hidden." Hermeneutics supposes that the text "hides" the intentions of the author or that it is possible to reveal basic contradictions, instincts, or different kinds of social, psychological, or cultural entities.

Interpreting the Text Literally

One kind of textual analysis emanates from interpretations of the Bible or other holy texts, but is also seen in legal and political connections. It is characterized by focusing (quoting or selecting) certain parts of a text in an authoritative way. The text interpreted is often seen as "holy," and the interpreter claims that his interpretation is the only correct one. Such an interpretation often presupposes that every linguistically correct text has one and only one interpretation and that the correct interpretation emanates from the wording of the text. Furthermore, it presupposes that words are monosemic and that ambiguity and vagueness on the whole do not exist and that the function and the meaning of a sentence are clear from a linguistic formulation. If explanation of a text is needed it is for pedagogic reasons or because the text is incomplete or has false or vague premises. Many interpretations of norm sources seem to work in this way. Since God has produced a text, He cannot readily be ambiguous or vague in His divine use of language. Several institutional norm sources similarly may not be interpreted by ordinary people: specialists must legitimate certain interpretations and do it with claims of monopoly founded on societal sanctions.

Such an idea of interpretation denies elementary facts: most words are ambiguous and vague and their meanings cannot immediately be determined by means of the linguistic formulation.

Analytical Semantics

Analytical semantics denies the idea of a "correct" interpretation of a text. Instead, it is possible to make reasonable interpretations of a text. The reasonableness is dependent on certain contextual claims, which can be linguistical, logical, semantical, or empirical. Semantics assumes a principle of reconstruction which replaces the principle of testability; and the principle of reconstruction shall answer such questions as "Which context has been considered?" "Which interpretations have been tried?" "Which criteria of interpretation have been applied?"

Sentences have different functions, and in principle every sentence can be interpreted in terms of these functions independently of the formal character of the sentence. Analytical philosophers, however, do not agree on the number of the basic functions. This depends partly on the different views of the character of value sentences. A common set of sentence functions are analytical, synthetic, expressive, prescriptive, and performative.

A sentence can be interpreted in terms of all five functions. The stages in such an interpretation would perhaps be as follows: Which possible interpretations can be found in terms of different functions of sentences? Which terms in the sentence are ambiguous and vague and can be interpreted in different directions? Which interpretations are reasonable? Which interpretation is most reasonable as to different contextual factors?

In the case of extensive texts, a systematic analysis of functions of sentences is not possible. In this case it is necessary to systematize the argumentation in one way or another. Strategically selected sentences can then be analyzed with the sentence functional method. One can also subordinate an argumentation to a formulation under which one constructs chains of *pro et contra* arguments. A whole argumentation can also be systematized according to a set of questions, answers, and arguments. They can be implicit in a technique which emerges from a line of thought based on the function of the sentence and gives the interpreter a more creative role in the process of interpretation.

Semantics presupposes that the language and thereby the text has an open structure, which always make it possible to create new perspectives and new precizations of the text. The original text is made more distinct essentially through precizations. Semantics makes a model of the text, which in a systematic way realizes the internal textual connection of meaning. Semantics makes the relations between different textual categories clearer and presents them in a more systematic way than the text itself.

Structuralism

When Lévi-Strauss analyzes myths, he rearranges them according to a synchronic pattern. The elements of the text are classified into groups so that different functional elements of the text—events, structures, persons, processes—are grouped according to similarity. The basic similarity in every set of elements Lévi-Strauss calls mytems. The text-functional elements can be combined in different ways. However, Levi-Strauss is of the opinion that only one of the possible combinations constitutes the timeless pattern of the text, the real structure. Furthermore, he draws conclusions regarding relations between mytems which are based on some form of structural similarity between these relations. Lévi-Strauss gives names to the mytems; that is, the structure by which a set of text-functional elements can be arranged. It is a procedure that may appear reminiscent of factor analysis: after having rotated a set of values in a certain way, values close to each other are clustered together and then given a name.

In *Sémantique Structurale* Greimas tries to analyze a text as a system of oppositions. The smallest units of meaning he calls sémes. Greimas maintains that combinations of sémes constitute the content of a word. But the words, or "lexems," as Greimas says, are dependent not only on the system of oppositions but also on the context of the lexems. The lexem is given meaning through the unity of sémes or the combination of sémes and the context.

Furthermore, Greimas speaks about a system of "actants." A message contains at least one actant and a predicate, giving the actant a concrete content. An actant seems to be everything that plays a "role" in a text; it can be one or more actors or objects. Greimas sets up basic actant schemes for the text: (1) an axis of communication—sender-object-receiver; (2) a conflict axis—helper-subject-opponent; and (3) an *"axe du désir"*—subject-object, which links the two horizontal axises. For texts with a diachronic content Greimas sets up models of transformation which he subsumes in the basic opposition between life and death.

Kristeva defines the textual model as a "formal system, the structure of which is isomorph or analogous with the structure in another system" (Kristeva, 1969: 29). Kristeva regards the textual reading as "*une lecture verticale*"; it begins with the manifest level and goes downwards, revealing codes on deeper levels. Thus, we have three levels: manifest, transformative, and generative. The text producer transfers certain ideological codes to a manifest text which, through narrative codes at the transformation level, receives its final "syntagmatic code." The different levels are said to be overdetermined, so that the text on every level is given characteristics specific to that level. The task of the interpreter is to roll up this sequence and reveal the ideological or generative code.

Other structuralists have criticized efforts to reduce texts to basic models. Eco claims that Greimas enlightens oppositions in a text from the point of view of a certain "reading hypothesis." Another reader with another key to the text may well find other oppositions. Every text has an openness and an ambiguity which make many interpretations possible. There is no timeless structure of a content. With the concept "the absent structure" Eco expresses his basic opinion that such basic models of texts "have no ontological stability." Eco is more interested in the structuring process than the structures.

Eco speaks about "cultural units"; these are defined by their position in a system of other cultural units, which surround or stand in opposition to each other. The meaning is the value of the position of the sign. The values can be defined as differences, not through their content but through the position in the system. Cultural units have a semantic field, they carry semantic and behavioral reactions. Within a certain culture there are contradicting semantic fields, which can be strengthened or weakened. A semantic field can be dissolved and restructured to form a new field.

In his book *S/Z*, Barthes analyzes a short story, "Sarrasine" by Balzac. There he criticizes the idea of reducing all diachronic texts to a single structure. The early analysts of tales imagined that it was possible, by means of an inductive method, to create a pattern and from a great number of tales build a "big, narrative model." Barthes maintains that this is not possible. There are differences which can never be resolved: texts, language, and systems have infinite ambiguity. The alternative is to relate every text to the factors working in connection within the text. The text is caught in "the infinite paradigm of differences." "To interpret a text is really something else than giving it a meaning, it is to assess its manifoldness" (Barthes, 1975: 11). There is nothing outside the text, and there is no "real entirety of the text." It is not possible to trace the text back to an "original internal order," where the oppositions are "reconciled" under a general textual model. The text is liberated both from its external image and its entirety.

Barthes denies the possibility of general textual models and emphasizes the textual ambiguity. He speaks about "the broken-up text." He does not cluster the elements of a text in order to subordinate them to a hierarchic textual model, but speaks of creating semantic material, divided but not categorized. It is not a question of making a structure visible, but establishing a structure. The interpreter must not remain at the level of the text itself and not construct an entirety, but just remain at the broken-up text. He is pleading for something of a "middle-range model" of textual analysis. The broken-up text will exhibit an associative space, an open structure, a manifoldness, an ambiguity which cannot be caught in a general textual model.

Hermeneutics

In *Wahrheit und Methode* Gadamer has established a hermeneutic theory of interpretation. Gadamer means that the text itself points to the method according to which it is to be interpreted. Our own methods have only a negative function: the text says nothing beyond what we knew before. The method blocks the truth, the possibility of an understanding of the text. It is an illusion to believe that a reader can understand a text in the same way the author understands the text. We cannot place ourselves outside history. An interpretation is influenced by all interpretations made before: it is an element of a *"Wirkungsgeschichte."* Every human being has a "horizon," certain knowledge and preunderstanding. To understand a text is to partake in a "fusion of horizons," where every new text extends the interpreter's horizon. The interpreter must have a genuine respect for the text. He does not create the meaning of the text, but is a receiver of it and the tradition it mediates. This textual "truth," the horizon-extending character, is something positive, while the "method" "destroys" the text.

There are two kinds of hermeneutic responses to Gadamer which can be represented by two authors: Hirsch, in direct polemics with Gadamer, reconstructs the intention of the author; Ricoeur discusses the methodological problems of the text in another way.

Ricoeur claims that we must construct the meaning of the text for two reasons (Ricoeur, 1974: 104-107). First, the text is written, which means an asymmetric relation between the text and the reader. Second, the text represents a cumulative, holistic process. However, there are no distinct rules for this construction. The construction relies on "clues" contained in the text and on a set of prohibitions and permissions. A probable construction is a construction which (1) has the greatest number of facts provided in the text and (2) offers a better qualitative convergence between the traits which it takes into account. Furthermore, Ricoeur posits a principle of "plenitude," which seems to signify a kind of synthetic interpretation of the same type as that of Barthes in *S/Z*: all possible connotations are included; the text means all it can mean.

For Ricoeur, the "world" of a text is the ensemble of references opened by the text. Ricoeur tries to liberate the meaning of the text from the "tutelage of the mental intention" as well as "the limits of ostensive reference." To interpret is to understand the world opened up by the nonostensive reference of the text—that is, to understand the world in its manifoldness.

Ricoeur's concept of interpretation expresses a shift of emphasis in the hermeneutical circle from the intention of the author to "the world of the work." The early idea of the hermeneutical circle implied some kind of circularity between understanding a text and understanding oneself. According to Ricoeur, there is a shift to an understanding of ourselves before the world of the work: it enlarges the horizon of our self-understanding. Thus, the meaning of the text is not subordinated to the interpreting subject. The hermeneutical circle is moved from a subjectivist to an ontological level.

Hermeneutics is a special case of a general phenomenology, emphasizing basic questions of thought. The practice of psychoanalysis is often seen as hermeneutical, as it tries to reveal hidden meanings. Hermeneutists have regarded psychoanalysis as a prototype of a hermeneutical-critical social science. A text is to be seen in the light of the *Weltanschauung* of the producer of the text. A text must not be treated as an object, but as an expression of a certain preunderstanding, which the hermeneutists try to articulate.

A text is subject-related in two ways: created by a subject with an aim of communicating something and interpreted by a subject with the aim of understanding the textual meaning. One has to "enter the language," engage oneself as a subject, be influenced by the text. We participate in a linguistic game, similar to the producer and the consumer of a text. The text is not autonomous; it is an open relation between sender and receiver, as a Swedish hermeneutist, Aspelin, says (1975: 258). The different elements in text and context are dialectically linked together: therefore, the textual meaning is difficult to handle because of the infinite combinatory possibilities.

Content Analysis

In content analysis there is a basic assumption of the relation between the frequency of the linguistic units and the interest of the text producer. In principle, the text producer is more "interested" in frequent units than infrequent units. In content analysis the manifest, objective characteristics are in focus.

In general, content analysis applies empirical and statistical methods to textual material. Content analysis particularly consists of a division of the text into units of meaning and a quantification of these units according to certain rules. An early content analyst, Berelson, defines content analysis as a method for objective, systematic, and quantitative description of the manifest content of a text. Holsti modifies this definition: content analysis is an objective, systematic, and general description of the manifest content of a text. Objectivity means that every stage in the research process must be based on explicitly formulated rules and procedures. The content of the text is to be emphasized, and the values and beliefs of the researcher must not influence the result of the examination. Some kind of reliability test must be undertaken, so that another researcher can obtain the same result from the same rules and data.

That content analysis is systematic implies inclusion and exclusion of categories according to consistently applied rules. The possibility that the researcher will use only material supporting his hypothesis is thereby eliminated.

Holsti means that there must be a principle of generality. The content analysis must have theoretical relevance; that is, one must be able to generalize from text data to other data of the components in a communication model. Holsti regards the problem of quantity or quality as a quasi-problem. The relevant question is, "Which is the theoretical relevance of the measures I use?" Isolated data are meaningless. Only by linking data together with theoretical questions is analysis meaningful. About the manifest/latent relationship, Holsti says that the stage of coding must be manifest. By searching for a latent content, the searcher reaches a stage of interpretation. Evidence of different interpretations must be found in sources independent of the content analysis.

TEXTUAL MODELS

I will regard textual analysis and interpretation as a form of model-building. A text is a reality, of which the textual analysis gives a model. Both theoretical and practical intentions can exist with a model: one can describe, explain, understand, ascribe, predict, express, and perform. Models can have different forms: verbal, schematic, and mathematic. They can be qualitative and/or quantitative. They may or may not be related to time factors. They can state different kinds of connections between factors in the model.

Thus, in the process of model-building, one begins by asking questions which define the problems of the text. With these questions one can establish the relevant factors of the text. The text is then reorganized according to the questions asked. The process presupposes an ideology of interpretation, theories about correlations between factors, and methods to establish these correlations in a given text. This process of interpretation will result in a textual model—a picture of a text with its characteristics given by the process of interpretation.

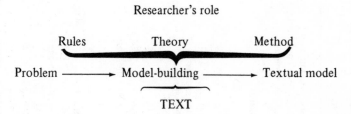

With this heuristic frame of reference we can summarize the approaches to textual analysis as to rules, problem, theory, method, and textual model (see Table 1.1).

TEXTUAL ANALYSIS AND THE ROLE OF THE RESEARCHER

How shall an interpreter treat the concept and terminology of the analyzed text? We can distinguish between an immanent and an objectivating way of presentation. If one does not want to accept the conception and terms of the analyzed text, it is common to use other terms with a different or the same descriptive meaning but with a neutral emotive meaning. An objection against such an objectivating way of presentation is that it may not be possible to translate terms from one emotive meaning to another without changing the descriptive meaning. There are several associations connected with a term, especially concepts with synthetic characteristics (that is, terms which are systematically ambiguous). Furthermore, it can be difficult to determine whether one's terms are neutral. In addition, terms have certain positions in a text, where the importance differs. If terms are changed, this position can be disregarded. In the case of immanent presentation, one tries to analyze a text from the point of

TABLE 1.1

	Rules	Main problem	Theory	Methods	Textual model
Semantics	External	Ambiguity	Sentence functions	Precizations	Structure of meaning
Content analysis	External	Manifest structure	Connection environment/ manifest structure	Quantitative	Communication model
Structuralism	External				
Lévi-Strauss		Patterns of Symbols	Mytem	Clustering	Synchronic pattern of symbols
Greimas		Oppositions	Sémes	Positional	General model of oppositions
Eco		Codes	Semiotics	Positional	Field model of codes
Barthes		Codes	Associations	Connotations	Broken up text
Kristeva		Codes	Ideologem	Transformation analysis	Level models
Hermeneutics	Internal				
Gadamer		"Wahrheit"	Horizon	Immanent	Immanent structure
Ricoeur		Textual reconstruction	World of the work	Immanent	Immanent structure
Literal	Monopoly of producer/interpreter	Formal textual organization		Quotations, emphasis	Immanent structure
Producer	Monopoly of producer	Producer's intention	Intention	Historical, psychological	Intentional structure
Consumer	Monopoly of consumer	Consumer meaning	Consumer image of the text	Sociological	Image structure
Interpreter	Monopoly of interpreter	Subjective	Personality of interpreter	Subjective	Subjective

TABLE 1.2

Type of Role	(1)	(2)	(3)	(4)	(5)	(6)
Type of Analysis						
Literal	0	–	–	–	–	–
Producer	+	–	–	–	–	–
Content	0	0	+	–	–	–
Hermeneutics	+	0	–*	0	0	–
Structuralism	0	0	0	+	0	0
Semantics	0	+	0	0	0	0
Consumer/Interpreter	0	0	0	0	0	0

+ obligatory
0 permitted
– prohibited
* impossible

view of its own prerequisites. But then, from the point of view of an objectivating presentation, it is possible to say that one cannot be objective and neutral, that one cannot transcend the limits of the perspectives and evaluations of the text, and that the text will be regarded as unique and thereby difficult to compare with other texts.

Below are listed six different roles the researcher can play when analyzing texts. Items (1), (4), and (5) are related to an immanent way of presentation; the others to an objectivating way:

(1) Immanent presentation, with the intention of emphazing what is regarded as the center and the periphery of a text;
(2) analyzing the text with a meta-language, with the aim of uncovering the different elements of the text in relation to external factors;
(3) an objectivating presentation, which neutralizes emotive meaning;
(4) immanent criticism, with the intention of demonstrating inconsistencies, on the basis of the meaning of the text itself;
(5) developing interpretations to make the text better; and
(6) a textual criticism with a point of departure in the conceptions and questionings of other systems.

We can relate these roles of the researcher to the different approaches, as shown in Table 1.2.

In intentional analysis and in literal interpretation everything except (1) is prohibited. In nonintentional hermeneutics (6) is regarded as impossible and (5) prohibited. In content analysis (6) is obligatory, (2), (3), and (5) are prohibited, and (1) and (4) are permitted. In semantics, (2) is obligatory; (4) is obligatory in structuralism; everything else is permitted.

In these relations between the text and the role of the interpreter the approaches emphasize different things. A combination between hermeneutics and content analysis seems to be difficult: what content analysis regards as obligatory, hermeneutics regards as impossible. For hermeneutics it is not possible to be neutral; one must occupy some position as an interpreter. For content analysis it is necessary to be value-free.

Other combinations of the approaches seem to be possible, and there are also some examples of such combinations. In addition, there are examples of what could be called a pragmatic view. When considering a concrete text different roles should be tried to see what they can offer. Instead of dogmas of interpretation one finds the supremacy of the text. However, this eclectic strategy also has disadvantages; the development of theories and methods may tend to be less efficient than in the case of a more limited idea of the relationship between the interpreter and the text.

MODEL-BUILDING AND
SYNTHESIS OF APPROACHES

The four main approaches discussed—semantics, hermeneutics, structuralism, and content analysis—have grown from a need to analyze specific textual types. Their original areas of analysis have then been extended to other textual types; and problems have appeared.

Hermeneutics is especially interested in ontological and epistemological prerequisites for interpretation. Ricoeur uses a structuralist text analysis as a prototype for his concrete textual analysis, while Gadamer uses the religious and legal textual analysis as a prototype. Hirsch is part of a long literary tradition of intentional interpretation. Other hermeneutists use psychoanalysis and Marxism as patterns for the analysis of symbols and societal phenomena. The texts analyzed are often historical, literary, religious, and philosophical. In terms of the communication model, hermeneutics is principally interested in the epistemological problems and prerequisites of senders, receivers, and interpreters.

Analytical semantics was originally used to analyze philosophical texts, especially to show that many philosophical problems are quasi-problems. It was then applied to argumentative texts in general and debates. In terms of the communication model, semantics is especially interested in the decoding process of the text: the internal connection of meaning.

Structuralists have examined the structure of tales, especially tales with symbolic content such as myths. This kind of textual analysis is then applied to every kind of diachronic text, but also to real events. The sender is constituted by the structure and not seen as determined in terms of intentions, decisions, and the like. Semiotics is interested in the structuring itself and the cultural codes and has a very broad area of interest: texts, events, rituals, cartoons, architecture, colors, and landscapes. In terms of the communication model, the text-situation relation is in focus.

Content analysis was originally used to draw conclusions regarding the sender from quantitative data. Senders typically have been collective, such as governments, organizations, and parties. Most texts analyzed have been extensive texts of mass communication. Lately not only texts of mass communication are analyzed but also literary, religious and other texts. The quantitative profile of the text has been in focus. The interest in factors outside the text has varied from a strong actor orientation to a strong situation orientation.

In her book, *Kontext och funktion* (Context and Function) Swedish content analyst Lagerberg discusses seven general problems of the field:

(1) The empirical problem: the difficulties in establishing the relations between content and facts.
(2) The syntactical problem: the difficulties in finding adequate recording units.
(3) The problem of substance: the difficulties in determining whether a unit has reference or coherence.
(4) The problem of completeness: what part of the content might be excluded and included.
(5) The problem of congruence: the general relations between phenomena to analyze and available content.
(6) The semantical problem: the fact that the recording units can have different meanings.
(7) The problem of importance: certain infrequent content characteristics have a decisive bearing upon the variable of analysis [Lagerberg, 1975: 292-295].

The empirical problem and the semantical problem can partly be solved by ideas of precization and reference within analytical semantics. The problems of importance, completeness, and syntactics can, I believe, be solved partly by structuralist ideas of positional meaning, semantic field, and cultural units. However, these also imply that content analysis should be ready to integrate new theoretical perspectives.

I have mentioned the contradictions among structuralists as to general models contra-"middle-range" models. General models must not be regarded as strait-jackets, but as a heuristic means of assistance. Barthes' alternative—the broken-up text—seems to be less fruitful: his analysis of Sarrasine is seven times longer than the text analyzed. Eco's perspective of structuring seems to be more interesting. The general problems of structuralism, mentioned by Eco, might be solved with the help of semantics and content analysis: the problems of analyzing trends and changes, extensive texts, structuring semantic fields, and so on.

Semantics would also be enriched by both structuralism and content analysis. The problem of importance can be deepened in semantics, I believe, using structuralist ideas of positional meaning and the ideas of the connections between sign and situation. Sometimes a quantitative analysis would offer a fruitful complement to a semantic analysis.

Hermeneutics may have an essential contribution to offer to the other approaches with respect to the prerequisites of interpretation and analysis. But it would seem that it has less to contribute to the concrete field of textual analysis in structuralism, semantics, and content analysis.

We have regarded textual analysis as a process of model-building. This process can be seen as a spiral of knowledge → problems → instruments, new knowledge → new problems → new instruments, etc.[2] The development of the spiral is linked to the development of the dialectics between text and textual model. The approaches are to be developed in this dialectic direction and not as isolated theories. Successful syntheses of approaches may eventually be developed during this process.

The contradictions between the approaches are sometimes real and sometimes predominantly dogmatic and prestige-bound. In the beginning the approaches were applied to special areas of interpretation. When their area of application expanded, internal problems and external confrontations appeared. The different approaches have developed from different historical conditions and have different profiles of interest. This opens rich possibilities in cases where the approaches are complementary. A fruitful convergent development, however, presupposes that textual analysts be undogmatic and have a broad knowledge of different approaches. There are some tendencies today among different approaches to transcend the limits of their own approach. One borderline, and perhaps the strongest one, lies in the use of quantitative or qualitative analysis. Within content analysis there are, however, tendencies toward using a qualitative approach much more than before. The negative attitude toward quantiative methods within hermeneutics, semantics, and structuralism is quite compact, but if the representatives of these approaches could bring themselves to use at least certain quantitative methods, the result might be worthwhile.

The potential of a fruitful integration between the approaches exists, as far as I can see, not as a General Method or Model, but as a battery of instruments with the capacity to start and develop the spiral of textual model-building. Such a development presupposes a pluralist role of the researcher, a "horizon-extending" ideology as to methods and models, and, finally, a broad knowledge of societal development as a whole.

Instead of searching for the Model, we could elaborate alternative textual interpretations and discuss their limitations and possibilities.

NOTES

1. For a discussion of this view as it is expressed by Weitz, Margolis, and Hungerland, see Nordin (1978: 61-64, 71-79).

2. This idea is elaborated in Törnebohm (1975) and Nordin (1978: 82-84); the latter transcends the hermeneutical circle and regards it as a spiral.

REFERENCES

ASPELIN, K. (1975) Textens dimensioner (Textual Dimensions). Stockholm: Norstedt.

BARTHES, R. (1975) S/Z. Paris: Editions du Seuil.

ECO, U. (1968) La struttura assente. Milano: Bompiani.

GADAMER, H.-G. (1960) Wahrheit und Methode. Tubingen: J.C.B. Mohr (Paul Siebeck).

GREIMAS, A. J. (1966) Semantique structurale. Paris: Librairie Larousse.

HIRSCH, E. D., Jr. (1967) Validity and Interpretation. New Haven, CT: Yale University Press.

HOLSTI, O. R. (1969) Content Analysis for the Social Sciences and the Humanities. Reading, MA: Addison-Wesley.

KRISTEVA, J. (1969) Sémeiotike. Recherches pour une sémanalyse. Paris: Editions du Seuil.

LAGERBERG, D. (1975) Kontext och funktion (Context and Function), Summary: Contribution to the Theory and Method of Content Analysis. Uppsala: Institute of Sociology, University of Uppsala.

NAESS, A. (1953) Interpretation and Preciseness. Oslo: Skrifter utgitt av Det Norske Videnskaps-akademi i Oslo, i kommisjon hos Jacob Dybwad.

NORDIN, S. (1978) Interpretation and Method. Lund: Institute of Philosophy, University of Lund.

RICOEUR, P. (1974) "Metaphor and the main problem of hermeneutics." New Literary History VI, 1.

TÖRNEBOHM, H. (1975) Inquiring Systems and Paradigms. Reports from the Department of Theory of Science, University of Gothenburg, Report No. 72.

Chapter 2

RELIABILITY AND CONTENT ANALYSIS

Gunnar Andrén

INTRODUCTION

Within the social sciences great stress is laid upon the reliability and validity of the research instruments, the raw data, the conclusions, and so on. There are numerous concepts of reliability and validity employed in these discussions, and it is not always clear what is meant by the terms "reliability" and "validity." This chapter deals only with problems pertaining to results of measurements—that is, raw data. Some proposals for conceptual reform are put forward. I will argue for three principal theses. Two of these are conceptual. The standard notion of reliability as consensus and the idea that something is valid when "it measures what it is intended to measure" (Berelson, 1952) are considered as unproductive; it is instead proposed that reliability is identified with truth, and validity with relevancy.

The main theme is, however, reliability and content analysis. Three different kinds of content analysis are discerned, and the requirement of reliability is applied to each of them. The main conclusion—and this will be the third thesis—is that the traditional position of content analysts that "regardless of who does the analysis or when it is done, the same data should be secured under similar conditions" (Berelson, 1952) is not tenable when applied to what could be called "content analysis proper"—that is, semantic content analysis.

AUTHOR'S NOTE: This chapter was written within a content analytical research program—Cultural Indicators: The Swedish Symbol System, 1945-1975—initiated and coordinated by Karl Erik Rosengren and financed by the Bank of Sweden Tercentenary Foundation. Kjell Nowak, Ragnar Ohlsson, and Karl Erik Rosengren read an earlier version and gave me some useful comments. During heated discussions on the meanings of "reliability" and "validity" Cecilia Feilitzen made several pertinent points. David Jones improved my English.

THE OBJECT OF SCIENCE

Science can be delineated in many different ways. Some definitions refer to institutional circumstances; others contain criteria that deal with the subject matter or internal characteristics of this kind of activity. Concepts of the first kind might be productive in sociological, historical, or policy-oriented contexts; but those which refer to subject matter and theoretical and methodological procedures are more adequate when it comes to judging the scientific status of individual efforts. In this study attention is directed toward questions of the second kind. What activities can justly be called "scientific," and what are the scientific grounds for assessing the results of such labor?

It is a difficult and controversial question whether it is necessary that a scientific result be *true*. On the one hand, the general opinion is that the object of science is to give us knowledge, and thus to produce true propositions. (Here I am assuming the prevalent notion of knowledge, according to which knowledge is justified and true belief; see Plato [1956] or Lehrer [1974].) On the other hand, we know that the history of science is to a large extent a narrative about delusions, fallacies, and mistaken or otherwise unsuccessful measurements. And it would be fanatical in some measure to prefer a true result which leads to human misery rather than a false result which has no effects at all or which happens to alleviate the human predicament.

One way of escaping this dilemma is to distinguish between the question of whether a result has any *value,* in itself or with regard to its consequences, and the question of whether it has any *value as science*. We could then maintain that truth is a necessary condition for a proposition to be accepted as scientific, and at the same time we can hold that a result that is false and thus unscientific has greater value than one which is scientific and thus true. This is simply to uphold the distinction between internal and external standards for the assessment of scientific work and its results. A result, when measured with an external standard, can be superior to one which is superior according to an internal standard.

This chapter, however, deals only with internal criteria, and, as such, the criterion of truth is certainly valid.

But truth cannot be the only criterion of whether an activity or a result is scientific or not. We must differentiate between science and *adiaphor*; scientific investigations cannot deal with trifles. *Relevancy*—that is, importance in relation to some theory or some practical, moral, or political problem—is also something that should be required.

The crux is, however, that it is seldom easy to know whether or not a result is true or relevant. In order to be *certain* that the results from a particular measurement (for example, a coding procedure) are true, one must, if not conduct the analysis oneself, replicate the investigation; and in order to *know* that the results are relevant, one must, in many cases, have an intimate understanding of the theory it is assumed to be relevant for, and master the theory as well as the scientist who maintains that it is relevant. As these requirements are seldom fulfilled, or even possible to fulfill, we must ordinarily try to trust the scientists and let future developments tell us whether the results were productive and trustworthy.

This actualizes the question of whether it is possible to find any practicable *criteria* which can be employed when assessing the truth and/or relevance of the results from a certain measurement. Within the social sciences, this issue concerning scientific trustworthiness and productivity has often been discussed under the heading of *"reliability and validity."* These discussions, however, have often been rather impenetrable. There are numerous conceptions of reliability and validity used by different authors, and it is sometimes difficult to grasp them in detail and to understand precisely how they are related to each other.

Moreover, it seems to be the case that the conceptions used in the discussions of reliability and validity in *content analysis* are taken from the theories and methodologies employed within psychology; and it cannot be taken for granted that the concepts constructed in order to solve certain problems connected with testing and interviewing are adequate instruments, in all respects, for the appraisal of the results of a content analysis.

Further complications are due to the fact that content analysis is a rather heterogeneous field of research. When discussing reliability and validity in content analysis, we should distinguish among three different kinds of content analysis: syntactic, semantic, and pragmatic.

We are thus confronted with at least three different tasks with great significance for the methodology of content analysis: (1) to discuss which concepts of reliability are adequate for the different kinds of content analysis; (2) to discuss which concepts of validity are adequate for the different kinds of content analysis; and (3) to discuss how these requirements are related to each other. Each of these questions is, however, a far-reaching one. In this article I will lay stress upon problems concerning reliability.

It is a common view that the requirement of reliability is weaker than the requirement of validity. It is assumed that reliability is a necessary but not sufficient condition for validity; validity is taken to imply (but not to be implied by) reliability (see Holsti, 1969: 142). Thus, it seems wise to begin with the problem of reliability. Is it really necessary that a content analysis is reliable?

MEANINGS OF "RELIABILITY"

Before we can answer this question, we must fix our ideas on what reliability is. This, however, is a difficult task in itself. The formulations of this requirement are often impaired by a certain vagueness. The following quotation from Kaplan and Goldsen (1965: 83) is a relatively early formulation of the requirement of reliability, as this requirement is usually understood within the mainstream tradition of content analysis:

> By the reliability of a measurement with respect to a given variable is meant the constancy of its results as that variable assumes different values. The variables usually considered are: the measuring event (e.g., the same person using the same ruler in successive measurements of the same object); the measuring instrument (e.g., different "forms" of an intelligence test); the person doing the measuring (e.g., different eyewitnesses of the same event).

Twenty years later the core of the same thought has found a more laconic expression in Holsti (1969: 135):

> If research is to satisfy the requirement of objectivity, measures and procedures must be reliable; i.e., repeated measures with the same instrument on a given sample of data should yield similar results.

In this passage we find a connection between the concepts of *objectivity* and of *reliability*. This is only as it should be; it is natural to assume that an objective result is independent of the subject who conducted the investigation. Here, however, we must distinguish between the factual or *ontological* problem—what makes the result true?—and the *epistemic* or methodological problem—how do we come to know that a result is true or false?

Ontological independence is a two-place relation. A datum is ontologically independent of its producer (for example, a coder) when it is not *about* the producer. The question of epistemic independence is more complicated and also more controversial. Epistemic independence is a three-place relation; it is a relation between a producer, P, a result, r, and a set of possible producers, S. Let us say that a certain result, r_1, produced by P_1 is epistemically independent in relation to a population of coders, S_1, to the extent that it is possible for the members of S_1 to *know* r_1 without first acquiring mental characteristics that P_1 already has. A datum is thus maximally independent, in this sense, in a certain population of coders if every member of this population would produce it. The epistemic independence is a matter of degree, insofar as more or less of more or less specific capacities and knowledges of the coder can be made use of in the process of measuring a message.

It is a matter of course that the results of a content analysis in most cases must be ontologically independent of the coding subject. This is due to the fact that the subject matter of the research is usually the contents of a certain text and/or picture and not the observing subject or his or her reactions. The exception to this is a certain form of pragmatical content analysis (see page 61).

A traditional endeavor within the field of content analysis has been to make the results as independent as possible, in the epistemic sense, in a population of coders which is maximally large. The ideal coder is a man who is a mass-produced machine. In the classic account of the method of content analysis (Berelson, 1952), we find, again, that "Regardless of who does the analysis or when it is done, the same data should be secured under similar conditions."

This endeavor to make the results as independent as possible has both good and bad sides. It has been possible, thus, to analyze large bodies of material; but the cost has been the impossibility of affording the coder more demanding tasks, which results in a certain kind of superficiality. What must be kept in mind when assessing this endeavor is that it is only contingent upon economic and other practical problems. There are no fundamental scientific reasons for a demand that the epistemic independence should be maximized. It is only ontological independence that is required by an adequate concept of objectivity. (As already mentioned, there is one exception to this rule—see page 61).

One difficulty with the formulations in the quotations from Kaplan and Goldsen (1965) and Holsti (1969) is their vagueness. When are two results "similar," and what does the "constancy" of the results of a measurement amount to, if we make this phrase more specific? The ground for this indeterminacy is that their conceptualizations of the requirement of reliability include references to the measuring event and to the person doing the measuring. We obviously cannot demand that a content analysis should be replicable by *any* person under *whatever* circumstances. This means that the formulae for their versions of this requirement must be open on vital points, unless we specify in detail which persons can, under what circumstances, replicate a reliable result; and that seems to be a rather forlorn enterprise.

The concept of reliability in most cases includes a requirement of *intersubjective testability*. One way of making these concepts more reasonable is to demand that only persons "properly equipped with intelligence and the technical devices of observation and experimentation" make measurements that yield similar results. Another way of making the concept of intersubjectivity less exacting and more feasible is not to prescribe that repeated measurements shall always, *in fact,* yield similar results, but that it is *possible* for one scientist to replicate the findings of the efforts of another scientist. Both these expedients are employed in the following passage from Feigl (1953: 11):

> *Intersubjective Testability.* This is only a more adequate formulation of what is generally meant by the "objectivity" of science. What is here involved is not only the freedom from personal or cultural bias or partiality, but—even more fundamentally—the requirement that the knowledge claims of science be in principle capable of test (confirmation or disconfirmation, at least indirectly and to some degree) on the part of any person properly equipped with intelligence and the technical devices of observation or experimentation. The term *intersubjective* stresses the social nature of the scientific enterprise. If there be any "truths" that are accessible only to privileged individuals, such as mystics or visionaires—that is, knowledge claims which by their very nature cannot independently be checked by anyone else—then such "truths" are not of the kind that we seek in the sciences. The criterion of intersubjective testability thus delimits the scientific from the nonscientific activities of man.

But what kind of possibility is involved in this concept of intersubjectivity and in the corresponding concepts of reliability? It cannot be a logical possibility, although Feigl's use of the term "in principle" suggests this interpreation. This interpretation would make the requirements of inter-subjectivity and reliability sheer trivialities. They will then only contain the proposition that it will not be a contradiction if two different persons produce the same result when using the same ruler in measuring the same object.

If the possibility referred to is some kind of empirical or factual possibility, we are again faced with the question of under which conditions it will be realized. Unless these are specified, the claim does not have much meaning. This means that the traditional concepts of reliability employed within content analysis turn out to be rather elusive when we try to pinpoint them.

As far as I can see, the best way out of these difficulties is to adopt a concept of reliability that is different from that usually referred to in discussions of content analysis in the social sciences but which is more directly connected with the object of science, as this was delineated in the first section. It is certainly not a new concept—I will refer below to its use within the humanities—and it is sometimes alluded to, at least implicitly, when social scientists discuss problems of reliability. Thus, for example, Krippendorff (1978: 4) distinguishes between the following three kinds of reliability:

> *Stability* is the degree to which a process is invariant over time, i.e. yields the same results at different points in time.

Reproducibility is the degree to which a process can be recreated under varying circumstances, different locations, involving different material forms, i.e. yields the same results despite different implementations.
Accuracy is the degree to which a process conforms in effect to a known standard, i.e., yields the desired results in a variety of circumstances.

The requirements of stability and reproducibility are again open to the charge of being too vague; and it is not possible to assess the scientific adequacy of the concept of accuracy until we know with which standard it is proposed to compare the results. There is, however, one interpretation of the requirement of accuracy, according to which it is identical with that notion of reliability which seems to be most productive in a scientific context; namely, that conception which identifies reliability with *truth*. We get this interpretation if we assume that the standard referred to in the definiens of Krippendorff's definition is *reality*. An accurate result is one that corresponds to reality, which means that it is true. (We should also omit the word "known" that occurs in Krippendorff's formulation; what is important is not that the results of our measurements correspond to a known reality, but simply that they correspond to reality.)

Krippendorff himself, however, holds that when reality is the standard, then the requirement of accuracy is turned into a concept of validity and thence no longer is a concept of reliability. It is difficult for me to see the justification for this conceptual jungle. At this point it seems urgent to reconsider the relations between reliability and validity.

RELIABILITY AND VALIDITY

There are, as was stressed in the first section of this chapter, *two fundamental questions* that can be asked from a scientific point of view concerning the results of a scientific effort. First, are the measurements *correct* and the results *true*? The second question pertains to the *importance* of the results. Are they relevant in relation to a hypothesis or scientific theory, or are they important in the sense that they shed light upon some problem or proposition of common interest?

As far as I can see, it is the *truth*, and nothing but the truth, that the requirement of reliability *should* be about. Many social scientists will react against a thesis like this. In fact, the motive behind the identification of reliability with some elusive kind of intersubjectivity, instead of identifying reliability with veracity, in too many instances seems to be the supposition that "truth" is an extremely difficult notion. But compared with other key notions within science, the concept of truth is not particularly difficult to grasp; what is difficult is to reach the truth—that is, to accept true propositions and reject false propositions about reality. And, as we have already seen, social scientists have a tendency to assign problems of truth to the domain of validity. But if we scrutinize these ideas of validity, we will find that, insofar as they pertain to raw data, they refer to the relevancy of the data. I have found one exception to this, predictive validity, which pertains to relevancy and truth at the same time (see below).

The subject matter of the humanities is in many ways even more evasive and difficult to penetrate than that of the social sciences. All the same, it seems to be more common among humanists than among social scientists to equate reliability with truth. We can, for instance, find the following statement (in Mandelbaum (1977):

> When the question of the objectivity of historical knowledge is raised, the issue is one concerning the accuracy or reliability of that knowledge; but not all uses of the concept of objectivity are equally concerned with this problem, *which has to do with the truth of what is actually affirmed or denied in the judgments we made* [p. 146; italics added].

Thus, the source of the proposal to equate *reliability* with veracity can be said to lie within the humanities. My second proposal is that we take the other fundamental problem—that of the relevancy of the raw data—to be the domain of the concept of *validity*. The standard formula for this requirement is "the extent to which an instrument is measuring what it is intended to measure" (see Berelson, 1952: 169; Holsti, 1969: 142; or Janis, 1965: 58). This formulation can be interpreted in various directions. Let us use the term "realism" as a label for the goal referred to by Berelson et al.

Realism is not the same as truth; a realistic description need not be literally true, but it must help us acquire an adequate or realistic picture of the world either by telling us straightforward truths or by offering us points of view, concepts, and the like which are fruitful in relation to this purpose.

Let us in this context consider a given instrument—for example, a thermometer—and apply Berelson's formula to it. This gives rise to two different questions: First, *what* does it measure; which variables is it assigning values to? The answer to this question is that it purports to measure temperature, that the values derived from its specific applications are various degrees of temperature. This is *minimal* realism, that a measurement or description is anchored in reality in the sense that it pertains to significant aspects of the world. But then we can go on to ask the further question of *how* it measures temperature; that is, if it measures temperature correctly and thus measures *the* temperature. This is *maximal* realism.

We can distinguish among three different interpretations of the requirement that the results of a measurement should be about "what it is intended to measure"—that is, three different meanings of "realism."

(1) The realism of a certain set of data consists of its *correspondence* to some facts—i.e., its truth.
(2) The realism of a certain set of data consists of its *connection* with some significant problem or with the purpose of the study—i.e., its relevancy.
(3) The realism of a certain set of data consists of its *correspondence* with precisely those facts that are *connected* with some real problem or the purpose of the study—i.e., truth and relevancy.

Discussions of validity and of the relation between reliability and validity are often somewhat difficult to follow, due to the fact that the meaning of the term "validity" oscillates between items (2) and (3).

In Krippendorf (1977) an elaborate discussion on problems of validity within content analysis begins with the following remarks:

> Generally, "validity" designates a quality that compels one to accept scientific results as evidence. Its closest relative is "objective truth." As such, this definition is too broad to be useful and finer differentiations are called for [p. 4].

Here Krippendorff seems to equate the meaning of the term "validity" with the interpretation given in (1); this is in accord with his proposition, referred to earlier, that the concept of accuracy turns into a concept of validity when "accuracy" is defined as correspondence with reality. Then he goes on to distinguish among eight different kinds of validity; and of these, five are forms of external validity or "validity proper." The first of these proper kinds of validity is "semantical validity":

> the degree to which a method is sensitive to relevant semantical distinctions in the data being analyzed. It is the degree to which processes in a content analysis conform to the semantics of the source language [Krippendorf, 1977: 6].

In Andrén et al. (1978: 44), this concept is described in the following way:

> There are several concepts of validity. According to one of them it is a measure of the correspondence between the meaning which is explicitly defined by the criteria of a classification system and the ordinary meaning of the terms used to name the categories.

And when Berelson (1952: 171) terminates his discussion on the problem of validity with the following words, he is likely to have this conception in mind:

> However, in most cases validity does not seem to be a major problem in content analysis. Most of the time, careful definition of categories

and judicious and alternative selection of indicators will take care of the matter.

This concept of semantical validity is, thus, rather often employed in the literature on content analysis. It has a natural application to that common form of content analysis which has the simple object of *describing* the contents of more or less large bodies of messages. The point of this claim is to secure that the results of such studies are realistic in sense (2).

A *translation* of a text, T_1, in one language, L_1, into another text, T_2, in another language, L_2, can be considered as the most primitive as well as most common form of content analysis. A translation of a text in L_1 in terms of L_2 will have *semantical validity* insofar as the concepts that are expressed in L_2 are identical to those expressed in L_1. To the same degree as a translation of T_1 into T_2 has semantical validity, it is related to the problem "what is said in T_1?" This means that the concept of semantical validity is an instance of (2); it claims that the results should be relevant in relation to the object of the investigation (for example, to depict the meaning of a certain message). And a translation can be an answer to the question "what is said?" without being the true or correct answer. Semantic validity does not guarantee that the results are true, only that the concept or variables employed in the study are adequate in relation to its purpose. Realism in the stronger sense of (3) is not claimed.

This also holds for the second concept of validity discussed by Krippendorff, *sampling validity*. This concept is described in the following way:

> sampling validity assesses the degree to which a collection of data can be regarded as representative of a given universe or as in some specific respect similar to another sample from the same universe obtained by the same method [1977: 26].

The requirement of sampling validity obviously does not aim at securing the truth of the data, but only their relevance in relation to hypotheses about a wider or another universe than that from which the data were collected. Again, we have an instance of (2).

This also holds for the third kind of validity discussed in Krippendorff (1977: 7)–*correlational validity.*

> *Correlational validity* is the degree to which findings obtained by one method correlate with findings obtained by another and justifies in a sense their substitutability.

The fourth example of a concept of validity given by Krippendorff is *predictive validity*; and it is delineated as "the degree to which predictions obtained by a method agree with directly observable facts (p. 7)."

Here, two different things are required: first, that the results can be used in a prediction; second, that this prediction holds. This means that predictive validity is an instance of (3); truth and relevancy are required at the same time. I also assume that a concept of validity of this strength is presupposed when it is said that validity implies reliability.

The last concept of validity mentioned in Krippendorff's account is *construct validity*. When writing about this concept he says:

> The argument underlying construct validation generally is again straightforward:
> — a valid theory, established hypotheses or at least some defend-able generalizations about the source are given,
> — The construction of the analytical procedure (method) is logic-ally derivable from that theory so that the analysis is in fact a valid operationalization of that theory,
> — therefore the inferences now drawn from data by the method may be accepted on account of the underlying theory's inde-pendently established validity.
> Thus, in construct validation of content analysis, *validity derives entirely from established theory,* tested hypotheses and general-izations about the source, whatever the evidential status of this knowledge might be at the time [1977: 51; italics in original].

If Krippendorff's account of construct validity is adequate, it seems quite clear that it has nothing to do with truth or correspondence between the results and the facts of the case; the truth of a certain datum or result cannot be established by relating it to a theory. To believe that would mean a regression to an old-fashioned rationalism that is foreign to the empiricist tenet of modern social science. What is at stake here is the productivity of the results. Results are not infrequently assumed to be interesting insofar as they are connected with some adequate theory. Construct validity, thus, does not lie in the correspondence between reality and the results, but in the relationship between the results of an investigation and some theory supposed to shed light upon the problems or questions behind the investigation. Again, it seems as if we are con-fronted with an instance of (2).

Let us now apply the concepts of truth and relevancy to that part of the methodological machinery of content analysis described by Krippen-dorff. First, validity is said to be basically related to truth. Then we meet four concepts of validity that are not related to truth but to relevancy; and one concept that is a combination of a requirement of truth and a requirement of relevancy. We have also met the prevalent notion that validity implies reliability, and this position presupposes a conception of a more complicated kind—for example, the third concept of realism given earlier.

When described in this way, the situation is, although puzzling, still comprehensible. But if we do not employ the concepts of truth and relevancy—and few content analysts do—and make use of only a mixed variety of concepts of validity and reliability, the situation must come near to *chaos.*

My two proposals are, then, that we identify the reliability of raw data with their truth and the validity of raw data with their relevancy. Thus, we achieve a conceptual apparatus that is maximally stringent. One distinct concept deals with the first aspect of realism (that is, truth); this is the concept of reliability. Another distinct concept deals with the second aspect of realism (that is, relevancy); this is the concept of validity. We can combine these concepts and thus cover the strongest concept of realism, (3). This is the *ideal*—a result that is both true and relevant, reliable *and* valid.

Let me end this section on reliability and validity by exemplifying what I mean by these terms and thus explain why I hold that there are no logical or internal relations between these concepts. Let us consider the result of a simple measurement, "the barometer has fallen ten points in the last two hours," and ask if this is a reliable and valid proposition.

The first question is, then, identical with the question of whether it is true or false that the barometer has fallen ten points in two hours. If it is a fact that the barometer has fallen ten points in two hours, then the result is reliable; otherwise, it is not reliable.

The second question is identical with the question of whether there is any interesting hypothesis or theory to which the proposition that the barometer has fallen ten points in two hours can be related. This proposition is relevant in relation to the significant hypothesis that there will be rain. The result has validity.

The conditional which says that *if* the barometer has fallen ten points in two hours, *then* it will be rain can be valid without it being the case that the barometer has fallen ten points in two hours. This means that the conceptions proposed here are such that the standard thesis that reliability is presupposed by validity is not true. Now we have two distinct concepts that deal with *different* subject matters; therefore there can be no logical relations between them. Perhaps this also means that it will be less difficult to grasp them individually.

Here the discussion about the meanings of "reliability" and "validity" and the relation between them must come to an end. Let us now return to the concrete criterion of reliability that has become a standard methodological requirement within content analysis; the demand that the results must be epistemically independent, that "regardless of who does the analysis, the same data should be secured."

CONTENT ANALYSIS AND EPISTEMIC INDEPENDENCE

It has already been mentioned that there are different kinds of content analysis—pragmatic, semantic, and syntactic. The answer to the question of whether epistemic independence is possible and desirable will probably vary depending on which kind of content analysis the question refers to. The next step in the argument will thus be to try to elucidate these distinctions.

Speech acts or pictures can be considered from different points of view. We can focus our attention on:

(1) the linguistic vehicle—the words and sentences used to express a meaning;
(2) the meanings—concepts or propositions—that, according to the linguistic conventions, are expressed by those light- or sound-waves that are the constituents of the linguistic vehicles;
(3) what the linguistic expressions are referring to, according to the conventions that define the language to which these expressions belong;
(4) the intentions of the communicator, the goals of the communication;
(5) the meanings and references which the communicator ascribes to the linguistic expressions;
(6) the meanings and references which the receiver or audience ascribes to the linguistic expressions; and
(7) the effects (individual or social) of the speech acts.

This list can, of course, be made longer. But it is always possible to classify a proposition concerning a speech act as belonging to one of three different categories, according to its subject matter. Insofar as a proposition refers to the linguistic vehicle used in a speech act, it is *syntactic*. A *semantic* proposition tells us something about which references or meanings the speech act has according to the linguistic rules. Finally, a *pragmatic* proposition contains some reference to the sender or the receiver of the speech act. This means that problems pertaining to (1) are syntactic; that those pertaining to (2) or (3) are semantic; and that (4)-(7) exemplify different pragmatic aspects of a communication.

We can, then, describe a content analysis as syntactic if it only results in or presupposes syntactic propositions; as semantic if it results in or presupposes at least one semantic proposition; and as pragmatic if it results in or presupposes at least one pragmatic proposition.

These distinctions are natural and are certainly implied in many passages in the annals of philosophy or linguistics. Modern formulations of these categories are based upon the works of C.S. Pierce. Morris (1938) contains the first, and perhaps still the best, systematic account of these distinctions.

Janis (1965) provides a classification of different kinds of content analysis that is seemingly identical with the distinctions drawn here between syntactic, semantic, and pragmatic content analysis.

1. *Pragmatical Content Analysis*—procedures which classify signs according to their probable causes or effects (e.g., counting the number of times that something is said which is likely to have the effect of producing favorable attitudes toward Germany in a given audience).
2. *Semantical Content Analysis*—procedures which classify signs according to their meanings (e.g., counting the number of times that Germany is referred to, irrespective of the particular words that may be used to make the reference).
3. *Sign-Vehicle Analysis*—procedures which classify content according to the psychophysical properties of the sign (e.g., counting the number of times the word "Germany" appears) [1965: 57].

What Janis calls "Sign-Vehicle Analysis" is obviously the same as syntactic content analysis. However, various passages in Janis' article imply that what he refers to as "semantical content analysis" is not semantic content analysis. This is because Janis employs a pragmatic concept of meaning; to say something about the meaning of an expression is, according to his conception, to make a proposition concerning its tendency to have a certain kind of response. He writes,

those procedures which take account of the *meanings* of signs (semantical content analysis) estimate the semantical signification responses of the sign interpreters [pp. 57-58].

He further states that the meaning of an expression is "an extremely complex and variable type of human response" (p. 59). This means that those propositions which Janis calls "semantical" because they deal with "semantical signification responses" in fact are pragmatical because they contain explicit references to the receiver or audience. Janis' conceptual scheme, thus, only allows for two forms of content analysis: syntactic and pragmatic.

Here we are confronted with a very difficult philosophical problem: is it feasible to analyze semantic entities (that is, concepts and propositions) without making use of pragmatic concepts or references to concrete uses of language? There do not seem to have been any entirely successful attempts to construe a behavioristic or otherwise pragmatic theory of meaning. Quine (1960) contains probably the most ambitious and ingenious effort of this kind, but there is no unanimous opinion that he has succeeded in his main ambitions. (Natural languages contain certain structures, called "opaque contexts," that Quine's theory cannot account for. Quine himself, however, seems to hold that this inadequacy of his theory is due to deficiencies within the natural languages and that his theory cannot be blamed on that account.) Let us, consequently, leave open the question of whether it is possible to eliminate every semantic element in a theory of meaning or language; therefore, we should not reject as meaningless or superfluous the employment of three different categories of content analysis.

It would be odd to demand indiscriminately that every content analysis should be epistemically independent. It would be equally odd to claim that the results of every investigation within the humanities or social sciences could have been accomplished by anyone. Scientific progress is sometimes contingent upon forms of creativity and/or perseverance that cannot be ascribed to every scientist (see Bergstrom, 1977).

From a strictly scientific point of view, the important question is whether or not a measurement is correct and whether the results are true or false; whether the results can be replicated by anyone is a problem with no fundamental scientific significance. But, as was already mentioned, here we meet with the practical problem that we are seldom in a position to know if the measurements of an investigation are correct or incorrect. In most cases we will nurture more or less well-founded doubts concerning the trustworthiness of the results.

One convenient way of assessing the trustworthiness of a result appears to be to replicate the measurement and then see if the results remain the same. There is, however, a certain uncertainty associated with this method. It is certainly true that a high degree of consensus is something positive. If two independent measurements give the same results, this is a strong indication of the correctness of the measurements and the truth of the results. But the converse does not necessarily hold; lack of agreement does not in itself imply that the results are flawed by serious errors. Let us assume that we have two different measurements of the same objects and that the results are not identical. What can be inferred from this is that it cannot be the case that both results are true; one of the results, or both, must be false.

The results that are presented in a research report must necessarily stem from one particular measurement. A coefficient of "reliability" pertains to two different measurements, and only one of these will be the source of the results presented in the report. Let us assume that we read a report from an investigation where the results are produced by A (A could be either an individual or a group of individuals) and with a coefficient that refers to the measurements of A and the measurements of another coder, or group of coders, B. This coefficient, however, does not enable us to assess how wrong the results presented are; we do not know if the disagreements revealed by the coefficient are due to the fact that A has made incorrect measurements or if the disagreements are caused by B's errors, or if they involve mistakes on both sides.

There is thus a possibility that the results of an investigation are completely correct or true at the same time as the coefficient of "reliability" is low because the control-coder has done a poor job. This means that the conventional coefficients are not informative enough. (In the last section of this article I will refer to a procedure which gives us more relevant coefficients.)

The prevalent belief that scientific measurements ought to be intra- and intersubjectively reproducible is connected with the notion of natural science as an ideal for all scientific activity. A distinctive feature of modern science is that it makes use of mechanical devices which, to a large extent, make the measurements and observations; and this means that the raw data of these sciences in many cases will be epistemically independent of the scientist. The question is, however, if it is possible and productive to try to make content analysis and natural science similar in this respect; or if this ideal will become a *Procrustean bed* for content analysis. Is it really an intelligent policy not to make use of the special talents—accuracy, acumen, discernment, creativity, and tenacity—that the coder might possibly possess?

When carrying out a *syntactic* content analysis it is not normally necessary (although it is practical) to derive advantage from the specific capacities of a human coder. The observations made within a syntactic investigation are often rather simple and the categories employed uncomplicated. How frequent do the words "freedom" and "justice" occur in the editorials of conservative and socialist newspapers? How extensive is advertising in different media? Tasks of these kinds can, at least in principle, be assigned to machines that are not human.

However, in this context it should be kept in mind that the coding process includes two different phases: observation and the classification of that which has been observed. Perhaps the observations of a syntactic analysis can always be done by a machine. But we cannot preclude the possibility that it will prove to be productive to adopt categories that are so complex that the investigator will not manage to define beforehand mechanically applicable rules for the classification of the observations. In such cases it is necessary to have a coder who understand the categories and thus has the capacity to transcend in a correct way the explicit rules of classification.

When it comes to *semantic* content analysis—analyses in which it is presupposed that the observer understands or correctly interprets the material of the investigation—it will in many instances be counter-productive to aim at eliminating the influences of the human skills of the coder; in this context it seems instead wise to exploit the linguistic and social competence of human beings.

Let us here consider an example of a rather trivial kind of semantic content analysis. The assumed object of the analysis is simply to count how many persons figure in various advertisements and to classify these persons according to their gender. Today there are no machines (and I doubt if there ever will be) that have the ability to decide accurately if an ill-defined structure of dots and lines refers to a person or, perhaps, a picture of a person or a projecting rock. And it may be even more difficult to decide the gender of the person the structure of dots and lines may be assumed to portray without having recourse to that specific sensitivity on these matters which are gradually acquired and developed during a long period, comprising decades, and which it is impossible to codify in all details.

To count heads is a comparatively simple task. It is usually more complicated to infer the semantic contents of a text and/or picture. A process of this kind necessarily involves *interpretation.* To interpret a text and/or picture is to identify those concepts or propositions that are expressed by it or to determine what the text or picture refers to. The latter task might appear less difficult; but knowledge about the extension of an expression, its references, presupposes knowledge about its intension or conceptual and propositional contents.

To interpret a certain text or picture is to apply to its syntactic surface those linguistic rules that define the language of the text or picture. This is indeed an intricate procedure. First, there is a multiplicity and a variety of linguistic rules; again, we can distinguish between syntactic, semantic, and pragmatic rules. Second, these rules are more or less indeterminate and more or less explicitly known within the linguistic community. Third, these rules interact in ways that are difficult to grasp and explain.

The process of interpretation can be compared with the procedure of proving or inferring a mathematical theorem (see Andrén et al., 1978: 46). Both of these processes involve the adoption of intuitively known rules—rules of interpretation and rules of inference.

It holds for every proposition that it is or is not expressed in a certain text or picture; and it holds for every mathematical proposition that it is or is not a theorem within a certain calculus. Sometimes it is possible to show that a proposition *is* expressed in a certain text/picture or to prove that a mathematical proposition *is* a theorem. But in many cases it is not possible to show that it is *not* the case that a certain proposition, p, is expressed or that a certain mathematical proposition, m, is a theorem. It could be that we have not discerned that which shows that p is expressed or that m is a theorem. Only if we can show that p is incompatible with some interpretation for which we have good grounds, or if we can prove that m is inconsistent with some mathematical proposition that can be proved, do we have good reason to assume that p is *not* expressed or that m is *not* a theorem. But even then we cannot be sure, the text or the calculus might be inconsistent.

The coding of semantic contents is thus, as is the proof of a theorem, a constructive process. If two coders produce different results—one of them records that the proposition p is expressed in the material of the investigation and the other does not record the presence of p—this must not be due to carelessness or laxity. Assuming that p was in fact expressed in the material investigated, we can say instead that the disagreement was contingent upon the creativity or sensibility of the first coder.

The moral to be drawn from this argument is that it will not always be feasible to prescribe that two independent coders must attain the same data, if their task is to record semantic contents. A requirement to this effect will sometimes be as misplaced as a requirement that Professor Cannonball's analysis of the poem "Death is My Harbour" will be acceptable only if Dr. Krapp gives an identical description of this poem.

Let us now turn to the problem of epistemic independence in relation to the third kind of content analysis. There are two different objects of a *pragmatic* content analysis: either to reveal the intentions or mental life of the communicator or to make propositions about the reactions of the receivers or the effects or consequences of the communication.

Content analysis rose in importance during World War II, since it was believed in the United States to be possible by systematic analyses of German texts and more or less official documents to detect the plans, thoughts, attitudes, and internal conflicts of the Nazis. Analyses of this kind require that the coder possess special forms of knowledge and/or sensitivity for nuances and the like; and thus it seems counterproductive to demand that different scientists must attain the same results. In addition, here we can apply the analogy from the analysis of literary works.

Someone will perhaps object that the creative aspect of the work of the scientist pertains to the analysis of the results of the measurements or to the process of inferring conclusions from them. This objection, however, presupposes that the coding procedures deal only with syntactic contents; otherwise, if the coder is required to record semantic contents, this objection can be rejected with reference to the discussion above. Syntactic data are not, however, as relevant as semantic data, if the pragmatic object of the investigation is to trace the beliefs and attitudes of the communicator. In a context of this kind, the form or surface of a message is not as pertinent as its content or deep structure.[1]

When it comes to the other kind of pragmatic analyses—those which have the purpose of gaining knowledge about the reactions in the audience or the effects and consequences of the communication—the case will be rather different. The object of such studies is often to obtain the ordinary responses to the various elements of the analyzed communications. This means that more particular and divergent readings are of no interest; instead, it is important to obtain converging data from different coders who are representative of the population whose understanding of the material analyzed is the target of the investigation (that is, data which are epistemically independent of but ontologically dependent on the coding subjects). The data are about the "signification responses" of the coders, but they should be about impersonal or generalized responses. That epistemic independence is considered as a strong *desideratum* within the Anglo-Saxon tradition of content analysis is perhaps to some extent due to the fact that the pragmatic object alluded to here is often presupposed. Can it, then, ever be reasonable *not* to make a pragmatic presupposition of that kind?

SEMANTIC VERSUS PRAGMATIC CONTENT ANALYSIS

One tentative conclusion of this study has been that it is not always productive to require that a semantic content analysis be epistemically independent. This actualizes the question of whether semantic analyses can have any value per se. Can a result which says that a certain proposition is expressed by a certain text and/or picture be of any interest, unless it can be assumed that the audience will interpret the text/picture in that direction? Is it possible to conduct an investigation that has no pragmatic elements? And if it is possible, will it be desirable or fruitful?

Janis would unhesitatingly answer both these questions in the negative.

In effect, content analysis procedures assume a one-to-one correspondence between certain sign-vehicles and certain signification responses (What is taken account of when the sign-vehicle is perceived). So far as I know, there are no techniques available for the direct measurement of signification response. There are a number of possible ways in which signification responses might be determined—for example, by means of a questionnaire which requires each subject to indicate the (semantical) category which is most appropriate for given sign-vehicles. If such a technique were available it would be possible to make a direct test of the validity of content analysis procedures by presenting a representative sample of the contents to a representative sample of the audience or the communicator [1965: 68-69].

It is, of course, to be expected that Janis would endorse the primacy of pragmatics. We have already seen that by accepting a pragmatic theory of meaning, he denies the existence of semantics as a distinct discipline. Furthermore, he belongs to a tradition within social science in which the interest is focused on the individual, on the intentions of singular actors or on the responses of individuals. Another significant feature of this tradition is the interest of that which is given. Below I will suggest that sometimes it will instead be productive to turn our attention on problems pertaining to what is *not* present in a given material and on *possible,* as opposed to actual, effects of a communication.

However, it will not be possible to discuss the productivity of semantic investigations that are not connected with pragmatic purposes unless we have an idea of what it means when a certain proposition is expressed by a given text/picture. This problem can be said to be *the* problem of an analytic linguistic philosophy as well as of the continental theory of meaning and interpretation called "Hermeneutics"; indeed, it is not possible to give an adequate account of this complex of problems in this context. Here it is only possible to make some rather rough statements.

The question of whether a certain proposition is contained within a given communication cannot be given an absolute answer; the answer will depend upon the *linguistic rules* that are applied to the communication. An interpretation is valid in relation to a particular set of conventions. Again, we can make use of the distinctions among syntactics, semantics, and pragmatics. Let us classify and describe a linguistic rule by relating it to one or the other of these three domains.

Syntactic rules determine whether a given string or sequence of words or other signs is possible or permitted within a certain language.

Semantic rules relate concepts to words and sometimes to longer expressions than words. Most words can express different concepts, and most concepts can be expressed by different words. Which concept a concrete instance of a word is expressing depends on the linguistic structure of the communication it belongs to and on the social context within which it is published. We can say that the semantic rules define a set of possible interpretations for every sentence or permissible string of signs.

When choosing between these possible interpretations in order to grasp that interpretation which is the most adequate, we will employ *pragmatic rules.* A pragmatic rule tells us which sentences it is *comme il faut* to use in a given context in order to express a certain belief or attitude. By the same token, they tell us which ways of understanding a given sentence are standard or normal in a given audience.

There is no natural language such that *one* interpretation of a given sentence is the true or correct one. There will always be a variety of possible interpretations; and quite often more than one of these interpretations will be plausible enough. But which of these plausible interpretations will be the *most* adequate? The answer to this question will be contingent upon the object of the interpretation; whether the aim is knowledge about the subject matter of the analyzed text/picture, knowledge about the beliefs and intentions of the communicator, knowledge about the social context of the communication, knowledge about long-range effects of the communication, and so on.

A semantic investigation into the propositional contents of a text picture always has *some* relation to intentions and effects. As was pointed out above, what is expressed by a text/picture is contingent upon a set of rules; and these rules hold for human behavior, the performance of a speech act, or the mental act of understanding or interpreting a speech act or set of signs. A semantic hypothesis to the effect that a certain proposition, p, is expressed by a given sentence, s, tells us how the audience *ought* to understand s according to exclusively linguistic criteria; or how they *should* understand s if they understand the language to which s belongs. By the same token, we could also say that the semantic hypothesis tells us which belief or attitude the communicator *ought* to have, from a purely linguistic point of view, when uttering s; or which belief or attitude he aims at expressing by s, if he is sincere and understands the language to which s belongs—namely, the belief or attitude that has p as its content.

With this sketch as a background, I will briefly discuss whether a semantic investigation can be anything but a means of attaining *empirical* knowledge—as opposed to the kind of *normative* knowledge mentioned in the foregoing paragraph—about the communicator or the receiver or audience. By pointing out three different areas of research in which semantic investigations seem to be pertinent by themselves, I will argue for an affirmative response.

In this context it is important to keep in mind the distinction between possible and actual responses to a communication and to remember that even if a result saying that a certain proposition is expressed by a given sentence does not give us any direct information about the mental life of existing persons, it is nevertheless true that this proposition *can* be the content of a mental act that is a response to this sentence, and it *will* be if the receiver understands the sentence.

First, investigations should be considered which have as their object the inquiry into whether a given communication, or set of communications, satisfies certain *normatively grounded criteria*. In Scandinavia, studies of this kind have been concerned with political as well as commercial communications (see Westerståhl, 1972; Asp, 1978; Andrén, 1978, 1980; Rosengren, 1979; or the article by Preben Sepstrup in this volume). These studies deal with the objectivity, informativeness, and rationality of communications. The task is not to find out whether the receivers in fact become more informed or rational; but to determine whether the communications analyzed offer the audience a real opportunity to become better informed.

Regarding *historical* studies it is, for practical reasons, not possible to attain precise and conclusive knowledge about the intentions, beliefs, and attitudes behind a given communication and its effects on the audience. But this does not mean that content analyses of historical documents and ancient pictures and writings will be of no interest. We have more or less comprehensive and well-grounded beliefs concerning which linguistic rules or conventions were in force at a certain time; hence it will be possible today to determine, more or less with certainty, which ideas or propositions were expressed by various historical items in relation to conventions of that time. Through semantic analyses of historical material we can thus attain knowledge about which ideas were available or current during a given period. It is obvious that they who lived within the society cultivating these ideas might have understood the ideas differently than we do. But this does not imply by itself that our conceptions of these ideas must be mistaken or inadequate, even when they diverge from the original conceptions.

Some authors advocate the thesis that an adequate understanding of a culture must be in terms of the concepts employed within that culture. (Chapter 2 in Pike, 1966, contains a lucid discussion on this thesis and its antithesis; see Rosengren, 1976: 669.) This position implies that research on alien, ancient, or dead cultures is pointless, since it will not be possible for us to understand the ideas and mores investigated in the same way as those who lived within the culture scrutinized. It is, however, an untenable thesis. One important goal of science is to construe concepts and develop theoretical constructs that can help us to penetrate deeper into reality than is possible for common sense. This means that a valid description or understanding of an idea must not be identical to a description of the idea that would be given by those who originally embraced it; the description need not even be intelligible for them.

Cultural studies concerning the ideas expressed within a society need not, of course, be historical. A fair and comprehensive account of an existing society should include a description of its *symbolic environment—* that is, the sum of ideas and concepts expressed within a society; it need not, in order to become interesting, be related to actual intentions or responses. The productivity of penetrating a certain phenomenon is not entirely dependent upon its causal powers with respect to human beings. Today no one would claim that astronomy became pointless when it lost its connection with astrology. Knowledge concerning which ideas are contained in a symbolic environment can be significant, irrespective of the tendencies to accept or reject those ideas that compose the environment. An objective appraisal of the beliefs of individuals presupposes knowledge about what is offered to them in this respect. The range of ideas and concepts available determines to a large extent which beliefs it will be possible to hold. And the normative status of a certain phenomenon (for example, a belief) can seldom be determined *in vacuo*; it must, *inter alia*, be related to what is possible; worth is seldom absolute, but instead relative to the relevant alternatives (see Bergström, 1966).

SEMANTICS AND RELIABILITY

Semantic content analysis is, as we have seen, an activity which often demands extensive knowledge and sometimes other rare capacities; in some cases the required knowledge can be acquired only through a long and laborious process of intensive studies. This means that it may be futile to demand that the task must be such that "regardless of who does the analysis or when it is done, the same data should be secured under similar conditions."

At the same time, it is certainly true that we want to be in a position where we can trust the results of a semantic content analysis; it is a strong desideratum that we have some kind of check on the results. We should not forget that science is a human activity and that it is always somewhat risky to trust a human being (see the discussion in St. James-Roberts, 1976a, 1976b). Thus, not only can the results of coding procedures be false; figures from reliability testings can also be false; we ought to have some kind of check on these; and so on.

When we make a conventional reliability test, we get a measure of the consensus between different coders; but we do not get any information about the source of the disagreements. The consensus coefficient has two defects. A poor coefficient can cast doubts upon reliable (that is, true) data. A high coefficient in certain cases may insinuate that a set of raw data is trustworthy, although it is unreliable (has a high frequency of false data). If we are interested in the truth of the data, we want instead to have a measurement of the tendency of the coder who is the source of the data to make inadequate interpretations and wrong classifications and hence to produce false data. This calls for a more qualified reliability test.

First, we should let another person recode a random sample of the investigated material. Then we can identify the disagreements and so reach the position where we can calculate the ordinary coefficient. Then we will be able to analyze each disagreement in order to determine if the disagreement is due to an error by the original coder or an error by the test-coder, or perhaps we will find that both have failed. Thus, we can attain a measure of the tendency of the original coder to produce false data. The more people we can engage in this process and the larger the amount of the material recoded, the more can we trust that the data are reliable.

This can be a time-consuming and costly procedure; and there is room for irrational as well as nonrational influences in the discussions that will tell us whose coding is the correct one. But, as this seems to be the only feasible way of attaining a measurement of the veracity of data concerning semantic contents, we must (at least tentatively) try to trust the results of such judgments.

I ought, finally, to stress one fundamental assumption for this reasoning. Interpretation is not, or must not be, a subjective process. It is here assumed that it is an *objective* fact that a proposition or concept is expressed by a certain set of signs: the question concerning what is expressed by a text/picture has *true and false* answers. This implies that I assume that semantic data are ontologically independent. And that means that intersubjectivity is not the ultimate arbiter.

NOTE

1. "The assertions found in a communication are the primary content indicators of the intentions and motives of the communicator" (Janis, 1965: 67). It is not evident what is meant by the term "assertion" in this passage; but other parts of Janis' paper make it clear enough that it does not refer to the garb of words in which the thoughts of the communicator are clothed.

REFERENCES

ANDRÉN, G. (1978). Media and Morals. Stockholm: Akademilitteratur.
——— (1980). "The rhetoric of advertising." Journal of Communication 30.
ANDRÉN, G., ERICSSON, L. O., OHLSSON, R., and TÄNNSJÖ, T. (1978). Rhetoric and Ideology in Advertising. Stockholm: Liber.
ASP, K. (1978). Kungstorgsockupationen i Goteborg (The Occupation of Kungstorget in Göthenburg). Stockholm: Beredskapsnämndens för Psykologiskt Försvar Rapportserie 91.
BERELSON, B. (1952). Content Analysis in Communication Research. New York: Free Press.
BERGSTRÖM, L. (1977). "Intersubjectivity in social sciences." Danish Yearbook of Philosophy 14.
——— (1966). The Alternatives and Consequences of Actions. Stockholm: Almqvist & Wiksell.

FEIGL, H. (1953). "The scientific outlook: Naturalism and humanism." In H. Feigl and M. Brodbeck (eds.), Readings in the Philosophy of Science. New York: Appleton-Century-Crofts.

HOLSTI, O. R. (1969). Content Analysis for the Social Sciences and Humanities. Reading: Addison-Wesley.

JANIS, M. (1965). "The problem of validating content analysis." In H. D. Lasswell et al. (eds.), Language of Politics. Cambridge: MIT Press.

KAPLAN, A. and GOLDSEN, J. M. (1965). "The reliability of content analysis categories." In H. D. Lasswell et al. (eds.), Language of Politics. Cambridge: MIT Press.

KRIPPENDORFF, K. (1977). "Validity in content analysis." Philadelphia: Annenberg School of Communications, University of Pennsylvania.

KRIPPENDORFF, K. (1978). "Reliability, the case of binary attributes." Philadelphia: Annenberg School of Communications, University of Pennsylvania.

LEHRER, K. (1974). Knowledge. Oxford: Oxford University Press.

MANDELBAUM, M. (1977). The Anatomy of Historical Knowledge. Baltimore, MD: John Hopkins University Press.

MORRIS, C. W. (1938). Foundations of the Theory of Signs. Chicago: University of Chicago Press.

PIKE, K. L. (1966). Language in Relation to a Unified Theory of the Structure of Human Behaviour. The Hague: Mouton.

PLATO (1956). Meno. Harmondsworth, England: Penguin.

QUINE, W. V. (1960). Word and Object. Cambridge: MIT Press.

ROSENGREN, K. E. (1976). "Malinowski's magic: The riddle of the empty cell." Current Anthropology 17.

ROSENGREN, K. E. (1979). "Bias in news: Methods and concepts." Studies of Broadcasting 15.

ST. JAMES-ROBERTS (1976a). "Are researchers trustworthy?" New Scientist.

––– (1976b). "Cheating in science." New Scientist.

WESTERSTÅHL, J. (1972). Objektiv nyhetsförmedling (Objective News). Stockholm: Läromedelsförlagen.

Chapter 3

ACTOR-RELIABILITY
Some Methodological Problems

Tom Bryder

INTRODUCTION

Let us assume, as some social scientists always do (and all social scientists sometimes do), that it is both valuable and possible to produce relatively reliable, valid, and precise policy predictions on the basis of communication contents derived from personal documents. By policy prediction I mean something like "anticipated decision behavior and decisions," their centrality, intensity, and shape, as opposed to "anticipated policy outcome," which I take to be the same as assessments of "environmental impacts" or "milieu-effects." It then follows that it might be worthwhile to consider to what extent we may suppose that the communicator is a reliable source of information—in particular, if the communicator is identical to the decision maker whose behavior is under investigation. In systematic content analysis, such evaluations may reduce certain methodological hazards encountered in the construction of coder directives, data-sampling, and in the empirical evaluation of inferences made by investigators.

As analysts, we usually approach a situation of information similar to that used by political actors trying to opt for the best decision in an environment of more or less close, dignified and, consequently, influential foes and friends. Briefly stated, like political actors, we wish to assess whether an actor means what he says and conveys what he means in

AUTHOR'S NOTE: For their comments, criticisms and suggestions, I wish to thank Viveca Ramstedt-Silén, The Swedish Business School of Helsinki; Lennart Lundquist and Gunnar Sjöblom, University of Copenhagen; and Karl Erik Rosengren, University of Lund. For remaining errors, omissions and obscurities I am, of course, solely responsible. Figure 3.1 is reprinted by permission of Lennart Lindquist.

various situations. In terms of the analyzed actor, it is necessary to make "credibility estimations" in view of the fact that politics to a considerable extent is more like a credibility game than a game of rational discourse and choice. As Djilas says (1966: 93): "In politics more than in anything else, the beginning of everything lies in moral indignation and in doubt of the good intentions of others." Provided this—rather than any "rationalistic" (see Vedung, 1978: *passim*)—interpretation is true, the argument to be elaborated in the following pages may contain a certain degree of (unintended) practical utility, in addition to its analytical purposes.

In negotiation studies, communicator-reliability is a central problem of empirical analysis. But, as one student of international relations has claimed (Jönsson, 1975: 86): "Just as there is no sure way for an actor to make a commitment credible, there is no unequivocal criterion by which the researcher—or another actor—can make credibility estimations. And yet the researcher often has the advantage over the actor, as he is favored by retrospection." In this essay I nevertheless take the issue to be that we ought to devise such criteria and make them explicit whatever their limitations (see also Axelrod, 1976: Ch. 10).

Dostojevskij (1974: 84) once remarked that there are things at the core of each individual that he does not reveal to anyone but his closest friends. He further maintained that there are similarly things the individual does not reveal even to his friends, only to himself and in secret; finally, there are things which a man is afraid of revealing even to himself. Goffman (1971: 141ff) similarily distinguishes between dark, strategic, inside, entrusted, and "free" secrets.

Simplified and translated into the vocabulary of content analysis, it becomes necessary to distinguish between text, information, and reality planes for various types of information of an actor/communicator. Lundquist (1972: 95) supplies the following illustration of the situation confronting us:

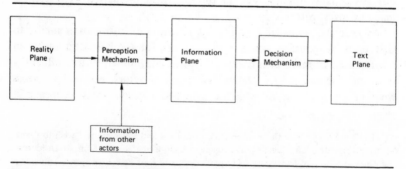

Figure 3.1 The Three Planes of Analysis
SOURCE: Lennart Lindquist, *Means and Goals of Political Decentralization* (1972: Fig. 11).

At the macrolevel of analysis, approached by means of decisional models containing assumptions of bounded rationality, it is quite sufficient to describe information and information trends at the text plane, within the traditional communication framework suggested by Berelson (1952). This approach has the well-known advantage that it allows for the use of large masses of texts, which are easily manipulated by statistical methods when categorized, coded, and quantified. In addition, the incorporation of contingency analysis in such studies will usually raise the level of theoretical relevance of what is coded, so as to supplement important aspects of the information and/or reality planes of the actor/communicator. This is evidenced in, for instance, Anckar's systematic analysis of foreign and international policy reports of 17 Finnish newspapers (Anckar, 1971: 275ff). While acknowledging this type of concise endeavor to be necessary for theoretical improvement of content analysis, in the following I shall nevertheless be limiting my pursuits to a somewhat less rigorous, but no less consequential, line of reasoning about method.

Gouldner has argued (1974: 311) that "there is no group of sociologists anywhere in the world today who, more than those in Sweden, have a clearer and more agreed-upon view of the standards and values to which good sociology should conform." According to his investigations, "Swedish sociologists are the people of, by, and for a formal methodology." He further claimed that this seemed "much more distinctly Swedish than American" and that it appeared as if American sociologists were somewhat less likely to use externalized models and more likely to use "paradigms" (in Kuhn's sense), to guide their work by means of identifying certain specific and concrete pieces of research as good and outstanding, and then using those ideas as guides for their own efforts (1974: 316ff; see also Bryder, 1975: 29ff, 1976: 361, 364).

More specifically, social science in Sweden—more than in any of the other Scandinavian countries at least—tends to follow what Kaplan (1964: 28ff) calls the "law of the instrument" which may be formulated as follows: "Give a small boy a hammer, and he will find that everything he encounters needs pounding." It is not surprising that scientists are prone to formulate problems whose solutions require techniques in which they are proficient. What is objectionable, however, is that, to the extent this is done at the price of excluding other techniques and methods as unscientific, we are likely to end up in one form or another of "Model 1" analysis (see Holsti 1976: 26; Lindblom, 1977: *passim*)—that is, a type of unitarian frame of methodological reference which is premature since it relies on the use of "rules of thumb and formulas" instead of intellectual reasoning in problem-solving (Kaplan, 1964: 29). I subscribe to Kaplan's idea: "It is less important to draw a fine line between what is 'scientific' and what is not than to cherish every opportunity for scientific growth. There is no need for behavioral science to tighten its immigration laws against subversive aliens. Scientific institutions are not so easily overthrown."

I. THE MEANING OF ACTOR-RELIABILITY
IN POLICY PREDICTION

Galtung (1969: 67) maintains:

> The most important thing about content analysis is that there is nothing particular about it at all. Texts about content analysis are apt to present methodological principles of very general applicability as if these applied to content analysis alone, probably because they are texts with a relatively untrained target audience.

He also says that "the only difference between content analysis and standard opinion analysis is that the former is based on cultural artefacts, the latter on individuals" (p. 71). A better distinction would be to say that the former is built on unobtrusive and the latter on obtrusive measures (see Webb et al., 1973; Axelrod, 1976). Sartre (1966: 738ff) says:

> Every investigation implies the idea of a nudity which one brings out into the open by clearing away the obstacles which cover it, just as Actaeon clears away the branches so that he can have a better view of Diana at her bath. More than this, knowledge is a hunt. Bacon called it the hunt of Pan. The scientist is the hunter who surprises a white nudity and violates by looking at it.

Unobtrusiveness is described in no less drastic formulations by Goffman (1971: 203ff): "When an outsider accidently enters a region in which a performance is being given, or when a member of the audience inadvertently enters the backstage, the intruder is likely to catch those present *flagrante delicto.*"

To some extent, content analysis of one kind or another always takes the shape of "unobtrusive" investigation since newspapers, political speeches, or whatever material is used is not constructed for the specific research purpose. Moreover, it seems fair to say that content analysis is a basic tool since it is often used in the final stages of any research after the data-making has been done.

Winter and Stewart (1977: 29) argue:

> The recent interest of political scientists in psychological techniques and modes of explanation and the growing interest of psychologists in studying politics and politicians will surely accelerate the reliance on some form of content analysis. . . . One simply cannot imagine that students will ever be able to administer Thematic Apperception

Tests, an F-scale, or a behavioral observation inventory to the President of the United States, a foreign minister, or a key political advisor. It is, therefore, important to take stock of the ways in which content analysis of written material can be used to make psychological inferences about political leaders.

In addition to this, paralinguistic analyses of televised speeches and similar types of records may prove helpful as yet another type of unobtrusive measure. Like Galtung (1969: 156), I think it is reasonable to posit that the social scientist who wants to describe, explain, and predict the behavior of political leaders in a contemporary setting in most circumstances will approach them "with his techniques ordered after decreasing frequency: content analysis (including all kinds of biographical data), formal questionnaires, informal interviews, and formal interviews."

POLICY PREDICTION

The establishment of invariance hypotheses is the business of any science. Pounding away at problems of how to establish stable patterns taking account of the ways strategically important decision makers reach their options or fail is a lot of fun, particularly when this pounding is done with the aid of unobtrusive observations (see Bryder, 1979). Depending on whether we refer to goals or processes when we speak of policies, the nature of predictions will alter because they are susceptible to self-alteration (Henshell, 1978: 99) in different degrees. In political analysis, the nature of predictions will also alter depending on the scope available for individual decision makers to pattern choices and decision behavior at their own will.

Axelrod, writing about the specific difficulties of prediction on the basis of schema analysis and cognitive maps, explained (1976: 257): "Limitations in the use of cognitive maps for research and prediction arise from the limited availability of source materials on which maps can be based." He nevertheless also maintains that, "While prediction of *policy choices* are still very difficult, predictions of *explanations of events* may be feasible" (p. 230).

It is hardly wise to deny that ours is, in many respects, a collectivistic world of politics, and important matters of public policy are usually determined by groups rather than by individuals acting alone. Therefore, some ideas of how beliefs and assertions of individual actors add up to collective decisions must be kept in mind. Here it is important to avoid anthropomorphisms and similar confusions of the analytical levels. As Hermann (Hermann and Millburn, 1977: 19) said: "It is easier to postulate a relationship between what a political leader is like and what he does politically than between what a political leader is like and what the political body of which he is part will do."

However, let us tentatively assume that if we are interested in prediction of decision-making behavior, which is part of policies for both influentials and influenced, we may reasonably expect that in the last analysis a certain degree of individual variability is likely to prevail. This consideration, I hope, will suffice to serve as a minimal requirement, legitimizing the following concern with actor-reliability as a problem of methodological validity.

RELIABILITY OF METHODS AND ACTORS

The discussion of reliability in most methodological accounts of content analysis seems to center on the absence or presence of observation and measurement failures. One way of approaching the concept of reliability from this angle is that of Hellevik (1977: 155ff; see also Rosengren, 1976: 85ff; Zetterberg, 1965). Hellevik suggests that we distinguish between two main types of reliability tests: those pertaining to the same phenomenon at different moments, taking into account the *stability* of the measurements, and those occurring at the same moment, taking into account the degrees of *equivalency* of results. In terms of reliability tests of the equivalency type, we may further distinguish between *instrument-congruency*, on the one hand, and *intersubjectivity*, on the other. The pursuit of methodological reliability on the basis of equivalency is seldom a substantial problem in systematic content analysis, as is often evidenced (Riley and Stoll, 1968: 375). Thus, Kronvall gained an 88 percent coding reliability by using a test built on a mix of instrument congruency and intersubjectivity, and Anckar (1971: 342) reports a reliability for his 14 variables ranging from 83 to 100 percent, based on intersubjectivity tests.

Reliability tests of the stability type, which similarly have two sub-aspects, *object-constancy* and *intrasubjectivity*, are somewhat more problematical. Of these two types, the problem of object-constancy is most difficult to control, since it deals with "arbitrary variations in the observed attribute of the research object (which in this context means the same as communicators/decision makers) even though the theoretical attribute is constant" (Hellevik, 1977: 160). To the extent that actors are reliable suppliers of information with regard to how they actually behave, object-constancy increases by definition. Note, however, that "reliable" here is not the same as "truthful according to the face-value of what is being said." The possibility of making reliable inferences about the systematically lying person is just as good as when we have a constantly truthful person.

Since reliability in the supply of information is not always the case for all actors at all times, and certainly not the case for some actors at any time (see White, 1966: *passim*), we must approach this nexus of reliability/ validity by the employment of some conception of psychologically intervening variables, as Figure 3.1 suggests and as Cartwright suggested in his essay, "Influence, Leadership, Control" (1969).

HOW UNPROBLEMATIC ARE STATEMENTS BY TOP POLITICIANS FOR POLICY PREDICTION?

Analysts of social behavior who tend to concentrate on role requirements sometimes exhibit a certain inclination to assure their readers that the relationship between operational and official opinions is of minor importance for the establishment of hypotheses about top politicians' decision behavior. This claim has been sharply criticized by Singer (1968: 145) and Holsti (1976: 33ff). Below, I shall attempt to scrutinize one such claim made by Brodin and set out an alternative, but simultaneously complementary, notion about how to cope with certain prevalent issues concerning the reliability of statements made by top decision makers.

Brodin's Personality-Dispensability Hypothesis

In her methodologically important work, "Belief Systems, Doctrines, and Foreign Policy" (1972), Brodin argues that the public statements made by a decision maker tend to limit his freedom of choice and actions in the future in two important ways, both of which contribute to the substantial reduction of personality influences among the reality, information, and text planes. Utilizing a statement by the former Social-Democratic premier in Sweden, Tage Erlander, as a point of departure, Brodin says (1972: 105, 1977: 30ff):

> In the first place, these statements contribute to a number of expectations both within and without the country. . . . The point of the argument is that the credibility of the holders of power, upon which legitimacy of power ultimately rests, is contingent upon a certain measure of consonance between word and deed, doctrine and decision. . . . Secondly, the official declarations influence the basis upon which other actors make their decisions, at least to the extent that alternative channels of information are lacking. This, in turn, is likely to have an indirect impact upon the freedom of action of the decision maker making these declarations.

To do Brodin justice, it should be noted that she is of the opinion that "postulating an identity between verbal statements and private beliefs is from many points open to criticism" (Brodin, 1972: 104).

Assuming the first part of the argument to be generally correct, we may proceed to inquire into its effect on the formulation of official statements. In the first place, this consideration would have the effect that official statements will then be drafted so as to gratify and comply with generally accepted norms and moral values, in order for the decision maker to have an ideological basis to fall back upon, legitimizing intentions and future behavior. As George (1959: 112ff) says: "It is well known that the propagandist . . . uses language habits, attitudes, and behavioral dispositions of the audience addressed."

In the second place, such statements seem likely to be so diffuse and ambiguous that they are useless for the more precise assessment of any future pattern of action. This objection implies that actors, generally, try to avoid becoming committed when not forced to do so. In the third place, such official statements are likely to contain a relatively high proportion of rationalization, postdecisional dissonance-reducing qualifications, and other justificatory points, related to past and anticipated future events, designed to bridge—consciously or unconsciously—any inconsistency in words and/or deeds. Hence, they are not a sure basis for predicting behavior. To the extent that these statements are drafted on a collective level of decision-making, they are, moreover, inadequate for the prediction of *individual* behavior, provided we wish to avoid the "ecological fallacy." In certain types of situations, such as new, complex, and constrained ones, the personal influence of top decision makers on policy formulation and/or promulgation is likely to prevail (see Greenstein, 1969: ch. 2; Hermann and Millburn, 1977: 19).

Aspects of Actor-Reliability and Collective Decision-Making

"Included among the ways of getting closer to a person's 'true beliefs,' " Axelrod (1976: 255) claims, "are the use of source material that is less likely to be argumentative (such as private interviews), and a systematic comparison of what a person says in different contexts." The substantial and very important issue of Brodin's claim is that the appearance of insincerity is costly for the elite decision maker. In von Sydow's voluminous empirical study of Swedish top Social-Democratic policy makers between 1955 and 1960, *Kan Vi Lita På Politikerna?* (1978, with an English summary), this issue is put into proper perspective by substantive participant observation, content analysis, informant-observer analysis, private interviews, and a rigorous inclusion of theoretical arguments about actor-reliability in collectivistic settings.

Following some suggestions made by Downs and Sjöblom about the political costs of insincerity, von Sydow discusses how program realization, vote-maximization, parliamentary influence-maximization, and party cohesion affect political leaders' propensity to act in ways that comply with public and private views where these may be distinct. Substantial parts of the empirical analyses are centered on five policy areas: foreign, defense, economic, social, and constitutional politics. Theoretically as well as empirically, vote maximization and the wish to maintain party cohesion were found by von Sydow to be the constituent explanatory factors for discrepancies between private and public views and behavior of his researched subjects. In foreign policy decision-making—the concern of Brodin—von Sydow was even able to trace a residual factor explaining discrepancies—namely, secretiveness.

By and large, I would contend that not only in view of the empirical evidence in von Sydow's analyses but also in view of the abstract arguments about collective decision-making in a democratic setting such as those outlined by Downs and Sjöblom, the postulate of actor-reliability formulated by Brodin must be drastically circumscribed. In this conclusion I agree with Holsti's criticisms of the Stockholm analyses of foreign policy doctrines (Holsti 1976: 22, note 7).

Aspects of Psychological Variables and Actor-Reliability

If the relationships between words and deeds, between inferences from the text plane to the contexts of action, are not unequivocally determined by the decision maker's/communicator's role requirements, as I suggest they are not, then it follows that a valid interpretation of the latency in messages must take into account a psychological dimension of the communication situation. For the sake of simplicity, we may conceive of a psychological conversion process between the information inflow of an actor/communicator on the one hand and his decisions and decision behavior on the other. This conversion process functions as a prism for the actor, simplifying and ordering the more or less unstructured reality stimuli of the environment, providing a "cognitive map" for his choice of policy (see Axelrod, 1976: *passim*; Lane, 1978a: 814). A task of primary importance for content analysis is to reconstruct the "map" as the actor sees it. As Axelrod says of cognitive mapping (1976: 223): "Its real strength (especially as compared to other formal approaches to decision making) is that it is able to employ the concepts of the decision maker who is being predicted, rather than the concepts of the person who is doing the predicting."

This assumption can be illustrated by the process outlined in Figure 3.2. The central point of the figure is that a determination of what is *important* and *efficient*, as seen by the actor/communicator, is structured by images of past, present, and future experiences. These images, as well as the substantial and procedural goals of the actor/communicator, may be obtained by means of, for instance, a relatively unsophisticated, small-scale trend analysis of themes and symbols on the text plane which is later correlated to actual behavior and the actor's explanation of this behavior.

Having assessed the priorities at the level of the text, the inclusion of the entire sample of texts to be analyzed proceeds. By relying on secondary sources it is usually possible to determine important thresholds in the process of politicization which give significant clues as where to start more or less impressionistic countings of themes and/or symbols. The amount of impressionism can be substantially reduced if the analysis is informed with some type of behavior hypothesis, such as the "compensatory hypothesis" (Lasswell, (1951) and/or the hypothesis of "power spheres" and the selective self (George, 1968; Bryder, 1975: 100ff). At this stage, however, general directives for continuing the analyses must ensue from the problem investigated: "in any content-analysis problem, the investigator designates as his indicators only those aspects of the communication which are relevant to his problem" (George, 1959: 98).

In many ways, this holds generally for both sampling of concrete cases to be analyzed and the parts of the communications that are used as indicants (Riley and Stoll, 1968: 374). Stratification of major policy areas, which is necessary for the detailed specification of behavior hypotheses of the type mentioned above, can then be obtained by ranking on the basis of simple frequencies and/or by the use of correlations between themes and

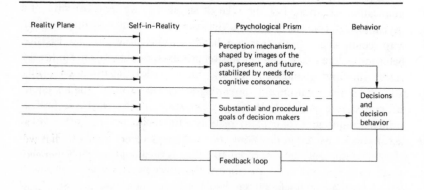

Figure 3.2   Threshold Components in the Process of Cognitive Mapping

symbols on the one hand and decisions and decision behavior on the other. The latter method, it should be noted, runs the risk of circular reasoning, but this is not inherent in the procedure, as Holsti has pointed out (1970: 153ff). This fairly conventional method for stratifying policy areas and ranking does not, however, adequately take into account the problem of "non-decisions," "mobilization of bias," and other forms of political tacit understandings (see the recent discussion of volitional short-circuits by Lindblom, 1977).

Cognitive consonance and complexity. The hypothesis about "power spheres" and the notion of the "selective self" says that decision makers tend to "carve out" a sphere of competence—a niche, some would say— constituting an "assumed field of power" where highly personality-specific behavior, including decision behavior, is likely to prevail. The validity of empirical inferences about such "assumed spheres of power" may be strengthened if tested on the theoretical basis of Festinger's theories of social comparison processes, and internal consistency in cognitions (Festinger, 1954, 1957). Lane (1978a: 814) says:

> Some of the most influential theories of cognitive processes stress the use of schemata (or vignette) which is tentatively "fitted" to observations to classify them and so give them meaning. The schema applied to leisure may be quite different from that applied to market activities. Finally, psychology, discovering that attitudes and even personality traits are often situation specific, now states that attitudes and traits must be considered in the context of functionally similar situations.

The validity of such estimations, however, must be understood in the light of what psychologists call "post-decision dissonance reduction": "After any decision involving conflict, there is a strong tendency to emphasize the better features of the chosen object or course of action and the less agreeable ones of that rejected" (Lane, 1978a: 809).

Having said this much, it should also be noted that individual tolerance of dissonance in cognitions may vary with personality so that "a person who is very decided concerning opinions, issues, and values also shows an inability to make decisions" (Festinger, 1957: 269). Rigidity in an actor's striving for a "continuity of standpoints" (for the party aggregate level of decision-making see Sjöblom, 1968), combined with firmness on issues of opinion, values, and attitudes, may not be so much a hallmark of a propensity to act in accordance with the expressive contents of what we infer from the text plane as an indication of what Freudians call super-ego needs. Frequent instances of expression such as "then I thought . . . now I know" and "I knew already then, but rudimentarily only . . ." (see also Berger and Luckmann, 1967: 160) may, then, reveal not so much the actor's real priorities as a slight instance of personality disorder. Self-references in political statements, generally, should be compared with the actor's projections in material which relates to others in less argumentative contexts, if used at all in policy-prediction on the basis of personal data. In short, the polaroid effect of the "self-in-reality," as represented by the actor's cognitive map and shown in Figure 3.2, must somehow be systematically taken into account and modified by other types of inferences than those obtainable from the face-value of self-descriptions, because any systematic difference in value interpretation that may exist between the analyzing actor, assigning magnitudes to his variables, and the meaning of these magnitudes for the particular piece of content analysis may be theoretically significant.

Empathy. In *Political Thinking and Consciousness* (1969: 61), Lane says: "The attention to cognitive balancing mechanisms should not be allowed to obscure the fact that in the long run it is the balanced condition, not the balanced sentence that will receive men's greatest effort and attention." If we allow the ontology of this balanced condition to include the way other people reason and argue, one can at least partially "get at" the condition by employing empathetic modes of thought. Lasswell (1958: 195) offers the following description of what this means:

> Empathy enlarges a person's perception of the subjective events whose focal position is the "consciousness" by an "other" of himself. By playing this role in imagination an individual comes to enlarge the primitive ego symbol and to include with it the symbols of other egos to constitute a self.

Empathetic thinking and behavior have long been matters of interest and speculation in the social sciences. However, social psychologist Cottrell is probably right when he says (1969: 552n):

> There is wide agreement that whatever is denoted by the term is of central significance in theoretical and practical understanding of the processes of interaction and communication. Relative to its importance it is still an underdeveloped area of theoretical and empirical inquiry.

Empathy is the ability to feel another's feelings in a situation while at the same time remaining aware of one's own identity. As a concept, it is analytically distinct from sympathy, "since it does not contain the element of condolence, agreement, or pity essential for sympathy" (Greenson, 1960: 423); similarly, it should not be confused with identification, since identification essentially is an unconscious and permanent phenomenon (p. 418). Moreover, according to the same expert source, "Empathy is essentially a function of the experiencing ego, whereas intuition comes from the analysing ego."

At the empirical level, however, empathy, education, intuition, and sympathy may very well interact. As Mitscherlich (1970: 233) says: "Where there has been education to independence, intuititive understanding, empathy is possible, because the overriding compulsion of taboos has been broken. When empathy is encouraged, tolerance follows as a consequence of insight." (For additional discussions and empirical evidence see Lane, 1978b, 1978c.)

George and George, writing about the role of empathy in psychobiography, claim that it is an iterative process involving the constant reexamination and revision of earlier empirical interpretations, and that it involves a mixture of diagnostic, psychological sensitivity and factual knowledge of the researched subject (1964: x). Allport (1947: 21) similarily stresses the importance of empathy so conceived for the interpretation of personal documents: "The process of interaction between theory and inductive material ... is the essence of the methodological problem of personal documents."

Among practicing psychoanalysts, however, it is generally held that adults' capacity for empathy cannot be taught, but, when available, its proper uses can be taught. According to Greenson (1960: 423),

> The capacity to empathize seems dependent on one's ability to modulate the cathexis of one's self-image. The temporary decathexis of one's self-image which is necessary for empathy will be readily undertaken only by those who are secure in their sense of identity. Analysts with too restricted an identity or with amorphous or multiple identities will probably be inhibited or unreliable empathizers.

This, of course, holds for both the level of interaction and interpretation. (For a general empirical treatment of empathy in developmental psychology see Piaget, 1974.)

Depending on this, according to psychoanalytic theory, the availability of empathy is dependent on whether or not the subject wishing to empathize has a certain degree of depressive propensity—of a nonpathological character. Therefore, it is also frequently noted that those politicians who strive for power in order to compensate for low self-esteem tend to be shrewd empathizers, in fact often to the point that they become unable to make decisions because their analyses of interpersonal relations are too complex. In combination with experienced high self-esteems—which is frequent in many leadership situations—high cognitive complexity produces apolitical tendencies (Ziller et al., 1977: 174ff). This combination of cognitive complexity on the one hand and euphoric feelings on the other has very little to do with the formal and purposeful training in politically relevant skills, and, as it has often been observed, extremely sensitive empathizers among behavioral scientists are often similarly caught in this phenomenon and consequently inhibited by hesitancy, sometimes with the disastrous result of little or no intellectual output.

II. PERSONAL DOCUMENTS

The foregoing methodological considerations may be seen to illustrate the observation, often made by content analysts, that when validity increases, measurement and observation reliability of the more systematic kinds tend to decrease, and vice versa. Zetterberg (1965: 123) has written about the type of endeavor proposed above: "Lack of validity because of false information is, in principle, possible to detect. In practice, however, it is very troublesome, and we generally prefer to discover other facts than the extent to which informants lie." Actor-reliability is something more than just a question of truth and lies; it also contains aspects of cultural bias, ambiguity, vagueness, and so on. Let us say that it is, above all, a problem of validity and, as such—as Zetterberg notices elsewhere (p. 115)—there must be a progressive process of continuously adjusting techniques of research to theorizing and of continuously adjusting theorizing to technique and research. I would like to add that this is particularly so in elite analysis.

The particular problems of data-gathering among elite members are well known to most social scientists and may be summarized as problems of interviewing access and the like (see Galtung, 1969: 154ff). In the same way as all other social creatures, however, members of the higher echelons tend to leave behind documentary evidence of their existence, and this can be studied systematically for the construction of invariance hypotheses which are necessary in policy prediction. As Hermann (Hermann and Millburn, 1977: 4) says:

> Only movie stars and music groups probably have more traces of their behavior in the public arena than the politicians. Speeches of political leaders are regularly transcribed, their votes—if any—are recorded, their biographical statistics are maintained and printed, their autobiographies and biographies are fairly commonplace, and television and radio news programs feature interviews with them. . . . These potential data sources have just begun to be tapped by social scientists.

In order to avoid stating the case for analyzing these sources too enthusiastically, we ought to remember that systematic measurement-validity will be reduced because of heterogeneous formats, contexts, origins, and so forth, so that quantitative comparisons are hindered. Before we can proceed to analyze the sources, similar types of action-contexts must be identified if we wish to increase validity; in addition, we must keep in mind that an actor's intended meaning in a specific instance is not safely inferred from the usual and most frequent way in which he uses words. Thus, to some extent, qualitative semantics is likely to prevail wherever content analysis is being used, despite its methodological restrictions.

ASPECTS OF THE ROLE OF PERSONAL DOCUMENTS IN ANALYSIS

Following Allport (1947: xii), I take personal documents to be "any self-revealing record that intentionally or unintentionally yields information regarding the structure, dynamics, and functioning of the author's mental life." Some advocates of quantitative methods are likely to concede that personal documents and their analysis may serve as a first step for delineation of valid problem areas but that their inclusion somehow is prescientific. For scientific purposes, they seem to argue, statistical methods, "big science" designs, and huge amounts of high-level data must prevail. For my own part, I have come to agree with Allport (1947: 140) that this is a narrow and too-conventional view of what scientific method must be. As we know, Newton did not require a pile of apples to develop his ideas. Moreover, recent developments in the methodology of political science seem to indicate that such a one-sided way of reasoning is increasingly being abandoned by its former proponents (see Pedersen, 1977). Besides, there is no inherent objection to the use of quantitative methods in single-case analyses. In fact, some of the pioneering studies in content analysis in the early 1950s were conducted on the basis of small samples of evidence, such as suicide letters.

REPUTATION OR INFORMANT ANALYSIS

It is commonplace that the relationship between political rhetoric and political practice is subject to a wide variety of complex influences that simply cannot be discarded by a reliance on simple and general rules of thumb.

Mitscherlich (1970: 118) says:

> The idea that one is a good model may derive from an interpretation of the self in which the truth is very well concealed; it may be confirmed by neighbors, colleagues, seniors, and the parish priest, because social contact with them is restricted to the "official" level. But members of a man's family and his close friends often have a picture of him quite different from that which he himself and the world at large have of him.

Taking this into consideration, I contend that to the extent that systematic content analysis is carried out on the basis of self-observation (letters, diaries, autobiographies, and interviews) a minimal requirement must be to include a developmental analysis of sincerity and honesty, such as the analysis made by Leites with respect to Communists' propensity to reveal the sources influencing their thought, which he found tended to decline in a six-step process (Leites, 1953: 371).

Reputation analysis, or informant analysis as it is sometimes called, may adequately aid such an investigation. Uses of informants and acquired interviews must, however, be safeguarded against the so-called halo effect (affective feelings, stereotypy, and so on), and it is probably wise to include into the research design information from those who both support and oppose the actor/communicator, as well as from those without strong convictions and emotions, in order to maintain some perspective (Hermann and Millburn, 1977: 7).

I suggest that a content analysis for the prediction of policy behavior of a specific type of individual politician could follow the path set out below:

(1) Set out the criteria by means of which we can identify some concrete actor/communicator who approximately would fit the theoretical type.

(2) Sample the official speeches on a variety of politically relevant topics and in a variety of contexts at different times of an empirical actor, fitting with some approximation the theoretical type.

(3) Construct a research design which is theoretically relevant for the analysis of the political type under investigation, and use some form of content analysis (quantitative or qualitative) to establish by means of systematic investigation the actor's outspoken priorities, their relative weight, and their contingencies (that is, their covariation at the text plane).

(4) If the political context is a democratic one with a free press, the previous findings should be compared with a politically heterogeneous sample of newspaper reports similarly content analyzed.

(5) These comparisons should, then, be further scrutinized to the extent that there is little or excessive correspondence between the types of sources, and supplemented by small-scale, preferably private interviews relating to anomalies in the comparisons. The IPs could be selected on a variety of criteria, but they should in some form or another be personally related, either presently or in the past, to the actor under investigation. Sometimes acquired interviews with such people are available in the form of journalistic accounts, which may suit the analytical purposes of the investigation.

At the more general level of methodological and theoretical argumentation, the last step in this procedure is open to the type of criticism which Dahl launched against Hunter's *Community Power Structure* (1953) in the late 1950s (Dahl, 1958: 463ff).

What Hunter investigated was the power base of communities by establishing, through interviews, who was reputed to have power and influence in local politics. Dahl's argument against these studies came down to the logically correct conclusion that mere reputation is not a sufficient condition for arguing that there exists a ruling "power elite," and that the localization of those who actually govern must be based on the analysis of a series of concrete cases of politically important decisions. As Bachrach and Baratz (1970) later argued, Dahl, for his own part, never specified with any scientific accuracy how one should define "important decision issues"; in substance, he was right in saying that formal possession of power combined with a reputation of being influential, generally, is not sufficient for determining whether a person is influential in the making of decisions. And it should be admitted that the difficulties in establishing the truth of propositions about reputed power are mainly the same as when one tries to establish, systematically, reputed actor-reliability. What is really needed is research into the specific types of instances, issues, and contexts where various types of political actors are prone to be reliable or unreliable suppliers of information.

III. In Conclusion

"One cannot fully grasp the political world", Berger says, "unless one understands it as a confidence game" (1968: 187). The ideas I have tried to set out in this essay about some methodological problems of actor-reliability derive from such an assumption. Moreover, the very nature of politics as a game of confidence will likely pose problems of reliability for both the analyst and the practically oriented actor in fairly similar ways. In the case of the analyst dealing with personal documents, the actor's reliability is a validity problem for the construction of invariance hypotheses that fit into a larger theoretical framework; whereas in the case of the actor, the reliability of co-actors is most often a question of more short-term considerations. For scientific as well as for strategic reasons, however, in both cases the process of *connaissance d'autrui* must be carried out with a temporal de-cathexis of one's self-image in order to avoid the "sympathetic fallacy"—the idea that the object of one's attention is also the object of one's affection.

Mitscherlich (1970: 198ff) said: "The mark of intelligent behavior . . . is a capacity in affective situations for simultaneous empathy and reflective detachment; decisions made are not totally dependent on the other party's advantage in strength." The political importance of empathy and its lack is well documented in White's lengthy essay, "Misperception and the Vietnam War" (1966), in which he found autistic hostility to be present not only among the Vietnamese Communists but also among the top decision makers at the time of the outbreak of the two world wars. The hazards of acquiring a capacity for empathy has been intensively researched by Piaget (1974: 409): "In all social behavior patterns of thought it is easy to see how much more easily the child is led to satisfy his desires and to judge from his own personal point of view than to enter into that of others to arrive at an objective view."

For the sake of inferential validity of the type of content analysis proposed in this essay, I have suggested that we take into account the actor's/communicator's "self-in-reality," which is roughly similar to, for-example, Goffman's (1971) "self-in-everyday-life" with analytically distinct "front" and "backstage" behavior patterns. But, as should be clear from the previous discussions, there is no point in being dogmatic here; and, like Goffman, I would like to emphasize the fact that behavior in a concrete situation is always likely to compromise between the formal and the informal styles.

Adequate intercoder-reliability tests abound, and although they do not exhaust the problems of actor-reliability as a question of methodological validity, they are at least necessary for the establishment of a truthful and fairly objective picture of the conditions and considerations surrounding the making of political decisions. My concern here has been similar to that of Winter and Stewart (1977: 33):

> While reliability is important, we must add the caution that the ease of training coders to be reliable should not completely override considerations of interest and relevance of the categories. Probably any person could obtain a high reliability by counting the number of occurrences of the word "the," but such a variable does not have a great interest or explanatory power.

REFERENCES

ANCKAR, D. (1971) Partipolitik och Utrikespolitik. Åbo: Acta Academiae Aboensis.

ALLPORT, G. W. (1947) The Use of Personal Documents in Psychological Science. SSRC Bulletin 49. Ann Arbor.

AXELROD, R. [ed.] (1976) Structure of Decision: The Cognitive Maps of Political Elites. Princeton: Princeton University Press.

BACHRACH, P. and BARATZ, M. (1970) Power and Poverty. New York: Oxford University Press.

BERELSON, B. (1952) Content Analysis in Communication Research. New York: Free Press.

BERGER, P. L. (1968) Invitation to Sociology. Harmondsworth, England: Penguin.

––– and LUCKMANN, T. (1967) The Social Construction of Reality. New York: Anchor.

BRODIN, K. (1977) Studiet av Utrikespolitiska Doktriner. Stockholm: Almqvist & Wicksell.

––– (1972) "Belief systems, doctrines and foreign policy." Cooperation and Conflict 2.

BRYDER, T. (1979) Slutreplik till G W Lartey. Statsvetenskaplig Tidskrift No. 3.

––– (1976) Svar Till Mats Bergquist. Statsvetenskaplig Tidskrift No. 4.

––– (1975) Power and Responsibility: Contending Approaches to Industrial Relations and Decision Making in Britain 1963-1971. Lund: C W K Gleerup.

CARTWRIGHT, D. P. (1969) "Influence, leadership, control." In R. Bell et al. (eds.), Political Power. New York: Free Press.

COTTRELL, L. S. (1969) "Interpersonal interaction and the development of the self." In D. A. Goslin (ed.), Handbook of Socialization. Chicago: Rand McNally.

DAHL, R. A. (1958) "A critique of the ruling elite model." American Political Science Review.

DJILAS, M. (1966) Conversations with Stalin. Harmondsworth, England: Penguin.

DOSTOJEVSKIJ, F. (1974) Anteckningar från ett Källarhål. Stockholm: Tiden.

FESTINGER, L. (1957) A Theory of Cognitive Dissonance. London: Tavistock.

––– (1954) "A theory of social comparison processes." Human Relations 2.

GALTUNG, J. (1969) Theory and Methods of Social Research. Oslo: Scandinavian University Books.

GEORGE, A. L. (1968) "Power as a compensatory value for political leaders." Journal of Social Issues 3.

––– (1959) Propaganda Analysis. Westport, CT: Greenwood Press.

––– and GEORGE, J. (1964) Woodrow Wilson and Colonel House. New York: Dover.

GOFFMAN, E. (1971) The Presentation of Self in Everyday Life. Harmondsworth, England: Penguin.

GOULDNER, A. W. (1974) For Sociology. Harmondsworth, England: Penguin.

GREENSON, R. R. (1960) "Empathy and its vicissitudes." International Journal of Psychoanalysis 41.

GREENSTEIN, F. (1969) Personality and Politics. Chicago: Markham.

HELLEVIK, O. (1977) Forskningsmetode i Sosiologi og Statsvitenskap. Oslo: Scandinavian University Books.

HENSHELL, R. L. (1978) "Self-altering prediction." In J. Fowles (ed.), Handbook of Futures Research. Westport, CT: Greenwood Press.

HERMANN, M. and MILLBURN, T. W. [eds.] (1977) A Psychological Examination of Political Leaders. New York: Free Press.

HOLSTI, O. (1976) "Foreign policy formation viewed cognitively." In R. Axelrod (ed.), Structure of Decision. Princeton: Princeton University Press.

––– (1970) "The operational code approach to the study of political leaders. J. F. Dulles' operational and philosophical beliefs." Canadian Journal of Political Science 1.

HUNTER, F. (1953) Community Power Structure. Chapel Hill: University of North Carolina Press.

JÖNSSON, C. (1975) The Soviet Union and the Test Ban. Lund: Student-litteratur.

KAPLAN, A. (1964) The Conduct of Inquiry. San Francisco: Chandler.

KRONVALL, K. (1975) Politisk Masskommunikation i ett flerpartisystem. Lund: Studentlitteratur.

LANE, R. E. (1978a). "Markets and the satisfaction of human wants." Journal of Economic Issues 4.

––– (1978b) "Interpersonal relations and leadership in a 'cold society.'" Comparative Politics 10.

––– (1978c) "The regulation of experience: Leisure in a market society." Social Science Information 17.

――― (1969) Political Thinking and Consciousness. Chicago: Markham.

LASSWELL, H. D. (1958) Politics: Who Gets What, When, How? Cleveland, OH: Meridian.

――― (1951) "Psychopathology and politics." In The Political Writings of H. D. Lasswell. New York: Free Press.

LEITES, N. (1953) A Study of Bolshevism. New York: Free Press.

LINDBLOM, C. (1977) Politics and Markets. New York: Basic Books.

LUNDQUIST, L. (1972) Means and Goals of Political Decentralization. Lund: Studentlitteratur.

MITSCHERLICH, A. (1970) Society without the Father. New York: Schocken.

PEDERSEN, M. (1977) "Om den Rette Brug af Historiske Materialer i Statskundskaben." In Festskrift til Erik Rasmussen. Århus: Politica.

PIAGET, J. (1974) The Construction of Reality in the Child. New York: Ballantine.

RILEY, M. W. and STOLL, C. S. (1968) "Content analysis." In International Encyclopedia of the Social Sciences. New York: Free Press.

ROSENGREN, K. E. (1976) Sociologisk Metodik. Stockholm: Scandinavian University Books.

SARTRE, J. P. (1966) Being and Nothingness (H. Barnes, Trans.). New York: Pocket Books.

VON SYDOW, B. (1978) Kan Vi Lita på Politikerna? Stockholm: Tiden.

SINGER, J. D. (1968) "Man and world politics: The psycho-cultural interface." Journal of Social Issues 3.

SJÖBLOM, G. (1968) Party Strategies in a Multiparty System. Lund: Studentlitteratur.

VEDUNG, E. (1978) Det Rationella Politiska Samtalet. Stockholm: Aldus.

WEBB, E. J. et al. (1973) Unobtrusive Measures: Nonreactive Research in the Social Sciences. Chicago: Rand McNally.

WHITE, R. K. (1966) "Misperception and the Vietnam war." Journal of Social Issues 3.

WINTER, D. G. and STEWART, A. J. (1977). "Content analysis as a technique for assessing political leaders." In M. Herman and T. W. Millburn (eds.), A Psychological Examination of Political Leaders. New York: Free Press.

ZETTERBERG, H. L. (1965) On Theory and Verification in Sociology. Boston: Beacon.

ZILLER, R. C. et al. (1977) "Self-other orientations and political behavior." In M. Herman and T. W. Millburn (eds.), A Psychological Examination of Political Leaders. New York: Free Press.

Chapter 4

RELATING PREFERENCES TO POLICY
Three Problem Areas

Dag Anckar and Viveca Ramstedt-Silén

INTRODUCTION AND FORMULATION OF THE AIM

The concept "democracy" is, as we all know, much disputed in contemporary discussions. This is so to such an extent "that the statement that the good society is good hardly appears so much more tautological any longer than the statement that the good society is democratic" (Westholm, 1976: 184). In general terms two main positions could be distinguished, one roughly maintaining democracy to be a form of government that is realized when the content of political decisions corresponds to what the citizens wish for; another roughly maintaining that democracy is realized when the citizens can effectively take part in political decision-making. The two positions are actually complementary, in that the latter is to be regarded as a prerequisite of the former (Anckar, 1977: 20). In this chapter we are interested in the first position; at this point, we will discuss some problems arising from the application of a content-analytical method to an analysis of this position.

However, we do not claim to have entered into a discussion of democracy. Instead, we prefer to talk about "responsiveness," and particularly "policy responsiveness," whereby we understand the extent to which political decision makers create policies which are congruous with manifest citizen demands (Schumaker, 1975: 494). Thus, we will relate our presentation to the problems of policy research and the question of agreement between policies and preferences behind policies. We shall leave discussion of democracy to others. We confine ourselves to pointing out that the task we have outlined here is obviously important, for instance, for a judgment of whether and how the manner of functioning of political systems has developed in the course of time—whether the system has developed in a responsive or an unresponsive manner. To this should immediately be added the fact that results of this type are controversial also at the normative level: if, for example, we find that policy responsiveness is present, it is natural to look upon this state of things as good, but it is equally natural to look upon this state as less good. In the former instance it might be argued that people get what they want; in the latter instance it could be argued that it may be dysfunctional if people get what they want—what they want may not be that which is best suited to meet their needs. But we shall skip the normative question and simply claim that it is interesting to know whether or not policy responsiveness is present.

By way of introduction, it should still be pointed out that this formulation of the problem also brings us face to face with the controversial question of policy determinants, about which it has been claimed, among other things, that politics (whereby the structures and processes of politics are to be understood) does not, even to a slight extent, function as such a determinant. This thesis has often been supported by statistical analyses in which sets of socioeconomic and political variables have been related to a set of policy variables; and on the basis of observations of explained policy variance it has been maintained that the socioeconomic variables, far better than the political ones, explain policy variations, and for that reason politics must be considered of secondary importance. The results have been far from unambiguous, and the state of knowledge has to be viewed as unclear. One way of working toward greater clarity is apparently to ask more concrete questions and thus to get answers that are less difficult to interpret. Such concrete questions may be, for example, the inquiry about where the preferences that possibly agree with the content of policy really are to be found. One possible way of arguing—here we can only touch upon it (see Anckar, 1978b—is to claim that if the preferences can be localized to the environment of the political system, then it is reasonable to conclude that politics has functioned in a transformative manner where the environment rather than politics has been a policy determinant. If, on the other hand, they can only be localized to the political system (that is, to actors within this system), it is reasonable to conclude that politics has functioned in a determinative manner, and consequently has been a policy determinant.

As should have become evident from the above, when talking about preferences, we here expressly mean *underlying* ones. We will not, therefore, discuss the question as to how the reactions resulting from a certain political decision agree with the content of the decision (that is, how the decision that has been arrived at is being received). Our interest in preferences is focused on an earlier stage in the decision-making process, more precisely to the different stages preceding the decision-making, and our question then concerns the agreement between the claim that a decision shall have a certain content, and the final content that is given to the decision. This difference between preferences "before" and "after" decisions is less sharp than a firsthand impression may reveal—preferences "before" decisions presumably have been at least partly shaped by the content of previously made decisions and so they are in this sense simultaneously preferences "after" (see Schaefer, 1972: 272-274). But the distinction is no doubt necessary to maintain for analytical reasons; and certain general problem areas having been pointed out within which our question can be placed, the distinction also serves the purpose of indicating still another such area: the problems of agenda-building. Where do the issues that become political decisions come from? What do the intermediary processes look like? Who initiates and runs issues successfully? Who does this less successfully? (Cobb and Elder, 1975; Cobb et al., 1976). A study of the agreement of different preferences with the contents of decisions is likely to shed light on issues of this kind.

With these introductory comments we shall leave the outline drawing of our field of research and pass on to pointing out the specific problems that this chapter will discuss.

The task we confront is thus that of comparing preferences (PF) with policies (P) along dimensions of content where the aim of the comparison is to establish the degree of agreement existing between PF and P. One way of approaching this task is evidently to resort to content-analytical approaches: PF and P are made the object of a comparative content analysis. Other procedures could include for instance, finding out about attitudes of policy by means of interview and survey research. The method seems useful and not particularly difficult when studying ongoing processes in which, for example, different kinds of panel procedures may prove fruitful. But it becomes useless if one is ambitious enough to study processes that have already occurred. (And if one wants to ask the very legitimate and relevant question of how such processes have varied in the course of time, it is exactly this kind of ambition that is required.) Asking for preferences when a policy exists is of no value; the preferences may have changed with the creation and implementation of this policy. Other methods must be considered, and the content analysis almost immediately suggests itself.

If, however, we choose to approach our problem by content-analytical methods, one condition is that PF as well as P have operational forms, which makes it possible to treat them content-analytically. PF and P should exist in the form of documents; this term is used in a narrower sense than, for example, that used by Veikko Pietilä when he defines documents as "those products of human activity and behavior that by their nature may be considered representative" (1973: 7). By documents we here mean records, minutes, contents of mass media, and other such written material connected with, and emanating from, policy processes. With regard to PF, this creates no problems—PF exists in the direct and manifest form as a document offering itself to content-analytical treatment. Examples of such documents could be a motion proposed by a group or a member of Parliament, a resolution from a party convention, a motion submitted to the same convention by some member of a party, an editorial or a column in a daily newspaper, an appeal or an address, an election advertisement, and so on. The policy component, on the other hand, is more problematic and offers a more restricted choice of alternatives. It is by no means obvious, in the first place, what should be understood by "policy," but we will refrain from discussing definitions and conducting a conceptual analysis—we confine ourselves to a definition of policies as decisions and actions emanating from political systems (see Kerr, 1976). The problem is, however, to find useful operationalizations of such decisions and actions. A quick glance at what one has concretely examined when studying "policies" reveals that these have often been expenditures, planning activity, redistributive ratios, rates of diffusion, and so on[1]—things that from the systemic point of view are rather different and in themselves well illustrate the variety of ways of understanding policy. At the same time, these are not P-forms that lend themselves to content-analytical comparisons with sets of PF, and that is why it is important to find more document-oriented expressions for P.

Evidently, law-making products constitute one such example. Laws have the form of documents, and it can hardly be denied that the making of laws is a relevant problem for political science to penetrate, even if this operationalization of "policy" has been neglected in the literature.[2] There are, however, very different types of laws, and not all of these are useful as objects of study for the context we are interested in here. In simple terms, the problem is that many laws are so "small" (in a technical or corrective sense) that it is difficult to find any set of PFs with which such a P might be contrasted. Examples of such Ps could be a law concerning the amendment of the law related to the right of schools of physical education to use subsidies for a certain purpose, and, more generally, such laws that could for instance be called "microcomplementary" (Anckar, 1978a: 18). The operationalization therefore applies to "bigger" laws— laws intended to introduce more radical and controversial societal changes. Examples of such Ps could be a general pension law or a building law, and, more generally, such laws that might be called "innovative" (Karvonen and Anckar, 1978: 24-55).

Our argument has thus brought us to a situation where we have as P an innovative law and as PF manifest preferences relating to the content of

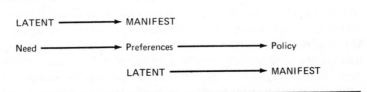

Figure 4.1   From the Latent to the Manifest: Visualization of Two Problems within the Study of Policy Determinants

this law. It is our task to establish, by means of content analysis, the degree of agreement of content between PF and P. Among the problems we encounter we will point out below two instances as a basis for our argument. In different ways the two problems deal with a distinction between the manifest and the latent; by "different ways" we primarily refer to different content-analytical aspects of validity. We have attempted to represent these two framings of the problem in the very simple illustration to be found in Figure 4.1.

The first problem concerns the knowledge we gain by content-analyzing PF—here, the question can be asked to what extent such an analysis has any validity. It is a question of bearing in mind that manifest preferences are manifestations of articulated demands directed against the decision makers of the political system, and that what is here articulated need not agree with what is desired. It is easy to imagine that the set of preferences under study only covers part of a greater and latent substratum of needs; and the question is then what representativeness the manifest possesses in reference to the latent: When studying the manifest do we also study the latent, and in that case to what extent?

The second problem concerns the relation between PF and P, where it might be argued that the structure of preferences—that is, the set of manifest preferences available for study—simultaneously forms a latent basis of the manifest decision to be made. The decision is thus in a latent way inherent in the structure of preferences and is transferred through flows from the latent to the manifest in its final form. The problem here, then, is to look for the manifest in the latent, to find categories that make a comparison possible and meaningful.

Of these two problems—it would probably be more correct to talk about complex of problems—we are concerned with the latter. This does not necessarily mean it is the more important one. In fact, the relation between needs and preferences is difficult to study and very worthy of discussion. But such a discussion would have to be more concerned with the problems of the conclusions themselves than with such operational and method-oriented questions as we are here interested in.

Our discussion will focus on three areas. First, we shall pay attention to a *problem of levels,* a result of the fact that between PF and P there may exist considerable differences in completeness of detail, formulation, and level of abstraction—in other words, it is a question of the latent and the manifest belonging to different levels, which makes comparisons difficult. Second, we shall pay attention to a *problem of transformation,* constituted by the fact that PF tends to change its appearance in the course of policy processes—as a consequence of learning, partial decisions, new perceptions, strategic factors, and other factors, the object of comparison, PF, takes on a different appearance, and such a change must be accounted for in the comparison. We choose to illustrate the considerations that are here brought to the fore by focusing on party ideology and its transformation. At this point we thus concentrate our interest on party preferences in policy processes. Third, we shall pay attention to a *problem of responsiveness,* constituted by the fact that all preferences do not look alike and that consequently a policy is responsive to different preferences in different degrees, which in its turn raises the question as to which degree of similarity should be stipulated.

PREFERENCES AND POLICIES: A PROBLEM OF LEVELS

We first discuss the problem concerning bad operational agreement. By way of introduction, it may be worthwhile to illustrate the problem more concretely.

Let us arbitrarily choose a law of a somewhat wider scope—the law relating to accommodation allowance in Finland, given in Helsingfors on June 4, 1975 (SBF, No. 408/75). Its text prescribes what is to be understood by a receiver of accommodation allowance, conditions of receiving accommodation allowance, the amount of the allowance, administration, redress procedures, and so on. The law thus identifies a problem, indicates ways of solving it, and prescribes certain procedural courses. However, behind this concrete legislation we find a richly varied set of manifest statements on different levels as to what such a policy action should contain. In a party program we may find a demand for the improvement of the housing conditions of less well-to-do citizens; in an election slogan we may find a general demand for creating greater social justice. Are preferences of this type to be related to the policy under consideration? And if that is the case, how is this to be done?

We do not believe it possible to relate preferences to policy in this way without an unacceptable degree of arbitrariness. The way from the latent to the manifest, therefore, is not practicable but must be abandoned. What is left is the opposite way, leading from the manifest to the latent, which involves comparisons on the conditions of the manifest. When looking for preferences we look for statements that are connected with the level of concretization dictated by the legal text before us. Here a different and more vexing problem emerges, however: from too general and diffuse preferences we encounter the problem of too specific and precise formulations of policy. We shall attempt to explain this more exactly.

Returning to our example of the law relating to accommodation allowance, we find that the law can be split up into what we might call *policy components* (Who may receive allowance? On which conditions? How much?). Let us represent these components by X. The law thus prescribes that allowance may be paid to families living as main tenants in a rented dwelling and to families living in their own dwelling, so long as the family includes at least one child and does not attain a certain threshold of income. This is the essential content of what we might call the *receiver component* of the law. However, the law specifies this component still further: it decrees, for instance, that childless married couples also may receive allowance for not more than two successive calendar years following the contraction of the marriage, so long as none of the persons concerned at the contraction of the marriage are over age 30. Let us represent this partial component of the receiver component by X_1. The problem is now that the further down we go in such a component hierarchy, the more we have to do with regulations that are so technical (also in the sense purely legally technical) or so exactly defined in relation to some more general wish that the principle mentioned above concerning corresponding levels of concretization becomes difficult to maintain. Preferences with this level of concretization are difficult to find; and if they can be found, false conclusions are easily reached. If, for example, one has the ambition—referred to in the introduction—to say something about agenda-building or the importance of politics as a policy determinant, one is compelled to decide which preferences can be attributed to which categories of actors. The question of whose preferences are to be counted and thus are to be found in the policy text under study has to be asked. It is, however, reasonable to imagine that different categories of actors act on different component-hierarchical levels. Different conclusions concerning the importance of the actors will be reached, then, depending on the level on which one chooses to operate. Figure 4.2 will illustrate our arguments.

Imagine a society in which sentiments and opinions are being articulated in demands for better housing conditions and a better housing level on the whole. Imagine further that the political system of this society wants to comply with such demands and therefore creates policies involving grants of accommodation allowances, the building of new houses, creation of funds for housing loans, and so on. These actions may thus be regarded as operationalizations of the demands mentioned above. Each of these actions can be broken down into policy components involving a

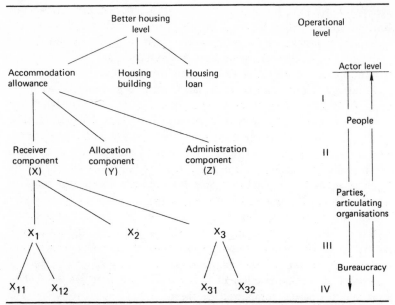

Figure 4.2 Policies, Preferences, Actors: Illustrating Problems of the Different Levels

further operationalization, and those components can be broken down into partial components involving operationalizations of policy components, and so on. Because we have found it impracticable, while preserving analytical cogency, to compare a statement of preference concerning a better level of housing with, for instance, a statement of policy that accommodation allowance must not be distrained, we have established the claim that the statements of preferences and of policy to be compared have to be on the same level of concretization (in other words, on the same operational level). The next question is, however, which operational level this could be.

As we already emphasized, it is a noteworthy circumstance that different actors appear on different levels. An unambiguous pattern is indeed not to be sketched out. It can probably be justified to say (1) that it is predominantly in the environment of the political system—that is, in the conglomeration of citizens, groups, and organizations we usually call "the people"—one generally finds preferences of a general and indefinite character; (2) that it is predominantly on the fringe of the political system—in fields where parties, large organizations, pressure groups, and other similar articulators of demands are active—one usually finds more elaborate preferences that are to be regarded as operationalizations of more general and indefinite preferences; and (3) that it is predominantly within the political system—in the fields where the political leadership and bureaucracy prepare, arrive at, and implement decisions—one usually finds more elaborate preferences that constitute specifications and elucidations of what we have here called policy components. Examples of typical documents within these fields may be a mass address, a government program, or a PM prepared by a civil servant.

As we said before, this pattern is not clear and unambiguous—it is easy to imagine situations where parties, for example, instead of taking in demands from the environment and cloaking them in operational terms, market and mobilize support "among the people" for initiatives that already have a certain operational form. The reaction of "the people" to such initiatives obviously then takes the form of preferences that are expressed on a more operational level than our argument above indicates. Likewise, bureaucracy in its concrete activity sometimes moves over wider fields than we have attributed to it above (Anckar, 1978b: 21-38). But the pattern must essentially be considered relevant, and the problem created by this cannot be disregarded. The risk is otherwise that in the study of, for example, agenda-building processes, final results are introduced into the very design of the investigation.

The question, then, is which strategy is to be considered optimal when we want to satisfy the demand for comparison according to the same level of concretization. It is favorable to stay near what we, in Figure 4.2, have called "operational level II"; that is, the level of the policy components. As we see it, this level offers at least two obvious advantages. As far as policy is concerned, it represents a degree of breakdown necessary to make the textual mass clear and manageable. Here it becomes fairly clear what the comparison involves (which manifest content is to be looked for in the latent); at the same time, the text is not broken up to the extent that the manifest altogether disappears in the latent. As far as preference is concerned, it represents the level on which different categories of actors act side by side to the greatest extent possible, and consequently the risk of false conclusions should be least. Here we probably find, more than on other levels, interaction between the masses and the elite by means of intermediary structures.

For reasons of space we cannot consider the question of *how* a legal text (a policy) can suitably be broken up into components. But earlier we pointed to the importance of aspects such as *allocating* (who is the receiver, to what extent, and on what conditions) and *regulating* (which administration, which institutional arrangements). In general, of course, different legal texts are differently structured and treat different things;

and the establishment of components, therefore, to a fairly large extent must be the result of individual decisions guided by discretion and thorough knowledge of the subject matter under study.

PREFERENCES AND POLICIES II:
A PARTY-DESIGNED PROBLEM OF TRANSFORMATION

When one has the ambition to analyze evaluations and preferences among political parties, one cannot escape the concept of ideology and the task of identifying the sources of one's ideological research, in principle extending all the way from the classical literature of ideas to the utterances of "ordinary people." In his investigation *The Profile of Party Ideologies,* (1969) Ralf Helenius distinguishes between the "sterile" program ideology, which he calls *manifest,* and the "living" latent discussion of ideas (see also Helenius, 1970). The latent ideology is more pragmatic as regards its content; it is a matter of the changing "ideology of the backyard" as opposed to the manifest "ideology of the facade." To Helenius, party programs and other corresponding literature are thus manifest ideology, while other collective representations—for instance, electoral manifestos or special programs—and individual statements, such as speeches at conferences, are considered to belong to the latent ideology.

Helenius further includes two dimensions in his "scheme of ideology"; namely, the underlying *ism* (political currents of ideas such as those originated by Marx and Burke) that influences the manifest and the latent ideology, and a dimension that he calls *practical politics.* To Helenius, party ideology can thus be found on different levels and can be either manifest or latent. In the latent ideology there are both collective programs of an "official character" and individual contributions to the political discussion; on the other hand, policy outputs (totalities of actions formulated by the party) fall outside this distinction.[3]

According to Martin Seliger, however, "the distinction between 'manifest' and 'latent' ideology is purely formalistic, pertaining in the last resort neither to what is argued nor to what is done, nor to the relationship between the two, but to whether an issue is argued in official or unofficial party quarters" (1976: 324). Furthermore, according to Seliger, Helenius' distinction is "not focused on the relationship between officially maintained principles and those actually underlying policies" (1976: 322).

Seliger also operates with a two-dimensional concept of ideology. In contrast to that of Helenius, however, his division is not based on the documents of program but on the structure of ideology. Seliger makes a distinction between *fundamental and operative ideology:*

> Thus, ideology applied in action inevitably bifurcates into two dimensions of argumentation: that of fundamental principles, which

determine the final goals and the grand vistas in which they will be realized, and which are set above the second dimension, that of the principles which actually underlie policies and are invoked to justify them. This second dimension of argumentation I have proposed calling operative ideology. In each, all the components of ideological thought are activated, yet with different emphases. *Description, analysis, moral and technical prescription, implementation and rejection* combine in any ideological argument, but the combination takes one of two particular forms that together constitute two interacting dimensions of argumentation. As against the continued assertion of principle in the dimensions of fundamentals, there developes a line of argument whose purpose is to devise and justify the policies executed or recommended by a party, whether or not they deviate from the fundamentals. In the justification of policy in the operative dimension, description and analysis exert greater influence through the enhanced consideration paid to the norms of expediency, prudence and efficiency, i.e. to *technical prescriptions,* which share in, or even replace, the centrality accorded to *moral prescriptions* in fundamental ideology [Seliger, 1976: 109].[4]

In agreement with this, we thus arrive at the conclusion that if one wants to examine the relation between ideology and practical politics, it is useful to penetrate the problem by means of such concepts as fundamental and operative dimensions of party ideology. Otherwise one runs the risk of, so to speak, separating politics from ideology, entirely disregarding policies: "Ideology is present wherever policy-making is present, and policy-making is the attempt to solve problems—or sidetrack them" (Seliger, 1976: 105).

Our real question has thus to do with the fact that preferences change their forms in the course of the policy process. When we associate this question with the argumentation above, the task will be to analyze the content of fundamental principles in relation to operative ideology. In other words, in compromises between different actors the actual application of the fundamental principles tends to be different from the intended one—between the two dimensions of ideology we find a conflict we should describe and analyze. A tool for this task is presented in Figure 4.3, where we have constructed a descriptive scheme of analysis in which the attitudes of "operative" party actors (party leaders, individual candidates for parliament, and the like) are contrasted with the collective attitudes of a programmatic character of the party. We thus distinguish between two different kinds of actors depending on which level of the political system these represent—namely, between actors on a *party level* and on an *individual level.* On the party level we find the party as an organization, as well as its leaders; that is, the party executive body, the party convention, or working groups of an official character appointed by the party. On the individual level we find the individual party representatives, the instrument

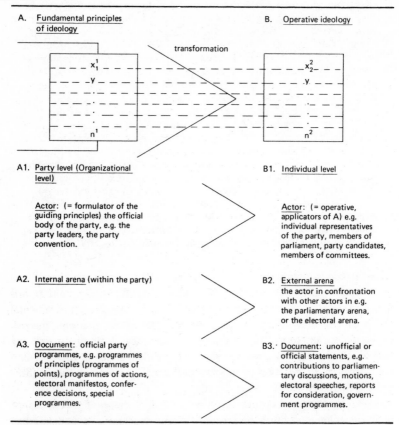

Figure 4.3 Transformation of the Content of Ideas of Politics: Outline of a Descriptive Scheme of Analysis

of the party, who are to act in accordance with the principles and the general outlines of the organization and to be responsible for the technical application of these. This separation is by nature analytical. It may well be that the same member of a party who has participated in the official body of the party and there drawn up the broad outlines, the fundamental principles, will also, in political field work, put these broad outlines and fundamental principles into practice. What takes place, however, is a change of arena. The individual actors leave the *internal arena,* where the objects of influence are constituted by the party's own members, and appear in the *external arena,* where the objects of influence are, for example, constituted by the electorate (*the electoral arena*) or by members of other parties (*the parliamentary arena*; see Sjöblom, 1968: 78-87, passim).

The scheme, of course, could be discussed in detail, but its main capacity is to serve as a basis for formulating a number of questions—for example the following: Were new issues, not present in A, included in B? Were ideas lost? Were innovative features in A transformed to B? Were important demands lost by the organization? Which interest groups were favored/not favored by the transformation?

It is obvious that by applying such a scheme one may arrive at answers to *what* is being transformed or not being transformed. The *circumstances* under which the transformation takes place, on the other hand, remain outside the scope of the scheme. Here we will not enter into such explanatory factors. (Arguments related to actor-oriented theories of party strategy and party tactics present themselves immediately.) Instead, for the sake of illustration, we will outline a conceivable case study applied to Finnish conditions.

The actors whose "ideological content" is the object of analysis are the political parties. Useful objects of study could then be, for instance, the Social Democratic Party (SDP) and the Coalition Party (CP)—suitable, among other things, because both parties are large and bound by close ties to different ideological camps, and useful because their economic and technical resources as a whole are fairly similar and because the party platforms are detailed and comprehensive (that is, comparable qualitatively as well as quantitatively).[5] It would seem suitable to locate the analysis in two different periods; for example, the years 1962-1966, when the Coalition Party was in cabinet position and the SDP was in opposition, and 1966-1970, when the parliamentary situation was the other way around. The purpose of such a division of time, of course, would be to see to what degree the treatment of the ideological content by the actors is due to the parliamentary position of the respective party. The importance of this question has been demonstrated several times in theoretically oriented literature (for example, Sjöblom, 1968: 272-278; Anckar, 1974: 31-37). Another interesting variable would be the area of political issues, and the concrete policies picked out for analysis could then be chosen from (a) the actual political sector of activity (such as the question of administration at the intermediate level); (b) the economic sector (such as price regulations and inflation-controlling actions); (c) the social sector (for example, the development of child care); and (d) the cultural sector (the comprehensive school reform; see Borg, 1965: 286-287).

Because verbal statements constitute the units of classification of content analysis, the empirical material would be composed of different political documents, from the literature of political programs to individual utterances. Programs of principles and actions, electoral programs, and other collectively created special programs, as well as decisions from conferences, can be said to constitute sources which are supposed to have a directing and normative influence on the attitudes of the individual party actor and which are considered to contain the fundamental principles of the party (A). The material forming the basis of the analysis of the operative dimension (B) is considerably more heterogeneous and has a different type of structure than the documents in A. It is important to find corresponding verbal units of analysis, as in A, for example, from minutes of political discussions such as the budget discussion in parliament, parliamentary motions, reports for consideration, and material from law-drafting boards and committees, as well as electoral speeches and contributions to electoral discussions.

PREFERENCES AND POLICIES III:
A PROBLEM OF RESPONSIVENESS

We shall make some comments on a third problem concerned with the relation between preferences and policies that we have called the problem of responsiveness. The starting point is that we are interested in the agreement of content between policy and preferences. We have treated the question on which operational level such a comparison should take place. The problem we now encounter has to do with the simple fact that the preferences may be—and very often are—incompatible among themselves. In addition, they are incompatible in different ways and to different degrees, and this entails content-analytical adjustments.

Let us by way of introduction consider the schema in Table 4.1, where we have indicated in a fourfold table some theoretically conceivable situations. In the first of them (1) we only find such preferences whose

TABLE 4.1   Responsiveness of Four Different Constellations Concerned with Content of Preferences and Content of Policy

		Authorities decide	
		According to preferences	*Deviating from preferences*
Preferences	Compatible	Responsiveness 1	Non-Responsiveness 2
	Incompatible	Partial Responsiveness 3	Non-Responsiveness 4

contents coincide; the policy emanating also corresponds to these preferences. The situation can be said to express policy responsiveness. In the
second situation (2) we also find only coinciding preferences, but the
emanating policy has a different content, and the situation is therefore
nonresponsive. The same is true of situation 4, where a policy emanates
whose content is different from any of the (mutually incompatible)
preferences. On the other hand, it is difficult to judge the third situation
(3), where a policy emanates whose content corresponds to one or several
preferences, but not to other preferences. It is presumably reasonable to
say that this situation is at the same time empirically also the most usual
one.

We will not, however, dwell upon how the analysis of this situation can
be further developed (see Anckar, 1979: 16-21). Instead, we will concentrate on the problem referred to above, a problem which must, on a more
fundamental level, underlie any empirical application of typologies of this
sort. What does it mean, concretely, that something "coincides" or is
"mutually incompatible"?

Let us illustrate the problem with a concrete and arbitrarily chosen
example, the law related to day care for children in Finland, given in
Helsingfors on January 19, 1973 (SBF, No. 36/73). When, as we did
before, we break down this law into policy components, we find that one
component encompasses the application area of the law—that is, the
question as to what day care for children really is. We could perhaps talk
about the area component of the law. The law says that day care for
children is care of children in institutions established for this purpose:
so-called day homes, care of children in private homes or in other family-
like conditions (family day care), and guidance and supervision of the
children's play and occupation—this is the essential content of this policy
component. If, however, we consider the manifest preferences that find
expression in the course of the creation of the law, we may find (1)
preferences which agree with this content; (2) preferences which in no way
correspond to this content (for example, demands that the problems of
day care for children should not be solved by establishing special institutions and forms of care but by means of entirely different actions of
family policy); and (3) preferences that partly correspond to this content
(for example, demands that society should organize child care exclusively
on the basis of institutions, and that family day care should as a consequence remain outside the law and the system of state subsidies it creates).
It is obvious that responsiveness occurs in the first instance and nonresponsiveness in the second, but what do we find in the third? And what
happens, for example, in the event of cross-preferences implying that
family day care should be the primary form of care, even if opportunities

for institutional care should also be offered? Is there "more" or "less" responsiveness than in the third instance? How much—if any—may a content of preference deviate from a content of policy for responsiveness to be considered to be present? Which is the rule of adjustment to be applied?

The first thing we can say here is that a demand for complete agreement between preference and policy is no reasonable point of departure. The demand is not reasonable simply because policies in parliamentary multiparty systems (and we have implicitly based our reasoning on such a conception of polity throughout this discussion) cannot as a rule be supposed to arise as a complete response to a demand while simultaneously ignoring other demands. That this cannot be the case can be explained in many ways; we shall briefly mention two. On one hand, decision-making is usually regarded as the result of an interaction between different decision makers, as an act of weighing together different standpoints. All actors involved in the compromise must give and take to a certain extent. On the other hand, there exist ideological and strategic considerations making the actors unwilling—at least in the early stages of decision processes—to include such considerations of compromise in the manifest preferences they give expression to (see Sjöblom, 1968: 104-106). To put it simply, one tends to claim more than one expects to receive. We thus have a situation in which the compromised content of policy does not completely correspond to any preference untouched by considerations of compromise; and if we stick to the demand for complete agreement, we experience nonresponsiveness down the line. This cannot be a reasonable interpretation, and so the demand just mentioned must be abandoned. The question is instead how much deviation we can tolerate and still talk about responsiveness.

This question can be reformulated to apply to the degree of *similarity*, and we shall here argue along such a line. The difficulty is that we have to deal with a continuum: the similarity between the content of preference and the content of policy may vary from complete agreement to no agreement at all. However, the demand for analytical manageability makes it necessary to do violence to reality and stipulate some reasonable cut-off point where responsiveness changes to nonresponsiveness. The second difficulty is that what we have here called policy components treat such widely different things that an argument supposed to cover them all must have a general form. The components may concern regulative, distributive, or redistributive activities; they may have different sectorial connections—the pattern is so varied that as a whole it can be encompassed only by extremely general categories.

With regard to this we can only suggest an operational procedure that is not free from elements of subjective judgment. The procedure is based on the idea of contrasting preference and policy with respect to two aspects connected with respective policy component. What aspects are to be chosen are impossible to determine because of the general variety we mentioned above; the decisions must be made from case to case. The aspects chosen must not be partial components, which would lead us into the difficulty we discussed in the previous paragraph. They must be retained on the operational level of the policy component, and they are then to be seen predominantly as elements in a key formulation of the content of the policy component. This procedure will offer *one* rule of thumb for the way policy components are to be constructed out of the textual material, even though they should represent clearly typical cases; the demand for clarity cannot be so strict as not to permit a separation of aspects.

For each aspect one makes a qualitative judgment of the degree of similarity along a constructed scale whose points may be, for example, "complete similarity," "strong partial similarity," "weak partial similarity," and "no similarity." The results of these judgments can subsequently be brought together in a matrix (see Table 4.2 below for an illustration) showing the total picture and the judgments of responsiveness emanating from this.

TABLE 4.2 Matrix of Responsiveness Showing Occurrence of Reponsiveness (R) or Nonreponsiveness (NR) in Ten Different Situations of Agreement

		Aspect II		
The similarity is:	*Complete*	*Partial, strong*	*Partial, weak*	*None*
Aspect I:				
Complete	1. R	2. R	4. R	7. NR
Partial, strong		3. R	5. R	8. NR
Partial, weak			6. NR	9. NR
None				10. NR

Regarding these judgments, it is true that they are also subjective. Situations 1-3 probably must be considered clear: here it is a question of more or less similarity. Likewise, situations 9-10 must be considered clear: here it is directly a question of a lack of similarity. The same thing may be said about situation 6, where we have a discernible, but yet not reasonably sufficient similarity. More problematic considerations appear, then, in situations 4, 5, 7, and 8. We have decided to classify the former two as responsive and the latter two as nonresponsive, on the grounds that the latter cases represent a balance where one of the aspects is not provided for.

One could, of course, discuss whether this is a reasonable way of stipulating a cut-off point. Especially the boundary between situations 5 and 8 may seem a matter of taste, and one could further ask whether situation 7, which involves complete similarity concerning one of the aspects, is not too severely judged. As stated before, such questions are by no means unjustified; and the fact that they may be answered in somewhat different but nevertheless equivalent ways provides a good illustration of the difficulties encountered when theoretically derived questions are contrasted in an operational guise with the empirical reality they are to illuminate and elucidate. In the present case, conclusions about responsiveness are thus at least partly dependent upon the classification decisions being made for the especially troublesome situations referred to above. The extent to which this is the case depends on the empirical frequency of the situations, and it is consequently to be recommended that attention be paid to this frequency. It should also be included in the conclusions eventually reached.

NOTES

1. A few examples in the literature are Cnudde and McCrone on expenditures (1969), Ståhlberg on planning (1975), Fry and Winters on redistribution (1970), and Walker on diffusion (1969).

2. A noteworthy exception is Damgaard and Eliassen (1978).

3. See Helenius (1970: 44). By "practical politics" Helenius refers to issues such as the "investment Bank" or "comprehensive school," which display a direct relation to manifest ideology and a visionary, indirect relation to latent ideology. However, "the surface layer of latent ideology already borders upon practical politics" (Helenius, 1970: 46; see also 1969: 285-287).

4. Further, Seliger claims:

I have also stressed that, to whatever degree policies conform with fundamental principles operative ideology denotes the argumentation of the policies actually adopted by a party. It is ideology because it devises, explains and justifies action. It is "operative" inasmuch as it is predicated on what is actually done or recommended for immediate action. Moreover, the explanations and justifications offered in operative ideology contain all the structural components of fundamental ideology. Operative deviates from or corresponds with fundamental ideology according to whether or not the specific contents (and the emphases of structural components) in one dimension are congruent with those found in the other [1976: 175].

5. See Borg (1965: 151-153), who demonstrates a striking similarity between object profiles in the platforms of the Coalition Party on the one hand and the left-wing parties on the other. However, the platforms express evaluations which are diametrically opposed.

REFERENCES

ANCKAR, D. (1974). "Analys av partiers beteende: en fallstudie i partistrategi" (Analyzing party behavior: A case study of party strategy). Åbo: Acta Academiae Aboensis, Humaniora, 48 No. 1.

——— (1979). "Arenaforing som politikmått: diskussion av kriterier" (Evaluating politics by analyzing agenda-building: A discussion of criteria). Paper delivered at the XIth Annual Meeting, Finnish Political Science Association, Åbo.

——— (1978a). "Att klassificera lagar: prolog till en policydiskussion" (Classifying laws: A prologue to policy research). Åbo: Acta Academiae Aboensis, Humaniora, 55 No. 4.

——— (1978b). "Politik, partier, policy: om modeller för arena-förande" (Politics, parties, policy: Models of agenda-building). Publications of the Research Institute of the Abo Akademi Foundation, No. 40.

——— (1977). "Lagstiftning, transformation, responsivitet. Skisser kring ett forsknings-program" (Law-making, transformation, responsiveness. Outline of a research project). Publications of the Research Institute of the Åbo Akademi Foundation, No. 16.

BORG, O. (1965). Suomen puolueideologiat (Party Ideologies in Finland). Porvoo: Werner Söderström OY.

CNUDDE, C. F. and McCRONE, D. J. (1969). "Party competition and welfare policies in the American states." American Political Science Review 63, 3: 858-866.

COBB, R. and ELDER, C. D. (1975). Participation in American Politics: The Dynamics of Agenda-Building. Baltimore: Johns Hopkins University Press.

COBB, R., KEITH-ROSS, J., and ROSS, M. HOWARD (1976). "Agenda-building as a comparative political process." American Political Science Review 70, 1: 126-138.

DAMGAARD, E. and ELIASSEN, K. A. (1978). "Corporate pluralism in Danish law-making." Scandinavian Political Studies 1, 4: 285-313.

FRY, B. R. and WINTERS, R. F. (1970). "The politics of redistribution." American Political Science Review 64, 2: 508-522.

HELENIUS, R. (1970). "Partiideologins kvalitet" (The quality of party ideology). Statsvetenskaplig Tidskrift, No. 1: 35-50.

——— (1969). The Profile of Party Ideologies. Helsinki: Scandinavian University Books.

KARVONEN, L. and ANCKAR, D. (1978). Om innovativa lagar (On Innovative Laws). Publications of the Research Institute of the Åbo Akademi Foundation, No. 33.

KERR, D. H. (1976). "The logic of 'policy' and successful policies." Policy Sciences 7, 3: 351-363.

PIETILÄ, V. (1973). Sisällön erittely (Content Analysis). Helsinki: OY Gaudeamus.

108   *Relating Preferences to Policy*

SCHAEFFER, G. F. (1972). "Policy analysis und politologie." In Sozialwissenschaftlichen Jahrbuch für Politik, Band 3. München: Günter Olzog Verlag.
SCHUMAKER, P. D. (1975). "Policy responsiveness to protest-group demands." Journal of Politics 37, 2: 488-521.
SELIGER, M. (1976). Ideology and Politics. London: George Allen & Unwin.
SJÖBLOM, G. (1968). Party Strategies in A Multiparty System. Lund: Studentlitteratur.
Statute-Book of Finland [SBF], Volumes 1973, 1975.
STÅHLBERG, K. (1975). Teori och praxis i kommunal planering (Theory and Practice in Communal Planning). Publications of the Research Institute of the Åbo Akademi Foundation, No. 4.
WALKER, J. L. (1969). "The diffusion of innovations among the American states." American Political Science Review 63, 3: 880-899.
WESTHOLM, C.-J. (1976). Ratio och universalitet. John Stuart Mill och dagens demokratidebatt (Ratio and Universality. John Stuart Mill and Contemporary Debate about Democracy). Kungälv: Rabén & Sjögren.

PART II

EMPIRICAL STUDIES

Chapter 5

MEDIA CONTENT AND
HUMAN COMPREHENSION

Olle Findahl and Birgitta Höijer

THIS CHAPTER PRESENTS an attempt to analyze radio and TV news items from the viewers' perspective. The analysis is based on psychological and psycholinguistic findings concerning the human comprehension process as well as findings about how people perceive and absorb broadcast news messages. The chapter includes a concrete example of such an analysis together with a brief summary of the kinds of conclusions that may be drawn from it.

APPROACHING THE TEXT
AND DESCRIBING ITS CONTENT

How does one describe a conversation, a story, a text, film, or television program? What is the content?

The last question may seem trivial, but it is not easily answered. Content analysis aims to do much more than simply relate or narrate a story or program. Rather, content analysis sets out to characterize, to condense and elucidate the content, to bring out the essentials or point out certain typical characteristics. It is a matter of describing the content not by itemizing all the words and clauses, but by revealing features that are not immediately apparent to readers, listeners, or viewers.

There are, however, numerous ways of describing content, and one's choice of method is determined by definite motives and assumptions, even though these may not always be made explicit. There are various theories and scientific traditions to choose from of which traditional quantitative content analysis—which has dominated the field of media research—is only one. The basic question is what approach to take. What features should be singled out? How? What level of analysis will produce satisfactory answers to the questions posed? These are vital considerations that face any researcher who sets about analyzing verbal communication.

According to the German philosopher Dilthey (1922), there are two ways of approaching a text, from without or from within. These two approaches derive from two separate scientific traditions—that of the natural sciences and that of the humanities. Natural science attempts to explain processes: dissecting the whole into its component parts, the natural scientist then tries to deduce the whole on the basis of the laws governing the interaction of those parts. Humanistic inquiry, on the other hand, seeks to understand: the humanist places a given whole in its context and then tries to identify its inherent function or goal (see Liedman, 1977).

The coming of the social sciences has rendered this classic boundary between the two traditions somewhat diffuse. Are explanation and understanding necessarily two essentially different processes, as Dilthey claimed, or can they be combined? Are they perhaps simply two different aspects of the same thing?

What, then, is understanding? Dilthey, for his part, distinguished two different kinds of understanding: ordinary understanding, in which subjective impulses and inspiration play a role, and strictly methodical interpretation, which is bound to a formal analytical procedure and schema. We are primarily interested in this latter form. However, what methodology, what analytical procedure should we use? The question is, how do we break the hermeneutic circle—that the whole must be understood on the basis of its individual components, while the components must be understood on the bases of the whole? Dilthey concluded that the problem was theoretically insoluble; only practical work on the part of a skillful and experienced analyst, well acquainted with his text, might resolve it.

The French philosopher Ricoeur (1970) offers an alternative solution, combining structural and interpretative analysis; that is, external analysis (from without) combined with internal analysis (from within). Ricoeur takes his point of departure in structural linguistics.

Both Dilthey and Ricoeur have pinpointed factors of vital relevance to content analysis: Dilthey, the necessity of thorough familiarity with the object of analysis; Ricoeur, the necessity of employing an external reference system, a structure one can impose on the text under study. It is only when one has an idea of the nature and the essential structure of the object of investigation that one can choose an analytical procedure and a method which will shed light on that object.

Traditional quantitative content analyses have started with a method and a procedure and forgotten to define their objects of study (Rühl,

1976). Behind that approach we find the empiricist doctrine that all that can be found is an accumulation of specific items. This corresponds to the naive psychological theory of the human mind as a storehouse into which incoming words are piled.

TWO TRAPS

Two main dangers are associated with the natural scientific and humanistic traditions, respectively, when it comes to the analysis of verbal messages. One is the temptation to analyze exclusively from the outside, to look upon the text in question as an abstract system unto itself. The other, opposite danger is the tendency to analyze totally from within, looking upon the text as a subjective artifact of the individual creator.[1]

Many linguists, philosophers, and structuralists have fallen into the former trap. Studying language as an abstract system unto itself, they ignore the fact that language assumes meaning only when it meets an audience whose members have experiences and histories of their own. Psychologists and literary scholars who are primarily interested in readers, audiences, or creators have fallen into the latter trap. Dwelling on the individual and the subjective features of the work, they forget that human language is a social product.

What people grasp of a text, however, is neither entirely individual/subjective nor a faithful copy of the words and clauses it is made up of. When, for example, we ask people who have seen a news program to relate what they have seen, their report is neither a transcript-like narration of the content nor the results of a linguistic analysis. Rather, their reports summarize and condense what they have heard and seen. The summarizing is not entirely individual or subjective. It is not arbitrary, but follows certain principles that apply to all who live under the same material conditions and share the same experiences and history.

ANALYSIS OF NEWS ITEMS
FROM THE VIEWERS' PERSPECTIVE

THE PROBLEM

Our aim is to study the news programs of the Swedish Broadcasting Corporation (Sveriges Radio) from the perspective of the viewing audience. What are the programs about? What do they tell people? Whom do they address? Are news items presented in such a way that the audience can understand what it is all about? Are the various conditions that permit viewers to learn about and comprehend events and processes in their surroundings satisfied?

Quantitative content analysis cannot answer these questions. It is inadequate here, as it is based on the often subconscious presumption that what the audience perceives and retains is identical to the text (or TV content) they are exposed to. However, it is hardly that simple. Identifying the features that are important to viewers demands other frames of reference.

One such feature is psychological relevance. This criterion applies to the level and units of analysis, to the descriptors, as well as to the concepts applied. It means that the mode of description must correspond to people's thinking, to their ideas and conceptual universe. The content is not "hidden" in the text, but develops in the interaction between the text and the reader, listener, or viewer.[2] Even if 100 percent of the population watch a news telecast, they have not learned much if they fail to understand what the news items are about; and even if they understand everything, the structure of the content will have influenced what they absorb. Three main factors are at play here: the human comprehension process, the program content, and the manner in which the content is presented. Any analysis of news telecasts from the viewer's point of view must take all three factors into account.

HUMAN COMPREHENSION

While there is no complete theory as to the specific mental functions involved in comprehension, certain basic principles have been established.[3] The comprehension process occurs on different levels (Luria, 1976). Processes on the lower levels usually occur automatically and unconsciously. If we confine our discussion for the moment to the spoken word, the impulses reaching us consist of words, intonations, and pauses. The next step in the process is one of grouping these impulses. The most important bits are sorted out and ordered hierarchically. Toward the end of this process, when grammatical and prosodic characteristics come into the picture, we are ready for the next phase of the process, which involves the reduction and condensation of the organized bits into a form of "inner language." It is on the basis of this condensed, inner register that we attempt to synthesize and grasp the gist of the message: What does it all mean? What is it about? In this process of interpretation we use our own previous experiences and our conceptions of reality as a framework or scheme for processing different types of news events.

Comprehension may be characterized as an active process in which the different phases interact and in which the elements of content are gradually linked together in accordance with overall organizational principles dictated by the context. The process then continues; once we have understood the messages, we proceed to draw conclusions as to what motives and purposes may underlie them.

Even though the lower levels in the comprehension process may be automatic, many problems can nevertheless arise due to the use of difficult, esoteric words or complicated grammatical constructions, or due to confusing visual accompaniment. Words and phrases, however, are not in themselves the decisive factor for listeners'/viewers' understanding of the messages. Rather, the decisive factor is the manner in which the words and phrases are organized into larger units. Two separate mental mechanisms are at play here: one, which is closely related to the short-term memory, involves linkages between, for example, the words of a sentence or the relations between successive sentence. The other mechanism deals with larger units—the logical or thematic structure of the news item—whereas the former has more to do with the manner or technique of presentation.

This leads us to conclude that we must focus our analysis on what links words, clauses, and pictures into meaningful wholes. Analyzing the verbal composition of a given text, we find it full of references backward and forward. New information must be linked to what has already been made known.[4] Repetition and references to antecedents play important roles in this regard.

Other linkages are to be found in the logical structure of the news items. How are the various elements or information linked to one another? These cohesive links may be found in the verbal and visual style of presentation. Is there an overall theme? Do sound and picture match?

THE PRECONDITIONS OF COMMUNICATION

Our analysis must also take into account one of the basic preconditions for communication; namely, what we might call the tacit agreement that must prevail between the speaker and the listener.

Human communication occurs on the basis of certain tacit preconditions. If a speaker wishes to be understood, he must adapt his manner of speaking to the person he addresses. This is a silent agreement, and as long as it is observed the listener will make an effort to understand what the speaker says. The communication between them rests on the basis of their shared knowledge. (In analyzing the news, we assume that the audience tunes into news telecasts because they want to find out what has happened in Sweden and the world. The main function of language in this context is thus to convey information about the real world.[5])

If the newscaster should start talking about something entirely foreign to his viewers, and does so without giving them an orientation or background information, the agreement has been broken. It is no longer a question of communication. The viewer/listener no longer feels like a viewer/listener, and may shrug his shoulders, saying "This means nothing to me," or "Words, words, words!"

Thus, we ask: "What knowledge and experience do journalists assume their viewers and listeners possess?" With whom has the "tacit agreement" been drawn up?

NEWS STUDY FINDINGS

So far, we have discussed some of the basic preconditions for communication and understanding. But the most important cornerstone on which the analysis rests is what we know about how people perceive and absorb broadcast news content. Here we refer primarily to the findings of a series of experiments undertaken to determine the importance of various verbal formulations and uses of visuals in television news (Findahl, 1971; Findahl and Höijer, 1973, 1975, 1976). First, we might start by summarizing the principal results on which we base many of our conclusions in the analysis.

Causes and consequences must be emphasized. What generally gets across to viewers and listeners is the location of the event and who or what is involved, especially concrete details like place-names, names of public figures and celebrities, and the names of firms: "rioting in Iran," "problems at Kockums steel." Often these elements automatically occupy the foreground of what people recall, while what caused the event and what it might result in remain in the background. The overall result is fragmentary recall, with viewers/listeners recalling isolated details but missing the context.

Mere mention of the cause of an event and its (likely) consequences is not enough. These elements must be emphasized and given a place in the foreground if they are to be recalled by the audience. What is more, only then will viewers/listeners be able to form a mental image of the news item as a whole and comprehend it in a broader context. One might even say that making the causes and consequences of an event clear is the key to making the event comprehensible to the viewing audience.

Visuals can compound fragmentation. Visuals are important in that they come across to the viewer, thrusting their content into the foreground. Unfortunately, what is easiest to capture in pictures is the more concrete aspects of the story—places, persons, and things—which viewers tend to recall best anyway. Panoramic shots of the location or pictures of the type of milieu involved and photo-portraits frequently serve as visual accompaniment in news programs. Such visuals may overshadow the rest of the content so that only the elements so illustrated are absorbed.

Sound and picture should jibe. Visuals that generally indicate what the event is about, but do not relate directly to the content (such as "postcard" pictures of Tour d'Eiffel or Big Ben) are seldom of any help to the viewer. Moreover, if the visuals are interesting in themselves—for example, if something new is happening all the time—they may attract most or all of the viewer's attention so that the verbal message is neglected.

However, when sound and picture correspond, so that the visuals support or provide cues to what is being said—or the reporter describes what is pictured—viewers' comprehension improves significantly (see also Wember, 1976).

Generally, the informational aspects of news presentation occupy our focus. Newcasts deal with happenings and ongoing processes in Sweden and abroad, with concrete events, places, people, and things, with causes and effects. We must check to see what of this content is emphasized verbally and, in the case of telecasts, what of the content is featured in the visual accompaniment.

Any analysis of comprehensibility must alternate between substantive and formal aspects of the text. Here we shall briefly indicate some of the more important formal aspects currently under study (for a review of the literature see Findahl and Höijer, 1977).

Complex pictures of fast-moving collages can cause difficulties, as a number of studies have confirmed.

Unclear or ambiguous visuals, the meaning of which is not immediately apparent, can also cause problems.

Tempo, too, is important. Too few pauses or too rapid delivery make it hard for many to grasp what the news item is about.

Undefined and abstract terms and concepts block and distract the viewers' ongoing process of decoding the news item, thus impairing comprehension.

A TWO-STEP ANALYSIS

We must approach our material with a holistic perspective. Such important aspects of the content as relations between various facts and other elements within a news item seldom can be classified and isolated in simple categories, since they are products of the whole and must be viewed in that context.

Traditional coding schemes are not suited to this task, since they serve only to carve the text up into pieces. Rather, in our analysis we carry on what might be called a dialogue with the material under study. Our methodology is rooted more in hermeneutic and structuralist traditions than in traditional content analysis, employing ready-made coding schemes.

In order to answer our research questions, it proved necessary to analyze the news items in two steps or on two levels. In the first step we ask what the item is about. What is the event? What are we told about it?

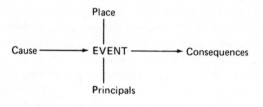

Figure 5.1   Structure of Events

Are other events mentioned? How is all the information interrelated? The answers to these questions form the content structure of the item—that is, a schematic description of the content of the item. We draw up what might be called an "ideal" description of the item content, analyzing the content without reference to the manner of presentation and the item's comprehensibility. We simply catalogue the information provided, noting how the elements are related to one another.

The structure of events. News texts are produced within a certain historical tradition and follow strict standard patterns. There are narrative rules for how a news story should be told.[6] News is about events, especially those which have recently occurred. Events, one might say, are a basic ingredient in practically every news item. The event involves actors and other principals to the event, who are fixed in time and place. There is a background of causes and motives, and the event has, or will have, consequences. These basic elements form a structure that may be illustrated as shown in Figure 5.1.[7]

Most news items contain, or make reference to, several events, principals, and so on. Different combinations of the basic elements are possible, and there are also temporal and geographic relations which give the news items a far more complex structure than that indicated in Figure 5.1.

In the second stage of analysis, we approach the material from the viewer's point of view, looking upon the news item as a process in which information is successively communicated to those who view and listen. Here we deal with aspects concerning both content and manner of presentation and the interaction between form and content. Our procedure is to go through the news item, element by element, and assess its "comprehensibility" with reference to the factors we know to be vital to viewers'/listeners' understanding of news information. The findings of this second step are recorded in the form of a possible message structure.

By way of illustration, we present a concrete example of such an analysis below. The analysis is very detailed—treating the content element by element. This is a consequence of our point of departure; it is on precisely such a concrete level that human comprehension takes place. However, before proceeding to the analysis, a few more words about our procedure are necessary.

It is difficult to formulate our procedure in any set of rules, and the reader hoping to find a recipe for assessing comprehensibility will be disappointed. Our guiding principle has been that each aspect or detail must be considered in context and in relation to a given content. Our analysis alternates between detailed analysis of, for example, a sentence, concept, or picture and analysis of the content as a whole.

This alternation between detail and the whole characterizes the comprehension process, and is also necessary in scientific interpretations of messages. The difference is that we as researchers analyze and discuss on both levels, whereas in actual comprehension, analysis of detail generally occurs unconsciously and automatically.

AN EXAMPLE–CRISIS IN THE LABOR MARKET

Crises in various branches of Swedish industry figured prominently in the news during the spring of 1978. The textile, steel, ship-building, and forestry industries all suffered acute problems. Unemployment gradually rose, hitting young people and the northern reaches of the country particularly hard.

As part of a series of analyses of Swedish radio and TV news programs, we studied one week's reportage about "the industrial crisis" in Sweden. The item treated below was among those studied.[8]

The time is Monday, February 27, 1978. Problems in the Swedish ready-to-wear clothing industry are treated as a major item of domestic news on one of the evening news telecasts. The headline, read at the beginning of the program, ran:

> AMS warns the government. In a letter to the Government today the National Labor Board [AMS] called for forceful measures to meet the current crisis in the ready-to-wear clothing industry. AMS is currently doing what it can to save textile and clothing firm Strands in Katrineholm.

Viewers were shown a photo of a seamstress at her sewing machine with a superimposed caption: "AMS WARNS THE GOVERNMENT." A dramatic headline. A cursory examination of the item shows it to consist of two main parts, both of which deal with the clothing industry crisis.

The former treats the industry as a whole, and the second treats the individual firm Strands.

But let us look at this item more closely. What is it about? How is it presented? (A detailed transcript of the item is presented on the following pages.)

THE CONTENT STRUCTURE –
WHAT THE ITEM IS ABOUT

Our first step to undertake is a structural analysis of the content of the item, a description of the facts included and how these facts are related to one another. In order to make this structure clear we have chosen to illustrate it in the form of a diagram (see Figure 5.2).

What does the diagram tell us? As noted earlier, the item consists of two main parts: one dealing with the crisis in general, the other with the the crisis at Strands. Both parts comprise several facts that are thematically or logically related. There are long chains of causal links, indicated by arrows.

Let us read the diagram beginning at the upper lefthand corner (1) with the crisis in the Swedish clothing industry. This had led AMS (the National Labor Market Board) to send a letter to the government. The letter calls for forceful measures. Alternatively, we might start at the lower lefthand corner (2). Unemployment in the Swedish city Katrineholm is above the national average. This means that it is difficult to relocate people in new jobs. The County Employment Board has therefore suggested that AMS convert the firm Strands into a relief work production unit.

In addition to these main parts there is an independent part not directly related to the news event: the mention of hospital trousers production, which is indicated in the center of the diagram at point 3. Background factors are mentioned with respect to both the crisis in general and Strands. The proposal of the County Employment Board and the prospect of cotton trousers production also have their own backgrounds. As seen in Figure 5.2, we have entered these background factors and motives to the left of the events mentioned in the news item.

Another feature worthy of note is the fact that AMS recurs as a main actor or principal in several connections. This may cause confusion. In one place the text states that AMS makes no specific proposals, while elsewhere AMS is reported to have placed a relief order to save Strands. Similarly, it is stated that AMS officials are not textile and clothing experts, while in the final interview an AMS official declares that Strands cannot respond to the need for hospital trousers. Meanwhile, another source suggests that AMS take over the management of the firm.

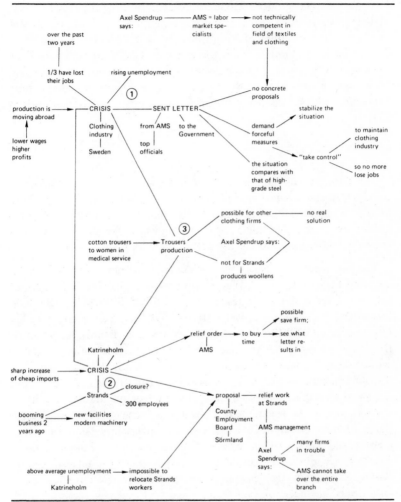

Figure 5.2 Content Structure of a News Item about the Crisis in the Swedish Clothing Industry

NOTE: The diagram includes all information offered in the item; lines and arrows indicate how the various bits of information are related. Arrows indicate causal relationships and should be read, "leads to" or "has led to." Lines represent other types of relationships.

A serious problem may reside in the characterization of Strands' present situation. The text states both that the firm has failed and that it has received a relief order "to tide it over."

Summary. The content structure is comprised of two main parts, related to each other by a common background. A third part is not directly related to either of the former two and "dangles" somewhat in mid-air. Each part contains facts that are linked in causal chains, forming independent cause-event-consequence sequences. One of the principals, AMS, plays a somewhat confusing role in several parts of the structure. Confusion also prevails concerning one of the main events—the crisis at Strands.

MESSAGE STRUCTURE

The next step in the analysis is to relate the content to the audience and analyze the comprehensibility of the news item and try to find out what information is foregrounded in the item and what information has little chance of being caught by the audience. We shall address this question by going through the news story point by point.

Leading headlines (read at the beginning of the newscast) cue viewers, directing their attention to the principal news items. The item analyzed here was given a dramatic presentation, with "AMS WARNS THE GOV-ERNMENT" superimposed over a still photo of a seamstress at work. The principal actor is AMS (the National Labor Market Board). AMS is mentioned three times in the headline, while it also figures in the superimposed caption. The headline stresses the urgency of AMS' actions: "warns . . . demands forceful measures . . . doing what it can to save . . ." But exactly what AMS has done remains unclear. The root of the problem lies in the last sentence of the leading text. Does this sentence refer to the subject of the caption, or does it not? Here is a seed of uncertainty. AMS has written a letter, and AMS is trying to save a firm—or is it one and the same thing? The audience, of course, has no opportunity to ponder this question in the dozen-odd seconds the headline takes, but somewhere "in the back of their heads" the uncertainty is there.

(1) The first sentence in the item itself refers back to the AMS letter mentioned in the headline, and it is now clear that it is about the problems facing the Swedish clothing industry. A long row of sewing machines is visible in back of the anchorman (see item 1 in Figure 5.3a).

That one-third of the garment industry labor force has been put out of work is mentioned in a single sentence. This fact shows the seriousness of the situation and explains the urgency of the AMS letter. But since it is mentioned only in passing, viewers have little chance to absorb this fact. Instead, the more or less glissando coupling of the industry as a whole (the

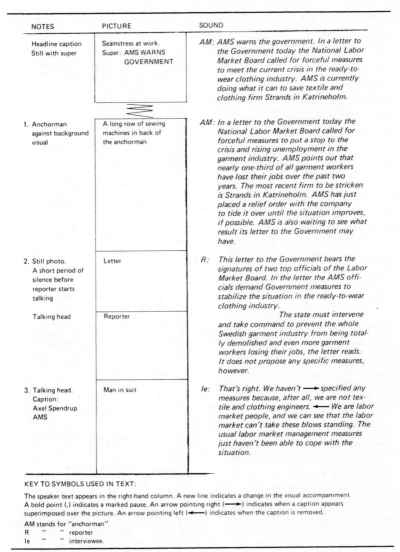

NOTES	PICTURE	SOUND
Headline caption Still with super	Seamstress at work. Super: AMS WARNS GOVERNMENT	*AM: AMS warns the government. In a letter to the Government today the National Labor Market Board called for forceful measures to meet the current crisis in the ready-to-wear clothing industry. AMS is currently doing what it can to save textile and clothing firm Strands in Katrineholm.*
1. Anchorman against background visual	A long row of sewing machines in back of the anchorman	*AM: In a letter to the Government today the National Labor Market Board called for forceful measures to put a stop to the crisis and rising unemployment in the garment industry. AMS points out that nearly one-third of all garment workers have lost their jobs over the past two years. The most recent firm to be stricken is Strands in Katrineholm. AMS has just placed a relief order with the company to tide it over until the situation improves, if possible. AMS is also waiting to see what result its letter to the Government may have.*
2. Still photo. A short period of silence before reporter starts talking	Letter	*R: This letter to the Government bears the signatures of two top officials of the Labor Market Board. In the letter the AMS officials demand Government measures to stabilize the situation in the ready-to-wear clothing industry.*
Talking head	Reporter	*The state must intervene and take command to prevent the whole Swedish garment industry from being totally demolished and even more garment workers losing their jobs, the letter reads. It does not propose any specific measures, however.*
3. Talking head. Caption: Axel Spendrup AMS	Man in suit	*Ie: That's right. We haven't ⟶ specified any measures because, after all, we are not textile and clothing engineers. ⟵ We are labor market people, and we can see that the labor market can't take these blows standing. The usual labor market management measures just haven't been able to cope with the situation.*

KEY TO SYMBOLS USED IN TEXT:

The speaker text appears in the right-hand column. A new line indicates a change in the visual accompaniment. A bold point (.) indicates a marked pause. An arrow pointing right (⟶) indicates when a caption appears superimposed over the picture. An arrow pointing left (⟵) indicates when the caption is removed.

AM stands for "anchorman"
R   "   " reporter
Ie   "   " interviewee.

Figure 5.3A

topic of the AMS letter) and Strands (the firm AMS is trying to save) is repeated.

(2) The letter is shown in the picture (see item 2 in Figure 5.3a). The letterhead reads "AMS." The audience is given a few seconds to read before a reporter begins speaking. He refers directly to what the viewers

NOTES	PICTURE	SOUND
3. Film-"collage"	Pressing. CLOSE-UP, ZOOM OUT to MED. SHOT	R: One-third of all garment workers have lost their jobs in the last two years alone, and the bottom hasn't been reached yet. Instead, more and more of Swedish production is moving abroad.
	Women sewing. PAN to clothing on conveyor	Wages are lower there, and profits higher. In the letter
	Still photo of letter	to the Government AMS compares the situation with that of high-grade steel.
	Facade of building. MED. LONG; ZOOM to LONG SHOT of whole b.	It is the failure of this company that has renewed the debate: Strands in Katrineholm, with 300 employees. Two years ago
	CLOSE-UP of sewing machine; ZOOM OUT to woman tending machine	business was booming and the company had to build new facilities and acquire modern machinery to keep up with its order book.
	Sports jackets in rows; workers in background	But, since then the volume of cheap imports has increased sharply, and it is this competition
	Needles sewing	that has beat Strands and other firms in this country.
	Sportsjackets in rows workers in background	As for Strands, the County Employment Board in Södermanland proposes that AMS
	Clothes conveyed away	save the company by making it a government-owned relief work.
	Woman walking in corridor. PAN, time-clock	The Board points out that unemployment in Katrineholm was well above average even before this crisis. It may prove impossible to find jobs for those now working at Strands, the Board says.
4. Talking head Caption: Axel Spendrup AMS	Man in suit	Ie: Many firms in many communities face ⟶ problems and may find themselves in Strands' position ⟵ and we can hardly take over the whole Swedish clothing industry.
		R: But you are planning measures clearly designed to save Strands?
		Ie: We will do what we can. We have already done something in giving them an order to tide them over a while.
Film	Woman models in hospital corridor	R: Female hospital employees are to be issued cotton trousers as standard dress. Doesn't that demand come just in time to help the clothing industry?
Talking head	Man in suit	Ie: As far as Strands is concerned it doesn't mean a thing. Strands sews Woollens, but what hospital personnel need is cotton trousers. There's a big difference. Strands isn't at all equipped for that; We've discovered that in our previous efforts to help the firm.
		R: How about other textile and clothing firms in trouble today?
		Ie: Perhaps. As I say, I don't think it solves the problem, but it may help.

Figure 5.3B

see before them (*"This letter to ..."*). The reporter proceeds to sum-marize the content of the letter. The wording is abstract: *". . . government measures to stabilize this situation," "the state must intervene and take command."* The summary surprisingly concludes with: *"It does not pro-pose any specific measures, however."*

At this point a man's face appears on the screen. Several seconds pass before he starts talking. Viewers must discover who he is and why he is commenting by reading a small caption shown briefly at the foot of the picture while listening to what he is saying. They are not allowed to hear the question he is obviously answering. In other words, viewers must simultaneously (1) find out who is being interviewed, (2) figure out what the question was, and (3) listen to his answer. How many viewers can perform this feat, especially when much of what is said assumes prior knowledge of the situation at hand: *"these blows," "just haven't been able to handle the situation"*?

(3) Next we are shown a film collage of glimpses from a garment factory assembly line (see item 3 in Figure 5.3b). In the first seconds of the collage the reporter repeats the vital information that one-third of the labor force in the industry has been put out of work over the past two years. Contrary to this statement, however, a presser is shown at work, and the camera zooms from a close-up to a medium-long shot to include a co-worker standing nearby. New scenes with new camera variation ensue. On the whole, if the camera is stationary, it is only because the picture is highly animated—for example, with long rows of garments passing by on a conveyor belt. Somewhere, seemingly far in the background, the reporter's voice continues, but his words are hardly likely to register in the minds of viewers.

The image of the letter reappears for several seconds, followed by a characterization of the problems facing Strands. The reporter says, *"It is the failure of this company ..."* and proceeds to describe the factors that have "beat" Strands. Earlier, however, the item mentioned a relief order and outlined ways in which the company might be saved. Does this mean relief orders to a closed-down factory? Or is the reporter assuming viewers known something they don't? Or is it simply a slip of the tongue?

The film collage continues its "action-packed" pace. To the accompani-ment of fleeting images, the County Employment Board of Södermanland proposes that Strands be converted into a relief work production unit. What that implies is not explained. This information creates some confu-sion in that it does not bear upon the AMS letter, while earlier it has been related that AMS was placing a relief order with the firm.

(4) The same "talking head" reappears (see item 4 in Figure 5.3b). There is no pause, no introduction, and once again viewers hear him responding to a question they have not been heard. The question must be deduced from three different sentences in the immediately preceding segment. The interview continues; viewers are now able to hear the questions as well.

Suddenly, the reporter brings up the need of cotton trousers in Swedish hospitals. The visuals show a woman modeling a white pant-suit in a hospital corridor. This film clip disappears as abruptly as it appeared. The reporter's manner of posing the question suggests either that he considers this new demand for cotton trousers a well-known fact or that, momentarily forgetting his audience, he engages in a personal conversation with the AMS spokesman. The latter is far from enthusiastic in his response, and the item ends up on something of a false note, coming to no real conclusion, with no "rounding off" or summing up.

Summary of the message structure. The initial headline at the beginning of the program presented the item with a dramatic caption, mentioning AMS, the government, a letter, the clothing industry, and Strands. All these elements were subsequently mentioned in various combinations several times. This repetition most likely resulted in viewers being well aware of who and what were involved in the news story. But how are the elements interrelated? What roles do the actors play?

That AMS sent the letter is made clear in several places, but what does the letter have to do with Strands? Viewers are left wondering. Just as the visuals were cut and rearranged, the interview with AMS spokesman Spendrup was also cut up and dispersed throughout the item. On the whole, the clothing industry and the individual firm, Strands, were discussed interchangeably.

Who was trying to save Strands—the government, AMS, or the County Employment Board? Who proposed a solution—the government, AMS, or the County Employment Board? And who had no proposal whatsoever—the government, AMS, or the County Employment Board?

That Swedish textile and clothing firms are in trouble would appear to be well known, but it is doubtful that the fact that one-third of all Swedish textile and garment workers have been rendered jobless in the last two years got across to the public. Much of the background information presented in the item was "illustrated" by a distracting film collage.

The situation of the Strands firm was also the subject of imprecise and apparently contradictory information. Much of the item treated proposed schemes to save the company, but this material was left "dangling" due to uncertainty as to the actual status of the firm. One week earlier 260 of the 300 employees had lost their jobs, and only the senior workers with their

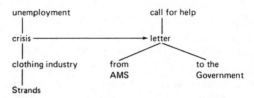

Figure 5.4 Message Structure

longer terms of notice were still working. This was never mentioned in the news item.

What got across to news viewers is most likely the following: UNEMPLOYMENT AND THE CRISIS IN THE CLOTHING INDUSTRY HAS PROMPTED AMS TO WRITE A LETTER TO THE GOVERNMENT. AMS URGES THE GOVERNMENT TO DO SOMETHING. STRANDS IS A COMPANY STRICKEN BY THE CRISIS. This may be summarized as in Figure 5.4.

What happened then? Two weeks later, Strands' machinery stopped once and for all. One hundred of its employees got new jobs at a clothing factory in the neighborhood. Two hundred were out of work. The problem for the Swedish clothing industry continued. Many firms were closed; others managed to remain functional with help from government subsidies.

We have similarly analyzed some 20 news items on the subject of crisis in Swedish industry, as experienced in the first quarter of 1978. The results of these analyses have been published in an initial report (Findahl and Höijer, 1979). Coming reports will analyze news coverage of proposed employee-controlled investment funds, atomic energy, central labor contract negotiations, and selected foreign news events.

What conclusions may be drawn from such an analysis? Let us now consider some of the conclusions we have reached.

MEDIATED REALITY—
SUPERFICIAL AND FRAGMENTARY

While the news made it clear that Swedish industry faced problems, this was done primarily in terms of a few key actors: major Swedish firms like

Kockums, SKF (Skefco), industries and manufacturers of high-grade steel on the one hand and the state, personified by Minister of Industry Åsling, on the other. Industry was in trouble, and the state was taking action. So far, so good. The specific news event was also made clear in many cases, but not always: for example, the government promises to extend credit guarantees, but no one explains what a credit guarantee is. Steel mills are to merge, but it is not made clear whether the decision is definite or simply one of several options. In some cases, the event at hand was hardly mentioned, knowledge of it being taken for granted. Viewers had to know in advance what the item was about.

What was the nature of the problems facing Swedish industry? What were their causes? What is the role of the state? What can government do? And, the prognosis: What is the likely outcome? Are there any alternative courses of action? These questions are vital at a time when the trade unions and the public debate in Sweden are dominated by the issues of employee-controlled investment funds and the pros and cons of state intervention in industry. Answers to these questions were, however, few and far between in the material studied. Radio and TV reporting remained on a superficial level, and the picture given the general public was spotty and out of context. While there were a few attempts to penetrate the subject more deeply, they were generally unsystematic and did not delve deep enough. Assessed from the point of view of the human comprehension process, the items presented many difficulties, which in fact deny many viewers the opportunity to be informed that news broadcasts otherwise might represent.[9]

The most serious fault is the fact that half the items studied either lacked all manner of background information or provided only sketchy references to underlying factors and motives. Causal factors were often hastily mentioned in passing, in dependent clauses, receiving no emphasis. Why was this so? Were the background and motives unknown? Hardly. When the same news item was treated in several news broadcasts, the cause might be mentioned in one report but not in the others. Was this related to item length? Was the program short of time? Apparently not. When we compared long and short items about the same event, we found that mention of causal factors was lacking in some long items, while causes might be treated in some detail in shorter ones. Indeed, some long reports were full of irrelevant "side-tracks" which in no way helped explain the situation.

How effective, then, were the items that tried to explain the background and motives behind events? In only a few instances were causal relationships made sufficiently clear. In many items this aspect of the story was "drowned out" by overwhelming, unrelated visuals or by fast-paced film collages full of zooms and pans.

Another common fault was the lack of a unifying theme. Some items contained information about several different events but failed to tell how they were related to each other. Others went off on tangents that had little to do with the main story. Faults like these can cause confusion; viewers mix up the details of the respective elements and, because of the lack of a unifying structure, fail to grasp the whole message.

Many items were not rounded off, but simply ended, followed immediately by the next story. This causes problems in that viewers are not given enough time to sort out the information in their minds and must either cast it aside unprocessed or miss the succeeding content.

Several of the items contained apparently contradictory information. In one item, for example, the reporter spoke of a risk that workers might lose their jobs. The next segment of the same item proceeded to discuss planned dismissals and how many workers would have to be dismissed. What is one to believe? A risk is one thing, but discussing the company's detailed plans indicates that the decision has already been made. Such inconsistencies naturally cause confusion among viewers, who are neither able to reconcile the two parts of the message nor given enough time to figure out why.

Another frequent source of trouble is when items fail to define key concepts and terminology. Credit guarantees, for example, were treated at length without being defined.

TV news visuals consistently failed to highlight what the items were about. Visuals are inherently powerful, and this failure has serious effects on an item's "comprehensibility." Some well-formulated texts were virtually devastated by irrelevant pictures that distracted attention from what was said. What, for example, does a ball bearing rolling along a conveyor belt tell the audience about the problems facing the ready-to-wear clothing industry in the form of stagnating sales, pile-ups in stocks, cutbacks in production, and lay-offs? What clues do pictures of a high-voltage power line and a pine forest full of wildflowers give the audience about billion-dollar losses, shrinking capital, and shortages of risk capital? What do whizzing sewing machine needles tell the audience about the problems in the ready-to-wear clothing industry regarding low-cost foreign imports and poor sales?

NEWS FOR THE INITIATED

We might sum up our findings in one phrase: News for the initiated. The lack of background factors in many items meant that they addressed themselves to people who already knew something about the news event and could thus place the information offered in context on their own. But for viewers unacquainted with the jargon of technology and bureaucracy, many items probably were poorly comprehended, if understood at all. Other factors contributed to this lack of understanding. Time and again, our analysis found implicit references in the items that only the initiated would be able to understand.

In the beginning of this chapter we spoke of the tacit agreement between speaker and listener in any communication situation. The speaker who would make himself understood must adapt his manner of expression to the needs and experiences of his listener. As long as the speaker makes this effort and keeps within the bounds of the knowledge they share, the listener will make an effort to understand. As for the news items dealing with the crisis in Swedish industry, our analysis amply shows that the tacit agreement observed by radio and TV journalists is one between them and a well-informed minority of Swedes. Any such agreement with the rest of the viewing audience was broken time and again.

NOTES

1. Volosinov (1973) labeled these two tendencies "abstract objectivism" and "individualistic subjectivism."

2. Students of literature have shown renewed awareness of the fact that litera- ture, too, is born of the meeting with the reader. According to this "aesthetic of reception," literature only exists dialectically, in the interaction between the com- municative structure of the text and the reader. This approach combines attention of reception with structural analysis (Jauss, 1970).

3. Kintsch and vanDijk (1974) have attempted to specify what such a global theory would entail. It would require theories of structure and comprehension concerning both the micro (proposition) and macro (discourse) levels. Further, a theory is needed that relates these structures and offers principles for the reduction of complex semantic information. A synoptical theory that relates history-specific structures to the logic and discourse of the document is needed. Finally, the body of theory concerning the relation of verbal and narrative structures to cognitive pro- cesses must be significantly augmented.

4. In linguistics and psycholinguists texts we can find different names for these bindings: "given-new" (Halliday, 1967), "old-new" (Chafe, 1970), "free-tied infor- mation" (Rommetveit, 1972), "cohesion" (Halliday and Hasan, 1976), "information- focus" (Halliday, 1967), "foregrounding" (Chafe, 1972), "staging," and "topic" (Grimes, 1975).

5. Sweden has only one broadcasting corporation—a single monopoly organization: the Swedish Broadcasting Corporation (Sveriges Radio). It is organized around the principle of broadcasting as a public utility and financed by fees for the possession of receivers. Commercial advertising is not allowed.

The legal framework is set by two radio laws—the radio act and the broadcasting liability act, an agreement between the state and the broadcasting corporation. Sveriges Radio is in this way an independent organization. It is not ruled by the government, but must fulfill government-imposed obligations.

6. We must here distinguish between narrative structures and content structures. Anthropologists, linguists, and literary theorists have used narrative structures to describe the rules for story-telling (Propp, 1968; also Labov and Waletsky, 1967). In recent years cognitive psychologists have also used narrative categories in studying traditional tales as problem-solving situations (Rummelhart, 1977). News is well suited for this kind of analysis, but our interest in this chapter lies more in the content of the news than in how the news is built up. There are, to our knowledge, no clear and comprehensive means for describing the semantic content of longer texts. The content can be represented by a semantic network (Lindsay and Norman 1972) or a propositional text base (Kintsch, 1974). But what we are looking for are not the linguistic relations between the sentence atoms, but the superior relations—for example, causal relations—that bind the different elements of a news item together. "Macro-structures" (Kintsch and Vipond, 1979) could be of help here, if they can be distinguished from the narrative structures.

7. There are philosophical and logical theories of action of a very detailed and formalized nature (vanDijk, 1977). The future will show how these mostly theoretical theories and descriptions will be used.

8. Radio and TV news reach four million Swedes daily. More than half the population (9-79 years) listen to a radio news broadcast on the average weekday, if we include the various five-minute news bulletins throughout the day. Roughly half the population view one of the evening news telecasts. Thus, news broadcasts play a central role as sources of information.

9. As mentioned in note 5, the Swedish Broadcasting Corporation has certain obligations to fulfill. One of these concerns the democratic values and the obligation to inform. Article 6 in the Agreement between the Government and Sveriges Radio states:

The Corporation shall uphold the fundamental democratic values in its programme services.

The programme services shall be conducted with regard for the central position of sound radio and television in the national life. It follows from the foregoing that the Corporation is required, inter alia, to disseminate, in suitable form, information on current events as well as information on important cultural and social issues, and to encourage debate on such issues.

REFERENCES

CHAFE, W. (1972). "Discourse structure and human knowledge." In R. O. Freedle and J. B. Carrol (eds.), Language Comprehension and the Acquisition of Knowledge. Washington: Winston.
——— (1970) Meaning and the Structure of Language. Chicago: University of Chicago Press.

DILTHEY, W. (1922) Einleitung in die Geistwissenschaften. Gesammelte Schriften Band I.

FINDAHL, O. (1971) The Effect of Visual Illustrations upon Perception and Retention of News Programmes. Stockholm: Sveriges Radio/PUB.

FINDAHL, O. and HÖIJER, B. (1979) Vad säger oss nyhetsprogrammen? Del 1. Krisen i svensk industri. (What Do the News Tell Us? Part 1. The Crisis in Swedish Industry.) Stockholm: Sveriges Radio/PUB.

——— (1977) How Important Is Presentation? Stockholm: Sveriges Radio/PUB.

——— (1976) Fragments of Reality. An Experiment with News och TV-Visuals. Stockholm: Sveriges Radio/PUB.

——— (1975) "Effect of additional verbal information on retention of a radio news program." Journalism Quarterly 52: 493-498.

——— (1974) On Knowledge, Social Privilege and the News. Stockholm: Sveriges Radio/PUB.

——— (1973) An Analysis of Errors in the Recollection of an News Program. Stockholm: Sveriges Radio/PUB.

GRIMES, J. (1975) The Thread of Discourse. The Hague: Mouton.

HALLIDAY, M.A.K. (1967) "Notes on transitivity and theme in English, part 2." Journal of Linguistics 3: 199-244.

HALLIDAY, M.A.K. and HASAN, R. (1976) Cohesion in English. London: Longman.

JAUSS, H. R. (1970) Litteraturgeschichte als Provokation. Frankfurt a.M.

KINTSCH, W. (1974) The Representation of Meaning in Memory. Hillsdale, NJ: Lawrence Erlbaum.

KINTSCH, W. and VIPOND, D. (1979) "Reading comprehension and readability in educational practice and psychological theory." In L.-G. Nilsson (ed.), Perspectives on Memory Research. Hillsdale, NJ: Lawrence Erlbaum.

KINTSCH, W. and VANDIJK, T. A. (1975) "Comment on se rapelle et on résume des histoires." Langages 40: 98-116.

LABOV, W. and WALETZKY, J. (1967) "Narrative analysis: oral versions of personal experience." In J. Helm (ed.), Essays on the Verbal and Visual Arts. Seattle: University of Washington Press.

LIEDMAN, S.-E. (1977). Motsatsernas spel. Vol 1. (The Games of Contradictions). Lund: Cavefors.

LINDSAY, P. H. and NORMAN, D. A. (1972). Human Information Processing. New York: Academic Press.

LURIA, A. R. (1976) Basic Problems of Neurolinguistics. The Hague: Mouton.

PROPP, V. (1968) Morphology of the Folktale. Austin: University of Texas Press.

RICOEUR, P. (1970) "Qu'est-ce qu'un texte?" In R. Bubner (ed.), Hermeneutik und Dialektik, Bd II, Tübingen.

RÜHL, M. (1976) "Vom Gegenstand der Inhaltsanalyse." Rundfunk und Fernsehen 24/4: 367-378.

ROMMETVEIT, R. (1972) Språk, tanke og kommunikasjon (Language, Thought and Communication). Oslo: Universitetsförlaget.

RUMMELHART, D. E. (1977) "Understanding and summarizing brief stories." In D. LaBerge and S. J. Samuel (eds.), Basic Processes in Reading: Perception and Comprehension. Hillsdale, NJ: Lawrence Erlbaum.

VAN DIJK, T. A. (1977) Text and Context. London: Longman.

WEMBER, B. (1976) Wie Informiert das Fernsehen. München: List.

VOLOSINOV, V. N. (1973) Marxism and the Philosophy of Language. London: Seminar Press.

Chapter 6

METHODOLOGICAL DEVELOPMENTS IN
CONTENT ANALYSIS?

Preben Sepstrup

INTRODUCTION

The last ten years have seen a tremendous growth in mass communication research in Scandinavia. However, when it comes to essential, practical
implications of this research, the results seem few and far between—with
the exception, perhaps, of advertising. Apparently, researchers have
learned a lot, although their results reflect themselves only insignificantly
in society, the society which is or ought to be the main concern of
research. Seen in relation to its intentions, research largely fails to have an
impact on the surrounding society. This holds for Denmark, I am sure, but
probably also for most other countries.

This lack of societal impact might be attributed to the choice of
research subjects; generally, however, this is not the case. It might also be
due to inadequate communication of results to politicians, administrators,
and the public. To a researcher this ever-present problem is not interesting,
since it is more a question of personal resources and will power than mere
capability. We are then left with the possibility that research itself—its
methods and theories—is insufficient.

The *first purpose* of this chapter is to contribute to methodological
considerations, aiming at improving the impact of communication research
on politicians, administrators, and the public. The discussion will focus on
content analysis, an important area within mass communication research.

The *second purpose* of this study is to describe an empirical application
of the methodological considerations, including the findings of the study
in question.

In order to illustrate the method, the presentation of findings is
more comprehensive than necessary. This should be seen in the light of

the study's *third purpose*: to outline male and female characteristics in advertising and thus account for a prerequisite of understanding the long-term influence on sex roles exerted by advertising.

The initial considerations of Section I are followed in Section II by a discussion of some methodological problems of content analysis and their relation to the impact of research in general. Section III presents a study based on the theoretical, methodological considerations of Section II. The method of the study and its findings are described. Section IV describes and evaluates the interpretation of the findings and their social impact in light of the methodological discussions in Section II. Section V draws conclusions on the content of advertising and the pros and cons of the method used in the study.

It is an assumption of this chapter that the ultimate goal of research in the social sciences is to describe and explain the structure and functioning of the existing society, the purpose being to advance a critique which can contribute to social changes/improvements.

II. RESEARCH THEORY AND METHODOLOGY:
SOME REFLECTIONS

MASS COMMUNICATION RESEARCH IN GENERAL

In my opinion one of the main reasons for the failing societal impact of communication research (and of content analysis in particular) is the total reliance on either one or the other of the two principal schools of thought in research theory. Each has certain strong points, but also very crucial weak points which limit their epistemological and administrative/political values, respectively.

One school is the Marxist or critical approach, with its highly developed theory of the social role of mass communication, its extensive comprehension of the coherence of individual elements, and its substantial critical potential. The Marxist/critical approach is found mostly in Europe, but is not predominant in any single country. It is a distinctive feature of this type of research that by and large only students and intellectuals are familiar with its results. Through Marxist/critical analyses these two groups have gained qualified knowledge of the functioning of mass media and society, with special emphasis on the social role of the media.

The most important reason for the lack of societal influence from Marxist/critical research is that the results of this research have not been considered reliable and serious. No one has felt compelled to act or react on the results. Researchers from other schools, among others, have perceived the results as individual examples, exceptions, subjective interpretations, and predetermined results.

The other type of research is positivistic, empirical research, which especially predominates in the United States. When dealing with matters relevant in decision-making processes, it often constitutes the point of departure for administrative and political decisions. An important reason for this is that the reliability of the findings in this kind of research is unquestioned. This may be due to the fact that the findings rarely put a spoke in the wheels of those in power, and—more important—that such findings are considered reliable because this kind of research corresponds to the commonly accepted ideas of research and its methods.

The findings in positivistic empirical analyses in social science are thus widely accepted and acted upon because of the status of the exact, empirical sciences as *the* science in the public mind. In the long run, however, the impact of such research results is rather limited since, in essence, they do not contribute to a greater *understanding,* but merely define and reproduce readily observable phenomena. In other words, we are faced with, on the one hand, a sophisticated, critical/Marxist theory and methodology containing substantial potential for comprehension and change, the results of which are, however, not readily understood and are even considered unreliable and too insignificant to call for any response. On the other hand, we have a positivistic theory and methodology which is closely related to a "full-fledged" empirical technique. Its results are highly esteemed, because (and this may well be the main reason) it can analyze and convey knowledge about substantial quantities of data, and because the methods applied comply with the traditional concept of science.

Hence, confidence in positivistic research results on the part of the establishment might be attributed to their not being critical of the existing political system. However, it is also possible that confidence in the results is caused by the *empirical method* and the techniques used. The next step is therefore to decide whether researchers showing critical, epistemological interests can maintain their theoretical and basic methodological starting point and be inspired and even apply parts of positivistic, empirical techniques and methods of analysis. Can results from critical content analyses be expressed as quantitative averages?

If, in the above, "critical" is synonymous with "Marxist," most Marxist researchers will undoubtedly hold the opinion that a combination of Marxist thinking and positivistic empirical methods is impossible. The present methodological research, however, has this in mind: to find out whether this apparent methodological hybrid under favorable conditions will possess the rare qualities of being able to systematize, quantify, and generate overall knowledge, insight, and understanding.

CONTENT ANALYSIS

Content analysis is—at least in Scandinavia—based on a positivistic content analysis tradition (see Ejbye-Ernst et al., 1975; Berelson, 1952; Holsti, 1969; Sexton and Haberman, 1974; Venkatesan and Losco, 1975), an ideological-critical tradition (see Bolvig et al., 1971; Møller et al., 1972; Williamson, 1978; Andrén et al., 1978), and an attempted Marxist tradition (see Qvortrup et al., 1979; Qvortrup, 1977; and to some extent Williamson, 1978; Fausing, 1973). There have also been attempts at Marxist criticism of the ideology-critical analysis (Madsen, 1977).

The considerable number of works on how to implement positivistic content analysis (for example, Kassarjian, 1977, Holsti, 1969; Berelson, 1952) can be seen as an indirect criticism of the so-called qualitative method, which is a widely used but not very appropriate common designation of Marxist, ideology-critical, nonquantitative methods. Marxist criticism of the positivistic content analysis has also been voiced (see Qvortrup et al., 1979).

Thus, there are many possibilities for the criticism of this present attempt. Its starting point is the criticism of positivistic content analysis, the purpose being to find a methodological variant which can be applied in connection with Marxist/critical epistemological interest and able to produce results which can

(1) be accepted by administrators and politicians and used in their decision-making processes (in other words, at least some of the results must appear as those quantified averages so often held in contempt by Marxists—and often rightly so); and
(2) be understood and have a liberating/activating effect on people who are exposed to possible suppression by the object of analysis.

In empirical quantitative research certain methodological and technical demands must be met. In positivistic content analysis such demands have often impeded epistemologically valuable analyses (Mortensen, 1977) because what have been conceived as methodological demands and possibilities have determined not only the objects of research but also the dimensions and characteristics used to describe and analyze the object.[1]

On the other hand, researchers whose roots are in critical/Marxist theory have been unable to develop empirical analyses exceeding the level of examples and/or establishing reasonable confidence in the replication of their studies and thus the general application of the results.

The following outlines a link between traditional quantitative positivistic content analysis and Marxist-inspired qualitative analysis, which attempts to meet methodological and technical demands on the quantitative analysis without assigning to them a superior determining role. First, some main points will be discussed in principle. Then the use of the principal consideration will be illustrated in Section III.

QUANTITATIVE CONTENT ANALYSIS
WITHOUT TYRANNY OF METHOD

Berelson's demands from 1952, of which the most essential elements are discussed here, are not in themselves inferior. But in their rigorous form and the rigorous tradition in which they are followed, they have developed tyrannically in relation to the research process.

On Category Formation and Manifest Content

It is outside the scope of this chapter to discuss whether knowledge of media content is useful for understanding media function and impact. Suffice it to say that content analysis is a necessary but insufficient condition for such understanding. In various forms the problem is shared by qualitative and quantitative analysis. With a large-scale quantitative content analysis the starting point will invariably be predetermined dimensions or categories. According to the Berelson tradition, category formation is conceived as an "objective" process outside content analysis. However, it is this process which is decisive of the results of the analysis. This does not mean, however, that the analysis can be left out; rather, it means that category formation is decisive of the theoretical or fundamental result *possibilities.* In case a category is not established in advance, the media content, of course, cannot be described in this dimension.

Consequently, category formation should not—as is often the case in positivistic quantitative analyses—be seen as a neutral/value-free phase preceding the actual content analysis. This is the decisive phase of content analysis, and it is imperative that category formation is determined by the purpose and hypotheses, and solely by these.

Thus, the object of analysis should be decisive, not in the sense that obviously observable phenomena in concrete media content are decisive of the category formation, but rather in the sense that what appears to be interesting when formulating hypotheses must be included in the registrations. In other words, the traditional, positivistic content analysis demand, only to register the "objectively" measurable manifest content, must be partly rejected, although this may imply an even more cumbersome quantifying process. Moreover, the categories used must include not only details but also integrated aspects of the overall content and aspects which reflect the societal role of the text or picture.

This starting point gives rise to at least two important problems. One is how to quantify such assumptions or how to empirically corroborate the correctness of various theory elements; for example, the assumption that commodity fetishism constitutes a decisive element in the argumentation used in advertising. The second problem is how to maintain the required traditional confidence in such measuring.

On Reliability

When rejecting the positivistic demand only to "measure" the manifest content, and at the same time demanding (traditional) credibility in measuring, the question about reliability becomes urgent. As will be known, the reliability problem concerns the question whether the same individual at different points in time (intrareliability) and/or different individuals at the same point in time (interreliability) reach the same conclusions concerning the text.

As will appear from the following, ensuring reliability in content analysis is in a certain sense merely a pseudo-solution, giving the researcher a false feeling of security. If the researcher's aim is not limited to merely describing what can readily be observed—that is, if he intends to use content analysis as a tool to comprehend function and impact of media content—the reliability demand is somehow artificial as well as misleading in that it can function only in relation to the direct form of manifestation of media content, and in that the perception of media content depends on both the social and psychological context in which the text is consumed.

If, on the other hand, it is held that in order to obtain credibility, it is meaningful (alternatively necessary) to quantify content categories in an attempt to grasp the character and function of media content, it also seems logical to demand inter-, as well as intracoder reliability. Moreover, it is unquestionably a prerequisite in gaining such credibility as to give the results a social impact.

The two views on reliability outlined above may be so contradictory that they constitute an insoluble dilemma. However, our purpose is to seek a solution in any case. One possibility is to develop, during the phase of formulating problems, hypotheses and categories, to rank the interest and relevance demand higher than the high-reliability demand.

Due attention to the narrow positivistic method demands (including, for example, the elementary and indispensable demand not to summarize observations measured on different scales) will then be paid through careful coding instructions (category descriptions), coder training, and reporting the reliability of each category in a traditional, positivistic sense.

It is also conceivable that reliability is analyzed in a broader and deeper sense by having groups of consumers of the media content in question evaluate the content with a view to the formed categories. Finally, additional qualitative analyses could be made in areas of high interest but low reliability.

It remains a crucial issue not to be misled by the methodological, technical demand to read too much into the results. High intercoder reliability only indicates that two or more persons have successfully been "educated" to uniform perception. High reliability to only a limited extent indicates high validity. *Reliability is a necessary but insufficient condition to be fulfilled to the widest possible extent.* The second problem, how to "measure," will be discussed in Section III.

On Atomizing Content

Traditional content analysis is further blamed for isolating and atomizing the text, and the procedure outlined above provides only a limited solution. Atomizing content means, for one thing, that the analysis is based on isolated observations of individual dimensions of the content, and thus it is not realized that an overall understanding cannot be found by summarizing the various subdimensions. Second, atomizing signifies that the content is analyzed independently of its social context; that is, society's existence in the text is not realized. The more comprehensive the theories behind the study, the less significant the problem, in that such theories ensure a considerable number of ways to approach the text and make it possible to incorporate categories which include the social context of the content.

CONCLUSION

The critical/Marxist, qualitative approach to content analysis and the positivistic, quantitative approach are applicable for various different purposes and problems, each in their own right. A combination of the two methods, however, seems to offer considerable possibilities for better understanding and more influence from research, the idea being to combine Marxist theory and its comprehension of social relations and the social role of mass media with the ability of quantitative methods to treat substantial amounts of material, to gain a more comprehensive view, to create credibility, and to ease the understanding of findings.

The crucial and difficult problem is to meet the basic demands on empirical analyses in general without being barred by the tyranny of method which is characteristic of positivistic, quantitative content analysis and which is especially reflected in the traditional demands on content analysis dating back to Berelson.

III. CONTENT ANALYSIS OF ADVERTISEMENTS: A PRELIMINARY ATTEMPT AT APPLYING METHODOLOGICAL REFLECTIONS

PURPOSE OF THE STUDY

Commercial advertising has a number of functions and consequences, which are systematized below. This research is directed toward the long-term ideological function and consequences of advertising.

Consumer norms, values, and attitudes are influenced by a number of factors. Socialization (channelling into acceptable behavior in society and groups) is a lifelong process, mainly taking place in the family, in small social groups, and in the educational system, but also through the mass media (besides, of course, in production and consumption). With the declining role of the family in society, the school and even more so the ever-increasing media supply will assume greater importance for socialization.

Advertising is part of the media supply and probably the part most consciously meant to have a direct influence. Advertising affects individuals in families and schools—that is, through primary socialization; it affects and increases the content of privately owned media; and it affects the individual person. Thus, its socializing effect is direct as well as indirect.

Advertising supposedly has a substantial socializing effect because of its scope and penetration into all walks of life. It goes without saying that it is almost impossible to quantify its impact on people's adoption of certain attitudes and norms, such as sex roles. It should be pointed out that irrespective of the advertising content opposing, agreeing with, or strengthening existing norms, it still has a socializing effect.

The purpose of the content analysis, the results of which are summarized in Section III, is to form a basis for assessing in which direction advertising is likely to affect sex role socialization. This is done by describing norms and values in advertising concerning this object and by comparing, when possible, sex role portrayals in advertising with the actual roles and conditions of society.

The findings may help to further the understanding of the functions of advertising, consumption, and the economic system. They might also lead to a reconsideration of possible control of advertising content in this

Advertising effects

	Economic	Ideological
Short-term	E.g. increased company sales; influence on consumer brand choice; influence on private media finances	E.g. influence on language; promotion of various fashion-like trends; influence on media content
Long-term	E.g. influence on competitive structure; influence on consumption patterns; influence on media structure	E.g. influence on consumer norms, values and attitudes; influence on mass media norms, values and atttitudes

respect if it turns out to contain elements contradictory to desired or desirable social and personal interests. In the light of the overall project, in which the content analysis forms an integral part, the findings may also trigger the following question: Is it reasonable that producers not only sell products, but also—via advertising and from capitalist motives—"sell" an ideology, if this can be demonstrated. Finally, the study may also serve the purpose of acting as a kind of feedback to advertisers, offering them a chance to reconsider the consequences of their overall impact and possibly modify or change this impact.

METHODOLOGY OF THE STUDY

With large-scale, quantitative content analyses like the present it is a sine qua non to formulate a number of assumptions (hypotheses) about the examined material in order to secure the necessary material through category formation. Such assumptions must be based on general and specific theories on the media content in question and on previous empirical studies.

At this point, it is important to note that it is hardly possible to implement content analysis according to the intended methodology without including qualitative analyses on a smaller scale to provide inspiration when forming the relevant categories.

Advancing Hypotheses

The hypotheses of the study spring from the background and purpose of the project, the "theory of the esthetics of commodities" (Haug, 1971;

see also Arnfred, 1975), from various advertising theories on creation of ads and on effect, and finally, from findings in previous analyses.[2]

The hypotheses are advanced through a hierarchy exemplified in the following. The hierarchical structure implies the possibility of proceeding from concrete findings (frequency of various categories in the content) to comprehension of these findings.

Basic Hypotheses

A: Each product has a use-value, constituting consumer buying motive. Similarly, producer motive to sell is the exchange-value of the product. In furthering producer interests, advertising will convey pseudo-use-values (esthetics), often focusing on certain values.

B: Closely related to A, it is assumed that advertising does not reflect reality but offers an incomplete (distorted) reproduction in accordance with its purpose, including its preference for *some* values and norms at the cost of others.

C: In connection with A and B, it is assumed that advertising treats men and women differently, and ascribes different values and roles to men and women.

These hypotheses are not meant to be tested in the study in a traditional sense. The purpose of advancing them, rather, is to use them as guidelines when advancing a number of more specific hypotheses.

Main Hypotheses

The transition from basic to main hypotheses is largely based on findings in existing, smaller studies.

1. Advertising depicts a young world of good-looking, happy people; a world of vacation, leisure, and entertainment, excluding work, poverty, old age, poor social conditions, conflicts, unhappiness and misery. It is a world of harmony which shows no signs of structural or economic problems.

2. Through advertising producers contribute to building up certain consumer attitudes and behavior of direct relevance to their consumption, such as greater awareness of people's bodies and sexuality, greater awareness of social togetherness, reification, suppression of buyer/seller conflicts, buying arguments, resource awareness, and so on.

3. A number of desires, interests, and behavioral patterns in advertising are attributed wholly or partly to both sexes. In addition to such nonfemale characteristics, females in advertising are generally young and beautiful, live a careless and self-centered life, are related to static elements in life, are confined to private surroundings and primarily defined as sex objects and, as such, objects of observation and erotic stimulus. A woman's main interests are

health, looks, housekeeping, and child care, while the predominantly dynamic active and ambitious man is depicted outside the family sphere, concentrating on hobbies, work, and career.

Specific Hypotheses

The following specific hypotheses are *examples* of hypotheses derived from main hypothesis 3.

3.1. Women are socialized by advertising into shopper and consumer roles, because women appear more frequently in ads than men.
3.2. Men and women are socialized through advertising into different fields of interest so that female interests will typically be hygiene, health, children, cooking, cleaning, shopping, and looks; whereas male interests will typically be technical, economic, social matter, public issues, hobby, and education.
3.3. The age distribution for persons in ads is more diversified for men than for women, and the age distribution for men largely corresponds to reality with a slight distortion toward younger age groups while for women it is grossly distorted toward younger age groups. Therefore, both sexes, through advertising, are socialized into believing that young age is more important for women than for men.
3.4. Considerable differences exist between men and women in working and recreational roles in and outside the home.
3.5. Women, to a higher degree than men, are shown in object-like roles in ads, such as decorative, eye-catcher roles, in erotic roles, and revealing no communication/connection with the reader.
3.6. Women in advertising give their looks high priority, they are attractive by traditional standards whereas the male look is somewhat more differentiated.
3.7. Advertising stereotypes male and female characters through their facial expressions (happy, smiling, serious, expressionless, and so on).

The specific hypotheses can be further specified until each hypothesis forms the starting point for a registration (category) in the coding sheet.

It is essential to understand that the hypotheses have not been advanced with a view to testing them in the traditional, positivistic, empirical sense. Their primary purpose is to act as guidelines when describing the content and when interpreting the quantitative result. Simultaneously, this interpretation must naturally be based on correct use of quantities; that is, traditional positivistic, empirical analysis rules should be applied when drawing conclusions on the basis of quantitative data.

Research Technique

The material examined consists of advertisements in all Danish newspapers and magazines over a period of one year (February 1977 to

February 1978). We examined 2035 advertisements in daily papers and 2203 advertisements in weekly magazines. The sample was taken as a probability sample, making it possible to calculate the sampling error.

The presentation of findings includes only differences which exceed sampling error. The confidence intervals applied ensure a 95 percent probability of true values, within the intervals applied. Differences between two figures are mentioned only in case of nonoverlapping of confidence intervals.

Selection of coded ads was made from a population consisting of all newspapers and magazines in a number corresponding to circulation multiplied by frequency of publication. All non-classified ads were analyzed.

Consequently, an advertisement in a paper or magazine with large circulation and frequent publication stands a greater chance of being analyzed than an advertisement in a paper or magazine with smaller circulation or less frequent publication. The same ad may appear several times in the study. Hence, the picture of the advertisements shown in the study corresponds in volume to the picture presented to the public by paper and magazine ads. In other words, the selection was made on an exposure principle rather than a production principle. In no way is it a picture of specially selected ads of special products or from special papers and magazines—which, incidentally, can also be produced by the studied material—but a picture of overall paper and magazine advertising.

The specific hypotheses have been transformed into 508 registrations formed as questions answered by five coders on behalf of the ads (see Sepstrup, 1979b). The ads have been given the choice of answering "yes," "no," or "uncertain." Picture and text were analyzed separately, but in principle in the same way. The 508 questions were tested and revised through four pilot studies. A comprehensive written coder instruction accompanied the coding form (see Sepstrup, 1979b).

The categories applied show great variation with respect to what in traditional content analysis is termed the possibility of value-free, objective evaluation of the appearance of the category in the material. This variation in its turn is related to the above principal reflexions on choice of categories.

The existence of some categories can be decided quite objectively (Is the person a female? Is the person engaged in cleaning? Is the person naked?). With other categories some interpretation is required (Is the person happy? Is the person young [20-35 years]? Is the person mothering?). With some categories considerable interpretation is required (Is the person good-looking by traditional standards? Is the face expressionless? Is the person basically romantic?).

Considerable efforts (comprehensive written instruction, practical training and so on) were made to ensure the most uniform interpretation possible. Repeated tests were undertaken to ensure that the coders followed the directions, coding identical ads identically and identically at different times (inter- and intracoder reliability). Only findings from questions not eliminated by these tests have been included in the presentation.

Calculation of the reliability coefficient for individual questions resulted in the elimination of findings from 29 questions (categories, registrations) from further examination because the questions did not reach a reliability coefficient of at least 0.80, which is the traditional lower limit of an acceptable coefficient. Three hundred thirty-three questions (66 percent) reached a coefficient of 1, 69 questions had a coefficient of between 0.90 and 0.99, and 77 questions had a coefficient of between 0.80 and 0.89 (all reliability coefficients are found in Sepstrup, 1979b).

Asking 508 questions regarding each ad is quite a task, but seems simpler than obtaining a thorough (verbal/qualitative) description of an ad. Many aspects, nuances, and overall pictures are neglected by the questions asked. This is the weakness of quantitative analysis and the price to be paid in order to be able to analyze extensive material. Thus, the following presentation of findings is not a complete description of print advertising in 1978, but an account of matters relevant to the 508 selected categories.

FINDINGS

A comprehensive presentation of findings can be found in Sepstrup (1979). The following conclusions on male and female portrayal in advertisements express the typical and most frequent content. Ads will show both men and women with many different characteristics. When, for example, it is maintained that women are passive and men active, it does not mean that active women and passive men are nonexistent in print advertisements, but that the predominant characteristics for men, and women in this context are passivity and activity, respectively, and that there is a significant difference.

It should also be pointed out that in various (individual) fields the differences between men and women are not in themselves very interesting. However, the trend in the findings is so clear and the findings form so consistent a pattern that these findings also contribute to justifying the following conclusions.

A. ADVERTISING DOES NOT REFLECT THE SITUATION FACING MEN AND WOMEN IN REAL LIFE. ADVERTISING CREATES, PERPETUATES, AND SELLS ITS OWN IDEOLOGY OF HUMAN SITUATIONS TO AFFECT CONSUMPTION.

The age distribution of persons shown is distorted toward younger age groups. Persons in the age bracket 20 to 34 years appear three times as frequently in ads as in real life, where four times as many persons belong to the age bracket 50 to 64 years, and the number of persons age 65 and above in real life exceed that shown in advertising 13 times. (Children are rarely shown in advertising.)

In advertising "occupation" is more insignificant than in real life and can be identified for only 18 percent of the persons shown. Advertising does not reflect the occupational pattern of reality. People in ads are more active and independent than in real life. The number of pensioners in advertising should be multiplied by four in order to correspond to reality. The number of independents shown in ads is twice that of real life.

The universe of advertising is one of leisure. Of the persons, 17 percent work, whereas 59 percent are clearly depicted in a recreational situation. In this context the situation of the rest cannot be identified.

Division of labor as to domestic chores underrepresents men and exaggerates female work compared with reality.

Speed in working of real life is high, but in the world of advertising 40 percent of the persons in working roles do nothing.

A number of leisure activities less well-suited for consumption of material goods are nonexistent in advertising, such as radio-listening, watching TV, reading, walking, bicycling, or attending a concert, theater, exhibition, or cinema.

All persons are unrealistically happy and in good form (55 percent and 77 percent). Anger, fatigue, and indisposition hardly ever exist. The majority of persons smile (64 percent).

Fifteen percent of all persons are depicted in extremely luxurious surroundings.

B. THE DISTORTION OF WOMEN IN ADVERTISING IS MORE PRONOUNCED THAN WITH MEN. IN THIS DISCRIMINA-TION THE IDEOLOGY OF ADVERTISING FOCUSES ON WOMEN IN PARTICULAR AND CONTRIBUTES ESPECI-ALLY TO ENTRENCHING WOMEN IN INDIVIDUALLY AND SOCIALLY UNDESIRED ROLES.

The age of females in ads is much more distorted than that of males. Twice as many men in ads than in reality are between 20 and 34 years, but with women there is a three-fold exaggeration. In reality, the 49 percent of women who are above 34 years, rarely recognize themselves in ads. Men above this age outnumber women by three times in advertising.

The female occupational situation—that is, the number of persons with identifiable jobs—is much more distorted compared with reality than that of men. Work, including household work, can be identified with 11 percent of the women, but with 27 percent of the men.

The occupational distribution shows far greater distortion for women than for men. Of women, shown in ads, 51 percent against 27 percent in real life are doing household work. Four times fewer women in ads than in reality are blue-collar worker, and 30 percent fewer are white-collar workers, whereas there is a five-fold exaggeration of independents in advertising. On the other hand, female pensioners of the real world outnumber those shown in ads by five times.

Distortion in advertising of the actual distribution between leisure and work is more pronounced for women than for men. The proportion of male and female depiction in recreational roles is the same in contrast to reality, where the dual role of working mothers is well documented. Of persons shown in a working role, 71 percent are men.

Women are happy more often than men (59 percent against 41 percent), and women smile more often than do men (70 percent versus 58 percent).

C. THE WOMAN IN ADVERTISING IS YOUNG, LESS DISTINCT, AND MORE OBJECT-LIKE THAN THE MAN. SHE BELONGS IN THE HOME AND WORKS THERE. THE WOMAN IS CONFINED TO PRIVATE MATTERS, WHEREAS THE MAN IS IN CHARGE OF PUBLIC MATTERS.

The woman in advertising is young: 90 percent of females in ads are young people. The woman is portrayed as less identifiable, less distinct than the man. Fewer female occupations than male occupations can be identified (11 percent against 27 percent). Fewer female than male social roles can be identified (46 percent against 56 percent). The environment of women is also less identifiable (40% versus 49%). Men are named more often than women when they appear in testimonials. Of men appearing in testimonials, 17 percent are well-known persons as against 3 percent of females in this role. Of women in testimonials, 89 percent are ordinary people against 55 percent of men in testimonials.

A woman's place is in the home: twice as many women in ads than in real life work in the home, and four times as few are blue-collar workers. Seven times more often than with women, men are depicted as colleagues. Of women in ads, 35 percent are shown in the home against 19 percent of men. Two percent of females in ads against 14 percent of males are shown in working roles. Twenty-five percent of women in ads are shown in their role as a mother, whereas 17 percent of the men are shown in their role as a father.

A woman's domain is the domicile: 52 percent of women in working roles against one percent of men take care of children, cook, wash, clean, or shop. When women (less frequently than men) are shown in a formal situation, it is in most cases (60 percent) connected to shopping. The corresponding figure for men is 20 percent.

D. THE WOMAN IS LESS QUALIFIED THAN THE MAN. SHE IS INACTIVE, SELF-CONTAINED, DECORATIVE, AND IS

DEFINED BY AND CONCERNED WITH HER BODY AND LOOKS.

The woman is less qualified than the man: in all registered fields of work men outnumber women, except for less qualified office work. In the working roles it is the men who do the talking. Only one-sixth of professionals and experts shown are women. Twice as many men as women are shown in a teaching/explaining role. More men than women appear in testimonials (21 percent against 15 percent). Of experts in testimonials, 83 percent are men. Three times as many men as women are seriously looking for jobs. Nine percent of women against 28 percent of men have an overall image of being competent and successful.

The woman is inactive and self-contained: 71 percent of persons in working roles are men. When men and women in working roles are actually not working, the men will most often have a regular break (often together with others). This applies to 69 percent of men against 27 percent of women. To a higher degree than men, women are inactive (53 percent against 40 percent). In working roles, women talk far less than men (14 percent against 41 percent), and they approach other persons less frequently than do men (19 percent versus 28 percent). In their spare time fewer women than men travel, fewer women than men are depicted in sports activities, and fewer women than men play with others. Women are predominant in the "activity" of total relaxation; 66 percent of these persons are women. Of persons concerned with health and hygiene in their spare time, 68 percent are women. Women equal men in love and family situations, but less frequently in formal situations (12 percent against 31 percent) and friendship situations (14 percent against 20 percent).

A woman's role is decorative: 71 percent of working persons are men, 29 percent are women. Of persons interested in their looks in their spare time, 88 percent are women. Seventy-one percent of women against 64 percent of men are used as eye-catchers. Among those who smile, 70 percent are women and 58 percent are men. Nine percent of women against three percent of men have an expressionless/machine-like appearance. Twenty-five percent of all female bodies (11 percent for male bodies) are shown in awkward, unnatural positions, solely for decorative purposes and impossible to maintain. Thirteen percent of women against one percent of men appear glamorized. Only 21 percent of less good-looking persons are women. Three to four times as many women as men can be characterized as handsome. Eighteen percent of women against 11 percent of men are placed in luxurious surroundings.

The woman is absorbed in and defined by her body: Women are immensely concerned with looks, health, and hygiene in their spare time, as shown above. Eleven percent of all women against one percent of all men shown are nudes or seminudes. An additional nine percent of the women against three percent of the men are dressed in a way which draws attention to their bodies (underwear, nightwear, bathing and beach costumes). Nine percent of all women touch or caress themselves as against two percent of all men. Eight percent of women against one percent of men can be characterized as sexy/sensual/erotic.

IV. INTERPRETATION AND
APPLICATION OF FINDINGS

As Section II has shown, the methodology applied is based on a desire to go beyond the descriptive level of traditional qualitative analysis as well as drawing attention to and obtaining a reaction on the findings outside the usual narrow research circles. To enable others to assess whether these goals have been attained, this section provides an exemplified answer to the question of *why* the described sex role ideology is implied in advertising, together with a description of nonresearcher reactions to the project.

INTERPRETATION: ILLUSTRATION OF
EXPLANATORY VALUE OF METHOD

The content analysis documents that advertising contains conditions of *passive* socialization within sex roles—that is, a socialization corresponding to the existing and predominant social situation. Passive socialization, however, is not tantamount to a neutral contribution to the sex role situation and the development of sex role patterns. On the contrary, it actively supports a status quo. In Denmark this is contrary to the official aim of the policy on equality.

As is also evident from the preceding sections, advertising implies conditions of an *active* socialization within sex roles; that is, a socialization contrasting predominant conditions, in that advertising implies possibilities of channelling women into a status and situation they have abandoned or are about to abandon—in other words, an even stronger opposition against official objectives and individual interests.

The description, resulting in the above statement, is interesting in itself, but not very useful since it does not explain *why* reality presents itself in the said way. It is the purpose of this section to suggest some answers, thus also demonstrating the ability of the method used here to go beyond what is possible in positivistic analysis. The analysis is brief and meant only as an illustration.

In the short run, the function of advertising is to look after the economic interests of individual companies. Many phenomena in individual ads can be explained from this purpose, but these explanations are found abundantly in marketing literature and are not to be repeated here. In order to give a more thorough explanation of the *aggregate* observations, it should be realized that advertising (both in the short and long run) is meant to ease and increase sales with a view to maximizing profits. In the long run, advertising (like all other commercial activities) must also contribute to the common interest of all companies in preserving the existing economic system—that is, a capitalist consumer-directed society. Advertising can look after these interests by (1) strengthening the ideological reproduction and continued loyalty toward the present social order and (2) contributing to maintenance and improvement of the conditions of consumption.

Advertising as a Contributing Factor in Ideological Reproduction

It is a contribution to ideological reproduction when advertising ranks the intimate sphere (family) higher than the social sphere (work), as is done with women in particular. Admittedly, work is fundamental to family happiness and prosperity (as expressed by consumption), but it should not be attributed an independent value or a predominant mental priority, since this is a prerequisite of possible wishes for changes in the social sphere, which, in turn, constitute a fundamental threat against the existing social order.

The basic idea in the above explanation may be expressed differently by considering the contribution of advertising to conceiving life as leisure to be a contribution to an ideology in which life is synonymous with consumption; people consume in their spare time, and when consuming, everyone *seems* equal. Production, with its strenuous, unpleasant work and its inequality, is a disruptive element in relation to loyalty toward the existing social order.

The false ideology that life is consumption entails a further falsification: that advertising singles out one type of leisure activity, one type of consumption—material consumption. Leisure outside the home and cultural consumption do not belong in the world of advertising.

Ideological reproduction also comprises concepts of social and individual division of labor. In this respect sex roles constitute an important element.

The ideological reproduction of women's (partly previous) self-conception—and men's conception of women—concerning women being confined to the private sphere is also a prerequisite of keeping women in the subordinate and, in relation to the labor market, inferior role, which makes her a flexible labor force reserve. The ideological reproduction of female tasks and interests is also necessary to ensure that a sufficient number of individuals consider consumption to be important and belonging to their most important field of responsibility.

From an overall point of view, the ideological reproduction of sex roles may also contribute to ensuring the existence of the nuclear family in its most basic form, thus ensuring substantial excess consumption in relation to other forms of cohabitation.

Finally, ideological reproduction of special female interests in home, body, and looks also conditions a tremendous consumption.

Advertising as a Contributory Factor in Maintaining Conditions of Consumption

With the last three statements in mind, emphasis on the explanation of advertising content by means of its contribution to ideological reproduction is being shifted to a somewhat different—but closely related—explanatory model, suggesting that advertising as an overall phenomenon contributes to maintaining the conditions of consumption. That the two explanatory models overlap is caused mainly by the ideological reproduction being one of the instruments in advertising to maintain the conditions of consumption.

That this is the case can be seen partly from the last three statements in the section on contribution of advertising to ideological reproduction, partly from the dual form, or dual function, of ideology in advertising.

On the one hand, an ideology is built up to idealize youth, for example. On the other hand, the instruments in this process shift into esthetics, functioning as supplements to the use-value of the product, a supplement which becomes increasingly imperative along with the increasing satisfaction of basic needs and with the decreasing amount of use-value of a vast number of products.

When, for example, so many deodorant ads show young people in pleasant surroundings, it helps to create an ideology idealizing youth. By the same token, "youth" in the individual ad becomes a supplement to the use-value of the product. It turns into esthetics, promises, and associations about youth when consuming the product, and, hence, a condition of such consumption.

Reality may even be so complex that the building up of certain ideologies, such as the ideology that women are primarily expressed or exist through their bodies, it is a prerequisite that the ideological "wrapping" in the form of aesthetics is conceived as a supplement to the product's use-value, and that certain products are conceived as having a use-value at all. If, for example, a woman is not "educated" to a false ideology leading her to consider herself primarily as an object of men's sexual interests (an object which must resort to all kinds of means not to lose in the competition about a sufficiently attractive look), she can hardly be expected to realize the use-value of a blackberry scented deodorant, nor to care much whether it is a blackberry scent or a raspberry scent.

The special type of socialization consisting in confronting people with (unattainable) ideals—this applies to women in particular as being especially responsible for consumption—and linking these ideals to consumption is also a prerequisite for keeping consumption at its present high level. Disappointment and frustration, encountered in the ever-present confrontation with experts in, for example, cooking, child care, cleaning, and beauty culture, are converted into consumption, seemingly the only possibility of attaining such ideals. This is a never-ending consumption, for the promises are never fulfilled.

If the major part of consumption entails a sense of disappointment, producers may risk stagnation in consumption. Such a situation is countered by providing many products with some real use-value, and through socialization into defining needs as the products and the related esthetics. Socialization into a general loyalty toward the existing social order is also an instrument in this context. Socialization to experiencing the needs as the supplied products and the related esthetics is the primary field of advertising and the secondary field of the surrounding editorial content. Socialization to loyalty toward the existing social order can be seen as the secondary field of advertising and the primary field of the surrounding editorial content.

Another, more technical, condition of maintaining consumption and a profitable production to satisfy consumption is a high degree of stability on the part of the consumer, since such stability is a prerequisite of mass production and large-scale selling with its long-range planning of production and sales. Advertising can and will contribute to this stability by preserving and entrenching consumer behavioral patterns as much as possible. This function emerges clearly as to sex roles, and it is evident that when using, advertising for this reason companies depict female characteristics in a totally reactionary way which, if realized, contributes to making most behavioral patterns extremely predictable for companies.

"But This Is Not The Way Admen Think"

The above reflections may not be part of the individual adman's short-term consciousness and logic, but they will be included in the long-term logic, in which the advertising industry is an integral part—capitalist logic. In other words, this means that when admen explain individual "unfortunate" ads by calling them errors or—in relation to portrayal of women—by saying that ads are mostly produced by (chauvinist) men, these explanations may have some validity in relation to isolated cases and in the very short run. However, they do not hold true in the long run, not in relation to the overall ad content, where economic factors manifest themselves and rectify or eliminate admen holding wrong views on the long-term interests of producers (capital).

APPLICATION OF FINDINGS: EFFECT OF
METHOD ON IMPACT OF FINDINGS

This section deals with social consequences of the content analysis. References will have to be made to a concrete society—in this case, Denmark.

The implemented analysis of magazine and newspaper ad content—illustrated here by the analysis of sex roles in ads—has produced no all-important results not already known from the many small quantitative analyses of single products or individual media, from the qualitative analyses which mostly treated a few ads, or from opinions and viewpoints expressed on different occasions by feminists and/or social critics.

Thus, in the Danish society, even before the publication of the present analysis, the conditions, activities and possible societal measures concerning the sex role pattern in advertising existed, but the subject has almost never been submitted to public debate.

The present analysis differs from already existing Scandinavian ones by covering the majority of findings in the various single analyses, by being representative of all products and media, by quantifying for the first time a number of observations, and by the scope of data quantifying previously qualitatively presented findings.

The publication of the analysis of sex role patterns in advertising triggered considerable public debate and activity, which continues with varied intensity.

Comprehensive mass media coverage after the publication of the analysis seems to have made many people aware of advertising and its possible influence on sex roles. The theme "advertising and sex roles" has been one of those most frequently discussed in the social debate and has caused many internal discussions in the advertising industry. The Danish Equal Opportunities Commission (Ligestillingsrádet) has requested the Danish ombudsman for consumer affairs to institute preliminary proceedings concerning a sexually discriminating ad and has made an application to the Danish Department of Commerce to consider the need for new legislation. It has also appealed to the advertising industry to change the sex role pattern through internal self-discipline.

The extremely strong public reaction to a mass communication research project may be due to an effective communication of the results; that is, through their use in a committee set up by the Danish ombudsman for consumer affairs. This does not rule out the justified assumption that also the method—quantifying, amount of data, representativeness—has played an important role. Women, sex roles, and advertising are popular subjects in the media, but without the other characteristics the media coverage would hardly have been so comprehensive, protracted, and serious.

Thus, the choice of method proved successful in that the analysis achieved the desired social impact in relation to the public, consumer and feminist groups, and administrators. In a wide sense it is also the merit of the method that easily available and understandable results with a certain explanatory and awareness-creating potential have appeared, triggering advertising and sex role criticism which, in turn, may be channelled into consumer and socialization criticism and in the last resort into economic criticism.

At the same time, the method also proved insufficient at the level of research strategy. The findings—and the use of these in a committee set up by the ombudsman for consumer affairs—have had a provocative effect in influential business circles. This is due, among other things, to the fact that just because of the method the findings cannot possibly be neglected; but at the same time it also turned out that research results are not accepted merely because traditionally acceptable methods of analysis are used—not even when elementary and self-evident matters are demonstrated. For at the same time, the study has been met with strong criticism from trade and industry, a criticism directed toward deviations and developments in relation to traditional methods. The application of content analysis results have been contested in general, and the theoretical starting points have resulted in the project being called a political project and not research.

In other words, the attempt via the method to make the debate focus on the results and their implications has been unsuccessful. In trade and industry, and to a certain degree also among administrators, the discussion has focused on the basis of the results. This may be seen as a step forward compared with research results merely being neglected, but obviously it is not satisfactory.

V. CONCLUSION

CONTENT OF ADVERTISING

By using sex roles as an example this content analysis has clearly demonstrated that advertising gives information not only about products but also about values and opinions. Advertising carries a distinct sex role ideology. It sells not only products but also opinions. The products are wrapped in certain viewpoints which, when it comes to sex roles, are conservative and have an entrenching and hampering effect on many women. In Scandinavia at least, the sex role views of advertising are in conflict with the official policy in this respect.

It may be assumed that the sex role ideology is only one of several examples of ideologies in advertising. It is also reasonable to assume that in the long run advertising will affect consumers in accordance with its content, especially since it is clearly a question of maintaining, enforcing or reestablishing existing attitudes and behavior, often in interaction with different media content.

A natural consequence of the study of advertising content is therefore to question the reasonableness in private, commercial forces usurping influence on individual and social attitudes and values and in the actual case on behalf of the activities of mankind. Similarly, the study gives rise to the question of why this is so with advertising, which sees it as its sole function to inform, to make the market transparent to consumers. The findings invariably must result in reflections on the economic system—its function and the reasonableness thereof.

METHODOLOGY

Qualitative analyses will always be necessary to produce actual understanding, to give detailed descriptions and analyses which are to describe and comprehend overall media content. But they will always be unable to cope with large amounts of data, and their results will be difficult to communicate and will have low general credibility.

Traditional positivistic quantitative content analyses will always be suitable for describing many simple forms of data, and their results are easily communicated and normally enjoy considerable credibility. But they are always inadequate when it comes to *understanding* the texts and *explaining* their content, especially in a broad societal context.

The attempt to combine in content analysis the "qualitative" and "quantitative" approaches has obviously not been fully successful. However, it does seem to illustrate the possibility of combining the advantages of the two approaches and of reducing their weaknesses, but just as a compromise between two extremes: more detailed and profound description implying better possibilities of fundamental apprehension of media content than offered by the traditional quantitative content analysis, but poorer than the qualitative. The latter, because of a certain tyranny of method, at least in the present case, is unavoidable and perhaps also because the actual administration of the project requires considerable attention and effort. The method applied is just as suitable as the traditional quantitative analyses to cope with substantial amounts of data and to communicate findings from analyzing these. Simultaneously, its general credibility and impact by far exceeds that of the qualitative analysis, but is not comparable to that of traditional analysis. The latter perhaps reflects the critical potential of the findings rather than the method itself.

NOTES

1. See for example the limited, somewhat uniform, and not always relevant selection of categories in the majority of quantitative analyses of advertising material (Belkaouni and Belkaouni, 1976; Courtney and Lockeretz, 1971; Dominick and Gail, 1974; Lundstrom and Sciglimpaglia, 1977; O'Donnel and O'Donnel, 1978; Sexton and Haberman, 1974; Wagner and Banos, 1973; and Venkatesan and Losco, 1975).

2. See also Andrén et al. (1971, 1978), Andrén and Nowak (1978), Bolvig et al. (1971), Fausing (1973), Flick (1977), Grønlie and Slettevold (1967), Hansen (1965), Jonsson and Jonsson (1970), Møller et al. (1972), Norgård (1975), Rasmussen and Korsgaard (1977), Togeby (1975), Warren (1978), and Williamson (1978).

REFERENCES

AARON, D. (1975). About Face. Towards a Positive Image of Women in Advertising. Toronto: Ontario Studies of Women Council.
ANDRÉN, G. and NOWAK, K. (1978). Gender Structures in Swedish Magazine Advertising 1950-1975. Working Paper. Stockholm: Business School of Stockholm.
ANDRÉN, G. et al. (1978). Rhetoric and Ideology in Advertising. Stockholm: Liber Förlag.
––– (1971). Argumentation och värderingar i reklamen. Lund: Studentlitteratur.
ARNFRED, S. (1975). "Kvinder, konsum og bevissthet." In L. Fåfeng (ed.), Kvinnens årbok 1976. Oslo: Pax Forlag.
BELKAOUNI, A. and BELKAOUNI, J. M. (1976). "A comparative analysis of the roles portrayed by women in print advertisements: 1958, 1970, 1972." Journal of Marketing Research, 13 (May).
BERELSON, B. (1952). Content Analysis in Communication Research. New York: Free Press.
BOLVIG, K. et al. (1971). Søndags BT. Rapport om en succes. København: Gyldendals Logbøger.

COURTNEY, E. A. and LOCKERETZ, S. W. (1971). "A woman's place: An analysis of the roles portrayed by women in magazine advertisements." Journal of Marketing Research 8 (February).

DOMINICK, P. J. and GAIL, E. R. (1974). "The image of women in network tv commercials." Journal of Broadcasting (Summer).

EJBYE-ERNST et al. (1975). Aalborg Stiftstidende i lokalsamfundet. Aarhus: Danmarks Journalisthøjskole.

FAUSING, B. (1973). "Sanselighedens byttevaerdi." Vindrosen 4.

FLICK, M. (1977). Kvinner i ramme. En innholdsanalyse av kjønsroller i ukebladsreklame. Bergen: Senter for Mediaforskning. Universitetet i Bergen.

GRONLIE, A. and SLETTEVOLD, A. (1967). "Å skape (kjøpe)-lyst. In E. Ryen (ed.), Sprak og kjonn. Oslo.

HANSEN, M. (1965). Reklamesprog. København: Reitzel.

HAUG, F. (1971). Kritik der Warenästhetik. Frankfurt am Main: Suhrkamp Verlag.

HOLSTI, R. O. (1969). Content Analysis for the Social Sciences and Humanities. Reading, MA: Addison-Wesley.

JONSSON, R. and JOHNSSON, I. (1970). Vad säger annonsen? 27 annonser ur dags–och veckopress analyserade med mitteraturvetenskapliga metoder. Lund: Prisma-debatt.

KASSARJIAN, H. H. (1977). "Content analysis in consumer research." Journal of Consumer Research 4 (1).

LAWRENCE, H. and FRISBIE, J. M. (1974). "Women's role portrayal preferences in advertisements: an empirical study." Journal of Marketing 38 (October).

LUNDSTROM, J. W. and SCIGLIMPAGLIA, D. (1977). "Sex roles portrayals in advertising." Journal of Marketing 41 (July).

MADSEN, P. (1977). "The intelligentsia, the critique of culture and mass media. Ideological critique in mass communication research in Denmark: Sociological and methodological aspects." In M. Berg et al. (eds.), Current Theories in Scandinavian Mass Communication Research. Grenaa: GMT.

MORTENSEN, F. (1977). "Massekommunikationsforskningens objekt og metoder." In P. Hemanus and T. Hujanen (eds.), Massekommunikationsforskningens vetenskapliga status. Tampere: Reports Nr.0 40/1977, Institute of Journalism and Mass Communication.

MØLLER, H. et al. (1972). Udsigten fra det kvindelige univers. En analyse af Eva. København: Røde Hane.

NØRGAARD, A. B. (1975). En undersøgelse af reklamens historiske udvikling og formidling–belyst gennem en konkret analyse af udvalgte danske reklamekampagner. Aarhus: Fagtryk.

O'DONNEL, W. J. and O'DONNEL, K. W. (1978). "Update: sex-role messages in TV commercials." Journal of Communication 28 (1).

QVORTRUP, L. (1976). Danmarks Radio og arbejdskampen. En analyse af DR's behandling af benzinkonflikten i november 1976. Odense: Bidrags skriftserie.

––– et al (1979). "Mediaanalyse–en foreløbig status." Odense Bidrag nr. 9.

RASMUSSEN, R. B. and KORSGAARD, E. (1977). Kvindeopfattelser i ugebladsreklame. Aarhus: Working Paper, Institut for Statskundskab.

SEPSTRUP, P. (1979a). "En undersøgelse af mands–og kvindebilledet i den danske magasin–og dagspresseannoncering." In Kønsdiskriminerende reklame. København: Rapport afgivet af en af Forbrugerombudsmanden nedsat arbejdsgruppe.

––– (1979b). Reklamen som socialisationsfaktor–teknisk rapport. Aarhus: Skriftserie E. Nr. 10, Handelshøjskolen i Aarhus.

Sexton, E. D. and Haberman, P. (1974). "Women in magazine advertisements.". Journal of Advertising Research 14 (August).

TOGEBY, O. (1975). "Sådan lever week-end generationen. Analyse af en annonce." In K. Kjøller (ed.) Analyser af sprogbrug. Argumentation. København: Borgen.

WAGNER, L. and BANOS, J. B. (1973). "A woman's place: A follow up analysis of the roles portrayed by women in magazine advertisements." Journal of Marketing Research 10 (May).

WARREN, D. (1978). "Commercial liberation." Journal of Communication 28 (7).

VENKATESAN, M. and LOSCO, J. (1975). "Women in magazine ads: 1959-71." Journal of Advertising Research 15 (October).

WILLIAMSON, J. (1978). Decoding Advertisements. Ideology and Meaning in Advertising. London: Marion Boyars.

Chapter 7

DANISH ELECTION CAMPAIGNS
IN THE SEVENTIES

Bo Fibiger

THIS CHAPTER is intended to give a summary of some preliminary findings in a project on which I am working in the Department of Nordic Languages and Literature at the University of Aarhus. The project concerns party-political broadcasting on Radio Denmark in the 1970s.

Several of the authors of the articles in the anthology *Political Communication* (Chaffee, 1975a) stress the necessity of widening the spectrum of the study of political communication to include not only single events but also wider relations in time and space. In Denmark a similar view has been held by the Danish Social Science Research Council, which has as one of its objects to initiate and support new areas of research. In a report, "Changes in the Interaction of the Political Institutions in Denmark" of July 1975 the council makes suggestions as to the initiating of surveys of the development in the manifest political communication, with a view to the legitimacy and strength of parties and organizations, the electors' understanding, interests, and possibilities, and the persuasivness and credibility of the media. "These trends in the messages of the media must be explained through systematic content analyses with a view to long-term changes (e.g. over 20 years)."

My project is an attempt to answer some of these questions. Together with Karen Siune (whose project is mentioned in another article) and with the support of the Danish Social Science Research Council, I have compiled a collection of sources from the election campaigns in Radio Den-

AUTHOR'S NOTE: The Danish Social Science Research Council has subsidized the collection of primary material. The Social Science Research Council and the Research Fund of the University of Aarhus have subsidized the transcription of tapes. Finally, the Research Fund of the University of Aarhus has subsidized the working-out of this article.

mark in 1971, 1973, 1975, and 1977. This material, which is available as
video recordings, sound recordings, and transcripts, forms the object of
this study. It has been confined to Radio Denmark only for pragmatic
reasons.

A study of the political communication over time in itself implies a
shift of the analytical interest away from the classic question of why a
certain party or a certain candidate was elected—that is, a shift away from
the instrumental character of the election campaigns toward their mental
implications. This can be related to O'Keefe (1975), who points out that
"campaign media have other effects than persuasive ones, and more
attention needs to be devoted to these" (p. 146). In this connection
O'Keefe puts forward some ideas as to the analysis of campaign media
content. "Content analyses may divulge more insights into voter communication orientations if they are directed at themes other than simple bias in
direction of one candidate or another" (p. 145). He continues: "Content
analyses could also examine the 'information content' of campaign news
and advertising, for example in terms of how well the content provides
voters with information explicitly drawing discriminations between candidates on relevant attributes" (p. 145).

On the basis of the Danish election campaigns in the seventies we shall
set up some broad themes for the analysis of the Danish development. It is
the hypothesis of this analysis that during this period there is a change in
the information content of the campaigns, a change which can be characterized in general as a shift from rational bias to emotional bias.

QUANTITATIVE AND QUALITATIVE CONTENT ANALYSIS

Berelson defined "content analysis" as "a research technique for the
objective, systematic, and quantitative description of the manifest content
of communication" (Berelson, 1971: 18). In a later chapter Berelson
mentions two types of qualitative analysis called "prequantitative." One of
them "refers simply to the selection of quotations and illustrations from
the content to be used in enlivening and humanizing the report of
frequencies by various categories." This is sometimes called "adding the
qualitative dimension to a quantitative analysis." All it adds, of course, are
"exemplifications of the categories used in the study, in the actual terms
appearing in the content" (Berelson, 1971: 115).

This analysis is also meant to add "the qualitative dimension to a
quantitative analysis," but in a way other than the simple method described by Berelson. The attempt is clearly determined by the fact that my

experience as a research worker within the humanities is confined primarily to the qualitative analysis of texts. However, in this analysis the attempt is also determined by the object analyzed.

Chaffee (1975b) mentions a number of problems in connection with studies over time. He states that "the meaning of a particular item of information can change as events occur that render it more or less relevant" (p. 114). Chaffee concentrates almost exclusively, however, on the problems arising in connection with surveys and not in connection with content analysis.

The problem of content analysis in connection with studies over time is the rigid system of categories. The categories we set up must be equally relevant during the whole period. Therefore, it is natural to set up fairly general categories. In order to establish the specific features of the individual points of analysis, the quantitative analysis has to be qualified, more or less as described by Berelson, not only through reference to "actual terms appearing in the content" but to themes conveyed structurally.

In addition to this function, the qualitative analysis is also a guarantee for the validity of the quantitative analysis. This validity test corresponds to what Holsti (1969: 143) calls "content validity": "Content validity is usually established through the informed judgment of the investigator. Are the results plausible? Are they consistent with other information about the phenomena being studied?"

The quantitative content analysis is based on the assumption that meaning can be transmitted through quantity. This implies that a quantitative configuration is a sign. In order for the analysis to be meaningful, the analyst must decode this sign. It is the validity of this decoding, not of the configurations themselves, which can be established through the qualitative analysis. We can regard this as a subdivision of Holsti's content validity and call it *contextual validity*.

The other object-defined problem in this analysis is based on the fact that it is a study of TV programs. Here the visual material plays an important role for the communication. The prerequisite for content analysis in Berelson's sense of the word is that the coding of the categories is based on conventional signs—those at word level. I do not wish to enter into the discussion of the science-theoretical problems related to the quantitative content analysis which can be raised in connection with this statement, but only to ascertain that pictures differ from words and sentences in that they are context-defined to a much greater extent. Furthermore, the visual material characterized by contextual signs presupposes the inclusion of a qualitative content analysis as a supplement to the quantitative content analysis.

HYPOTHESIS

During the seventies political scientists in Denmark conducted a number of surveys in connection with the election campaigns. These surveys have produced a rather extensive knowledge of the Danish elector: his attitude toward the political system, his reasons for party change, his use of the mass media, and so on.

This study has as its point of departure some of the facts known about the Danish elector in the seventies.

First, we know that the electors become more and more faithless to the parties. This is mirrored by a sharp increase in the gross movement taking place in 1973, after which it remained stable at a level somewhat above that of 1971 (1971: 18 percent; 1973: 36 percent; 1975: 23 percent; 1977: 26 percent). At the same time, there is a marked increase in the number of electors who do not make up their minds until during the election campaign (1971: 16 percent; 1973: 32 percent; 1975: 25 percent; 1977: 27 percent).

Second, there is a marked change in *the electors' reasons* for their choice of party. During the seventies there was an upgrading of short-term factors (confidence and topical issues) at the expense of long-term factors (group interests and partisanship).

Thus, there is an apparent overall tendency toward a weakening of the traditional party allegiances. It is the thesis of this study that this change of the electors' loyalty to the parties is closely connected to a change in the communication between politicians and electors, and that this change can be described within the framework of a general conflict between rationality and emotions.

However, the survey does not reveal anything about what can be said to be the dependent and the independent variables in this connection. A discussion of this is bound to be as meaningless as the debate about the chicken and the egg. Both tendencies, however, must be seen as factors in an overall network of trends in the seventies, of which the following brief outline shall be given.

During the sixties *the economy* was characterized by upward tendencies, and in this connection the society and the state were characterized by expansion. The political problems concerned primarily the distribution of the increasing wealth and the regulation of the economy, especially with a view to preventing overexpansion of the economy. Finally, the period is characterized by attempts at long-term planning.

Following some minor fluctuations in the late sixties the crisis made itself felt in 1973-1974, resulting in curtailment of the social and governmental expansion. The economic policy was marked by cuts, incomes policy, increased duties, and the rate of unemployment rose from one percent to approximately ten percent. This period is also characterized by a number of short-term crisis deals.

The political spectrum also changed radically. In the period up to 1971 the Danish Parliament (The Folketing) was generally composed of representatives of five parties. At the 1971 election nine parties ran, but only the five parties already represented got in. In 1973 11 parties ran for election, and 10 of them were represented. In 1975 11 parties ran again, and again 10 of them were represented. In 1977 12 parties ran for election, and only one new party did not get in.

The development is marked by a significant number of defections from the old parties. Three ideologically based parties, which have been represented previously at different times during the last decades, are now represented simultaneously. Moreover, this period saw the formation of four new populist parties, of which three were represented. One among these is the Progress Party, which obtained 15.9 percent of the votes when it first stood for election in 1973, and which has since remained more or less stable at this level.

Finally, *the general picture of the media* must be considered as one of the prerequisites of the development analyzed. The introduction of television in Denmark began in 1953, and the proliferation follows the classic S-curve. The evening out of this curve takes place between 1965 and 1970, so that TV from this time clearly must be said to have taken the role of the most important means of communication in Denmark. However, the central point here is not television's role as a vehicle for election propaganda but the general and gradual TV-socialization. During the seventies the program pattern was homogenized; this can be generally described as a "McCloudization": medium-close and close, tight-cutting with tension and action as the central, narrative elements. In another analysis I have tried to demonstrate how these narrative elements make up a central point in the media coverage of the crisis deals of the seventies mentioned above.

Another important media factor is no doubt the change in the printed media. Around 1970 the last remnants of the classic Danish party press disappeared, and regionally only one monopoly paper survives. The daily paper's importance as a factor of political socialization thus moves away from party-socialization toward a more general political socialization.

I do not wish to discuss the relationship between the various basic variables mentioned here, and others could also be included. They are mentioned only to give a rough outline of the social reality in which the object of the analysis is a factor.

THE ANALYSIS

As mentioned at the beginning, this is an overall analysis of the development in the party-political mass communication in Radio Denmark in the seventies, which is still far from being concluded. Therefore, in the following I will present only some of the results which have been used for a preliminary test of the relevance of the hypothesis and for a test of the analytical influx. The central point of the following analysis is a study of the development of the introduction program on TV produced by the Social-Democratic Party. The reason the Social-Democratic Party has been chosen as an object in this phase is that this party, except for a few short interruptions, has been the leading power in Danish government since the 1920s. The Social-Democratic Party is both the largest party and the pillar of the state in the political center.

Before entering into this part-analysis, however, a rough outline follows of two other part-analyses forming part of the testing of the hypothesis put forward. It is the general development of the election campaigns in Radio Denmark and some preliminary results arrived at in a study of the tendencies of panel discussions.

PARTY PROGRAMS IN RADIO DENMARK

In the period preceding an election, Radio Denmark, which is a state-owned monopoly institution, provides broadcasting time for the parties running. These programs are broadcast both on TV and over national and regional radio stations. All the parties running are allotted equal broadcasting time irrespective of size and previous representation. However, the exact hour of broadcasting is determined on the basis of party size. In general, the time closest to election day is preferred. This makes it possible to deal with problems arising during the election campaign.

Before 1975 the biggest party always was the first to choose in all program distributions. Since 1975 this principle has changed, so that the small parties are allowed to choose first in the national radio. This can be interpreted as an indication that the national radio is no longer considered to have crucial importance as a medium for party-political programs. This is due partly to a sharp drop in the number of people listening to serious radio programs, but no doubt also partly due to the fact that the radio is no longer an adequate political means of communication. In a description of the radio in relation to TV, it can be said that the radio is primarily a reasoning medium, whereas TV is primarily a narrating medium. These media characteristics are contained in the general paradigm constituting the hypothesis of the analysis: the relation between rationality and emotion. Thus, here we notice a shift of priorities away from rationality toward emotion.

We can take a closer look at this relation by considering the overall distribution of broadcasting time for the political election programs in the seventies (see Table 7.1 and Figure 7.1).

Thus, especially after 1973 we notice an upgrading of TV and the regional radio. TV has been characterized as narrative; and we can characterize the regional radio by the term "intimacy," which has again become an element in the emotional pole of the paradigm.

There is thus a development in the overall distribution of broadcasting time on media which is at the same time an *element in* and a *support of* the development in the political communication in the seventies.

PANEL DISCUSSIONS

In principle, an election campaign in Radio Denmark is composed of the following types of programs: introduction (produced by the parties themselves), any-question (questions by journalists), audience-participation (voters calling the party), and panel discussions with one representative from each of the parties running.

A preliminary analysis of the panel programs indicates that there are a number of general trends which can support the hypothesis put forward. The contributions in a panel discussion can be divided into five basic types: (1) introduction of the party platform, (2) questions, (3) answers, (4) comments, and (5) direct appeals to viewers. The results indicate that dialogue (categories 2 and 3) is gradually reduced for the sake of monologue. As far as dialogue is concerned, there is a tendency toward more and more unanswered direct questions; and as far as monologue is concerned, there is a tendency toward more direct appeals to viewers.

On closer examination of categories 2 and 4, which indicate relations between parties, another tendency can be seen. If we place the parties on a right-left scale, there is a change from close contact to remote contact. The differentiation in relation to neighbor parties has been replaced by a tendency of maximum profiling. This is also a feature supporting the hypothesis of a development within the basic paradigm set up.[1]

THE SOCIAL-DEMOCRATIC PARTY'S
INTRODUCTION PROGRAMS ON TV

As will have appeared, the basis of the analysis is the Social-Democratic Party's introduction programs on TV in connection with the elections of 1971, 1973, 1975, and 1977. The texts are available partly in the form of

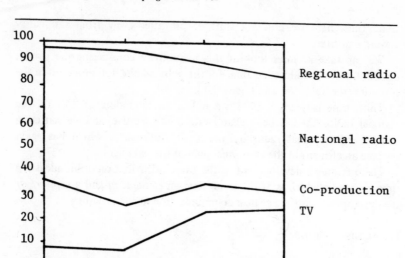

Figure 7.1 Broadcasting Time Distributed on Media, Relatively

TABLE 7.1   Broadcasting Time Distributed over Media

	1971 Total	%	1973 Total	%	1975 Total	%	1977 Total	%
TV	135	7	165	5	600	23	590	25
Co-production TV/national radio	630	32	600	21	360	14	180	8
National radio	1125	58	2035	70	1435	55	1260	54
Regional Radio	60	3	90	3	220	8	300	13
Total	1950	100	2890	99	2615	100	2330	100

video recordings, partly as transcripts of sound material. For practical reasons I have chosen to base the quantitative content analysis on the transcripts of sound material.

How is one to design a content analysis which can test the hypothesis put forward on an introduction program? I have chosen to design three quantitative basic analyses, each of whose contextual validity is then examined by means of supplementary qualitative analyses. The three quantitative analyses are based on the following theses:

(1) A movement within the paradigm of the hypothesis from rationality toward emotion will be mirrored in the subject matter of the text through a movement from information width toward focusing. Moreover, we can expect a qualitative shift of the subject matter from the political platform toward the political situation (persons, constellations, voter appeal, and so on).

(2) A movement from rationality toward emotion implies a change of the time perspective from present + future toward preterite + present.

(3) A movement from rationality toward emotion implies an upgrading of visual elements at the expense of verbal elements in the introduction program.

Thus, the content analyses are based on the following unfolded paradigm:

content	*manifestation*
RATIONALITY	information width presentation of platform present + future verbal priority
EMOTION	focusing political situation preterite + present visual priority

The first part-analysis examines what themes are being dealt with in the individual introduction programs. It may give rise to problems here to base the analysis on the transcripts of the sound material because the program's allocation of time to the themes does not necessarily correspond to the volume of sound material alone; however, since the material reveals a clear tendency, I have chosen to disregard this uncertain factor. Therefore, I have used sentences as an analytical variable and number of lines as the unit of measurement in the material transcribed. The analytical categories have been determined on the basis of the material in question, the aim of the analysis being only to test the information width, but roughly they follow the lines of the traditional political division of themes (see Table 7.2).

This part-study shows clearly that in this period there is a significant reduction of the number of themes included. This in itself reflects a higher degree of situational constraint. At the same time, there is another very

TABLE 7.2   The Coverage of Themes 1971-1977

Percentage Figures	1971	1973	1975	1977
Fiscal policy	8	18	–	6
Macroeconomics	9	6	38	29
Labor-market policy	14	24	10	–
Housing policy	8	16	–	20
Educational policy	23	–	–	–
Social-security policy	4	16	–	6
Regionalization	15	–	–	–
Foreign policy	7	2	–	–
Ideology (equality)	5	–	–	–
The party/persons	–	–	14	–
Other parties/persons	–	–	15	–
The election/Parliament	13	19	22	38
Other	6	–	–	–

clear tendency toward upgrading the election as such and the parliamentary situation. Therefore, this analysis seems to confirm the hypothesis put forward; at the same time, these tendencies clearly sustain the electorate's propensity to attach more importance to short-term factors/the situational constraint.

However, the other study of *the time relations* in the introduction programs raises a number of problems which can be solved only by means of a more detailed qualitative analysis, because the analytical categories turn out to have been modified in the meantime. If we take a look at the raw data first, however, applying the same analytical variables and analytical units as in Table 7.2 but applying backward, forward, and actually ascertaining analytical categories, the picture will appear as shown in Table 7.3.

To a certain extent the result of the analysis confirms that the preterite dimension is upgraded—in 1973 and 1977. Its absence in 1975, however, makes it problematic to draw an unequivocal conclusion on the basis of this part-study alone, one of the reasons being that the elections of 1973 and 1977, unlike those of 1971 and 1975, followed upon a period in which the Social-Democratic Party had been in office. Therefore, there might be a connection between the result of the analysis and this fact, which can only be finally disproved or confirmed when other parties have been subjected to the same analysis.

The reason some importance can be attached to the result is both the quality of the preterite statements (that is, that they do not concern the governmental period in particular but the historical role of the party in general) and that a similar general tendency can be demonstrated in the party's programs of principle and action from the seventies.

Furthermore, we can compare Table 7.3 with Table 7.2. The latter shows that in 1975 the argumentation oriented toward persons plays a prominent role. In Table 7.3 this material has been registered as actual, since it is an argument for Prime Minister Anker Jørgensen's personal qualifications. Compared with the voters' upgrading of the factor of confidence (one of the short-term factors of the election analysis), both history *and* actual persons may be of importance; and in relation to our overall content paradigm, both are expressions of an emotional presentation. The result from 1975 can thus be considered a different order of priorities among several variants of expression.

The orientation toward the preterite and persons can be considered a result of the party's problem of justification. In connection with the appearance of the new parties in the seventies, the Social-Democratic Party lost some of its traditional partisans. Both the upgrading of history and the focusing on persons took place at the expense of the presentation of a specific future policy which may be an impediment either to new parliamentary constellations or to the support of the traditional voters. Moreover, Table 7.3 shows, contrary to the thesis put forward, an apparent growth in the number of forward statements. A qualitative analysis of the statements registered indicates, however, that this result does not conflict with the overall hypothesis. One of the themes reappearing in the four introduction programs is economic democracy, which in each of the four years is given the following mention:

1971
The plans for economic democracy must be realized through workers' funds. It increases savings and brings more balance to the distribution of incomes and wealth. The funds must be extended to the individual enterprises, and the shopstewards and the cooperative committees are going to represent the worker capital in the management. And each worker is going to have a personal share in the fund. In all enterprises, private and public, there must be worker participation. We must pursue a modern labour-market policy.

1973
We have worked out a proposal for security and health and wellbeing. It was stopped by the election. So was the proposal for economic democracy. It is all right to discuss the final framework for the management, the central fund, and the placement of the money. The crucial point is that the proposal means participation in the management of the individual enterprise.

1975
Economic democracy is new thinking.

1977
We must provide the necessary capital for the investments of trade and industry. This is only possible through economic democracy.

TABLE 7.3   Time Orientation—1971, 1973, 1975, 1977

Percentage Figures	1971	1973	1975	1977
backward	–	17	–	15
actual	64	72	62	42
forward	28	11	38	44
other[x]	8	–	–	–

[x]In 1971 some of the statements of principle are difficult to place.

This example demonstrates how the actual description of economic democracy as a system is being reduced to a noncommittal mention leaving all possibilities open.

The example serves to illustrate another fact. In 1971 the central, loaded concept was the word *modern,* whereas in 1973 the central concept was *participation.* Thus, the example also serves to illustrate how words whose meanings can be contained by or border upon expansion are replaced by concepts whose meanings lie within the intimate, the warm and the secure.

The continuation of this development in 1975 and 1977 is further illustrated by other examples from those years:

1975
We must think ahead and we must think new thoughts. We must control development, development must not control us. We must humanize society. We must create good jobs together, make them safe. We must find new forms of housing together, new forms of togetherness which bring us closer to each other, do not estrange us. We must make solidarity something concrete.

1977
Denmark is a good country, a good home, and so it must always be; but we must take care that self-sufficiency does not catch hold of us. We must take care that selfishness does not influence our actions too strongly.

Therefore, the analytical result appearing from Table 7.3 as to the amount of forward statements must be seen in relation to a qualitative change in these statements. What seems to be an improvement of the electors' possibilities of making their political choice—more forward statements about the party's goals—is outbalanced by the fact that the statements become less precise and qualitatively can be characterized as expressing human goals. Although the result of the analysis conflicts with the thesis put forward, a more detailed qualitative analysis reveals that the result is in harmony with the paradigm of the basic hypothesis.

Let us follow up the tendency uncovered here at the stylistic level. The style applied in 1971 can be characterized as "modern technocratic style," in which the rhetorical element is inherent in the apparent rationality of the simple syntax. The 1973 platform is characterized as containing colloquial phrases; for example, expressions such as "face the problem," "at the grass-roots," and the like. This tendency continues into 1975, in which year we are presented with the following closing remark:

1975
We must join hands, town and country, east and west, north and south, everywhere hands must be joined. We must refuse selfishness, and then together we must create the security we are all longing for.

Not only do we find a metaphor, but also an instance of the classic rhetoric: parallelism and chiasmus. In the 1977 platform this use of metaphors continued—"riding our own hobbyhorse," "Getting out of hand," and so on, used here in combination with a significantly colloquial syntax and frequent use of adverbial insertions ("you know" and "of course") to mark the common interest.

Whereas the mental correlate to the 1971 modern technocratic style is rationality, the mental correlate to everyday speech and the metaphors is emotion. Thus, the content paradigm of the hypothesis can be correlated in the tiniest linguistic detail in the texts. At the same time, this qualitative analysis has a methodical function as a validity test of the interpretation of the quantitative analysis.

So far we have only analyzed the textual material, but now we will extend this analysis by studying the relation between textual material and visual material, and the visual material as such. To test the thesis that visualization increased during the seventies, we can assume that the volume of textual material can be measured on the basis of the number of typing units in each transcript. This presupposes equal talking speeds in the four programs, but the result is so clear that this uncertainty must be rejected. This quantitative part-analysis has the result shown in Table 7.4.

Thus, the number of typing units in the transcript indicates a significant decrease in the volume of speech from 1971 to 1975. But apparently there is an increase in the textual material in 1977. However, this contrast must be seen in relation to the reduction of broadcasting time in 1977, the actual volume of textual material in fact being smaller than in 1975 (approximately 7500 typing units). Therefore, the contrast can be ascribed to a certain degree of inertia, because a continuation of the previous

TABLE 7.4   Textual Material 1971-1977

	1971	1973	1975	1977
typing units[x]	12,000	9,500	8,000	11,000[xx]

[x]The figures are approximate because they are calculated on the basis of average length of lines.

[xx]The figure has been corrected for the fact that the 1977 program lasted only 10 minutes as compared with 15 minutes in 1971, 1973, and 1975.

tendency would have meant an even more drastic decrease in the volume of textual material.

A comparison between the visual material and the textual material also indicates that in 1971, 1973, and 1975 there was overall synchronism between visual material and textual material; that is, the interaction has a redundant function, whereas in 1977 there were many instances of asynchronism between visual and textual material. Thus, in 1977 the visual material stands out as an independent narrative element. Therefore, it would be more appropriate to conclude that in 1977 the visual elements of the program were given a still higher priority.

This preliminary study of the volume and function of the visual material points to the same results as the analysis of the subject matter of the textual material—a change from rationality to emotion.

As far as the visual material is concerned, this interpretation is supported by the changes occurring all through the period in the narrative structure of the programs. The 1971 program was built around a speaker talking sporadically in the program. His role was primarily to provide continuity by passing the floor to a number of social-democratic politicians acting as experts. Accordingly, the visual matter was dominated by medium-close shots of ex-ministers whose predominant variation is zooming variance (remote: outlook; close: appeal).

The 1973 host of the program stood out more distinctly in the program. Light was focused on him as he sat at a desk (outlook), and the last pictures of the program zoom gradually to close-up (appeal). All through the program the studio host was the dominating person as far as the visual material is concerned. Compared with the 1971 program, therefore, this program was characterized by a higher degree of unity. Moreover, the politicians were replaced by persons representing different social groups (the worker, the pensioner, the tenant). The program thus applies figures of identification while appearing in interiors that increase the authenticity. All through the individual's contributions, cuttings are made from person to illustration. This lends a more rapid cutting rhythm to the program.

The 1975 program is composed largely according to the structure used in 1973, except that the studio host's role was enhanced to dominate the program completely. Again, the other persons are figures of identification, but they appear in much shorter glimpses. In this program the extension of speaking time allotted to the studio host is outbalanced by increased use of redundant illustrations, including cartoons. This intensifies the cutting rhythm.

Thus, the 1973 and 1975 programs show an overall tendency toward a more general, narrative structure and a higher degree of visualization at a more rapid cutting speed. In terms of perception psychology, there is a shift of interest from the level of the statements in the textual material to the general impression and the aesthetic sense stimulus. Finally, the politicians are replaced by figures of identification.

The 1977 program is made up of two parts: one layer forming the framework of the program (the Prime Minister at his desk) and one layer constituting the introduction program "proper." At the visual level the interior represents the Prime Minister as the statesman keeping everything together, whereas at the verbal level he is "the common man" telling about his childhood. We are here presented with the double (asynchronous) communication in the two layers of the text: competence and identification. If we probe the introduction part "proper," we find that it consists of a number of stills which have been cut in such a way that a person is gradually brought into the focus of the picture. Very often these pictures are only peripherally connected to the statements in the textual material (asynchronism). The linkage is brought about, however, in such a way that the movement of the textual material from situational description toward change is accompanied by movement in the picture from remote via medium-close to close, whereupon the last change to close-up is supplemented with a face showing smile/happiness. The visual material therefore has the function of identification and also adds positive value to the textual material.

Although the 1977 program changes its style, it is, however, externally a departure from the previous trends. The overall development from 1971 to 1977 in the narrative structure and in the visual material is thus an additional indication of the general tendency toward a shift from the rational pole in the paradigm toward the emotional pole.

EVALUATION

This preliminary analysis has been confined to the Social-Democratic Party. The extent to which the tendency uncovered can be claimed to be a general tendency is, of course, dependent on studies of the other parties, but the analysis of the overall distribution of programs and the panel discussions suggest that the tendency can be claimed to be distinctive of Danish political mass communication in the seventies.

A couple of times in the analysis we have touched upon internal matters in the Social-Democratic Party which could also be used in support of the understanding of the development described. For this party, these internal matters no doubt contribute to intensifying the tendency described, and therefore they must be given a brief mention. The basic variables in question are party strength, party relations, and relationship to the trade unions.

On the face of it, *party strength* can be measured on the basis of the number of votes at each election—1971: 37.3 percent; 1973: 25.6 percent; 1975: 29.1 percent; 1977: 37.1 percent. Thus, during the seventies the party moved from a peak in 1971 via an absolute slump in 1973 and then upwards again in 1975. This surface movement, however, hides another movement—decreasing adherence by the middle-class. The party is thus divided in a dual interest in keeping the loyal voters and at the same time capturing and keeping new voter groups.

In the mid-sixties the Social-Democratic Party had begun a cooperation with the left which was continued from 1971 to 1973. From 1973 to 1975 the party was in opposition to a liberal minority government. When, in 1975, the party took office again, it was supported by the new populist center-parties, a line which was followed in the summer of 1978 through the formation of a coalition government with the liberal party. After 1973 we see a departure from a socialist line toward a center-right line. This development forced the party to face some problems of justification vis-à-vis the voters.

Moreover, these problems of justification were aggravated because of worsening relations to the *trade unions*. Historically, there has always been a close connection between the trade unions and the Social-Democratic Party. The worsening relations are caused by, among other things, the entry into the EEC in 1972. Especially after the party's formation in 1975 of a government dependent on the center, the problems were aggravated, both in connection with the many crisis deals and with incomes policy and the incrimination of the trade unions' traditional weapons.

These internal problems of justification no doubt contributed considerably to predisposing the party to a modified strategy of communication in which rationality is eliminated for the sake of emotion. But the basic hypothesis of the entire analysis is that other things than pure party-political calculations apply, and that it is a question of a general tendency which the individual parties can be more or less predisposed to follow.

EVALUATION

So far the analysis seems to prove a close connection between changes in the attitudes of electors toward the parties and the attitudes of parties toward the electors. As mentioned before, it is hardly a question of a simple relation of cause and effect, but of a more complex relation with the general social development as the driving force. However, there is hardly any doubt that the two tendencies are mutually reinforcing.

This "Americanization" of the political public sphere in Denmark no doubt results in a serious weakening of the political system as such and also its ability to continue a controlled regeneration. From this point of view the analysis relates itself to Jürgen Habermas, the German social philosopher, who has demonstrated how in the entire history of the bourgeois society there has been a development from a reasoned public to a consumer public (Habermas, 1962). However, Habermas' analysis is a glorification of the classic bourgeois public sphere, which is presented as a "paradise lost." The problems raised by the development in the political public sphere described here cannot be coped with by means of nostalgia, however, but through fundamental changes in the political system. Thus, instead of being built downwards from the top, it is built upwards from the bottom through a real popular revolution.

The purpose of this chapter is not, however, to give a total presentation of the sociopolitical problems raised by the results of the analysis, but primarily to demonstrate methodologically an interaction between quantitative and qualitative content analyses different from the forms mentioned by Berelson.

In more concrete terms, this model analysis concerns the risks of interpretation which may be met when the quantitative analysis is applied in connection with studies over time. The quantitative content analysis embodies analytical categories whose original value of statement is converted during the analysis into its own opposite pole. In certain cases some of these problems can be solved by making more extensive use of subcategories, but frequently a qualitative content analysis at a thematic/structural level proves necessary.

Another problem lies in the possibility of interpreting a given result in a quantitative content analysis in different ways. The validity of the interpretation in question may be ascertained here by means of the qualitative analysis; that is, by relating the result of the analysis to other structures of meaning in the overall context. To illustrate this, it would hardly seem reasonable to uncover the change in the paradigm from rationality to emotion only on the basis of the quantitative content analysis; however, by virtue of the qualitative content analysis we are able to interpret the results as expressions of and factors in this process.

NOTE

1. The fundamental thesis of the above-mentioned analysis of the McCloudization of the political communication is that the differentiation between neighbor parties is made in the media coverage of the current political practice instead, which, by virtue of the narrative character of the media, create heroes and villains, a subparadigm of the emotional pole.

REFERENCES

BERELSON, B. (1971). Content Analysis in Communication Research. New York: Hafner.
CHAFFEE, S. H. [ed.] (1975a). Political Communication: Issues and Strategies for Research. Beverly Hills, CA: Sage.
––– (1975b). "The diffusion of political information." In Political Communication: Issues and Strategies for Research. Beverly Hills, CA: Sage.
HABERMAS, J. (1962) Strukturwandel der Offenlichkeit. Unterzuchungen zu einer Kategorie der bürgerlichen Gesellschaft. Darmstadt: Hermann Luchterhand Verlag.
HOLSTI, O. (1969). Content Analysis for the Social Sciences and Humanities. Reading, MA: Addison-Wesley.
O'KEEFE, G. J. (1975). "Political campaigns and mass communication research." In S. H. Chaffee (ed.), Political Communication: Issues and Strategies for Research. Beverly Hills, CA: Sage.

In addition to these references, a number of analyses of Danish voter attitudes and the Social-Democratic Party have been applied.

Chapter 8

BROADCAST ELECTION CAMPAIGNS
IN A MULTIPARTY SYSTEM
Denmark as a Test Case

Karen Siune

POLITICAL COMMUNICATION does not occur in a vacuum. In this chapter a general model is proposed for factors influencing the content of mass-media-transmitted political communication. Hypotheses are put forward about politicians and journalists as agents in the campaign situation in a multiparty system. Three Danish general elections are used as test cases. Before the model and the hypotheses are introduced some different approaches to research in political communication will be discussed.

RESEARCH APPROACHES

"A great deal can be learned about the political content of a society by examining the structure and forms of programs in which political material is transmitted" (Smith, 1976: 208). For hundreds of years political communication has been transmitted by the printed press, while the broadcast transmission is relatively new. In relation to both printed and broadcast transmission of political material it is relevant to ask what determines the content of the transmission. If this question can be answered we will have come a step further in the understanding of the content.

Is the political content given by the political character of the society, or by the economic system, as argued by Marxists? Is it given by the actors communicating, the journalists, the political parties? Or is it given by the medium used for the transmission, as McLuhan said: "The medium is the message"?

Some will argue that the answer must be found on the individual level; that it is determined by the individual actors, who participate as communicators of the messages.

The answer which can be reached is dependent on the level of analysis used in a given context, and to a very high degree is dependent on the theoretical point of departure. This can be illustrated by means of a short review of the many analyses of political communication conducted over the years.

In Scandinavia there is a tradition for research in party political communication. This is partly due to the newspaper structure, which basically was party-affiliated (Thomsen, 1965; Kronvall, 1972; Vallinder, 1974; Høyer et al., 1975). Research on political communication on radio and television has concentrated more on the problem of balance in news-reporting (Westerståhl, 1972; Rosengren, 1979).

American traditions such as analysis of individual speeches of political leaders (for example, Nixon and Kennedy; see Kraus, 1962; Lang and Lang, 1968), analysis of television coverage of conventions (Kraus and Davis, 1976), and other events (Kraus et al., 1975) have not influenced Scandinavian research very much. Individual politicians do not play the same important role in Scandinavia as in the United States, and this is mirrored in the research. Because of this difference between the political systems, the level of potential explanation will more often be found at an institutional level in Scandinavian analysis compared with the individual or event level focused on in America.

The purpose of much research in political communication has been to look at the impact of the communication, the effect on the individuals in the society, on political cognitions in general (Becker et al., 1975), and especially the effect of political campaigns (O'Keefe, 1975). Another approach has been the uses and gratifications of political communication (Blumler and McQuail, 1968; Blumler and Katz, 1974).

The main concern in this study is not the effect of political communication but the factors influencing and forming the content. In addition, a discussion about the function of broadcast political campaigns will be raised.

A GENERAL MODEL

In Figure 8.1 an attempt has been made to put forward a general model intended to cover media-transmitted political communication. The basic idea behind the model is that the content of media-transmitted political communication is influenced generally by the political and the economic system as well as by the actual situation in which the interaction between the mass media and political actors takes place. The model implicitly assumes that it is possible to separate the impact of the situational variables—that is, the short-term effect—from the long-term impact of the

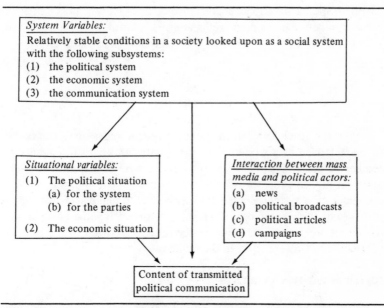

Figure 8.1 Model for Factors Influencing Mass-Media-Transmitted Political Content

system variables, where the system variables in a given society can be treated more like parameters (variables in comparative research) but relatively stable from situation to situation in a given society. Thus, the model applies to comparative research based on several political and economic systems with different media structures, as well as to dynamic research which test the value of the situational variables.

In the model the interaction between the mass media and the political actors is influenced by the system variables as well as by the situation in which it occurs. The system characteristics relevant to the interaction are relations among the political system and the media organization. These specify the intentions and the limitations of the interaction. The structural result of the interaction can be characterized by the different forms in which it can be found. News coverage is the most continuous interaction. Reporting of political news during nonelection periods with normal party activity is not the least interesting to look upon as a result of system characteristics and situational circumstances. How is the agenda for news transmission made up? Comparative research of newsbroadcasts like those done in Scandinavia (Bakke and Siune, 1974) is a special case, which raises opportunities for testing the model.

An election campaign is another special kind of political communication, creating material to which the proposed model can be applied. A campaign can be defined as occurring in a given political system at a given time with special situational characteristics. The structural possibilities for interaction between the mass media and the political parties can be listed, and the content of the transmitted political campaign can be analyzed.

HYPOTHESES

Within the general model, the political system under consideration can be characterized as a western democracy with free competition among a number of political parties. The economic system is a market economy based on private property combined with heavy state intervention. The communication system is a system with a limited number of mass media outlets and with some degree of state control. Hypotheses about the content of an election campaign can be raised in relation to the behavior of the different agents acting in the campaign.

POLITICAL PARTIES AS AGENTS

Political parties in a multiparty system (defined as a system with three or more parties) can be conceived as agents in different arenas. Sjöblom (1968) refers to strategies on the parliamentary as well as in the electoral arena. Mass-media-transmitted political communication is an arena with a potential mass audience, classified primarily as voters.

The main goal for a political party participating in an election in a multiparty system with free competition among several parties is to maximize the number of votes given to the party. How this goal is pursued is a matter of strategy and allocation of resources. One method is to turn all communication potentials into a party platform; from that platform the party can communicate, to a large number of people, the message which is intended to give the image of the party as party leaders want it transferred to the electorate. One aspect of the image is reliability, a party in which voters can have confidence.

The assumption that vote maximization is the goal for every party participating in a parliamentary election must be perceived as realistic for the majority of political parties in western democracies. There are modifications insofar as some parties put a higher priority on nonparliamentary than on parliamentary actions; but when the object of analysis is an election campaign, the assumption should be valid. Another problem is that ideas about future parliamentary behavior can act as a limitation on campaign behavior. But even taking this into consideration, the expectation is that every party will search for a platform in the campaign situation.

Based on these assumptions, we can put forward the following hypotheses for campaign behavior:

1. A political party will, through its communication, try to convince voters of its own abilities to solve society's problems.

From this hypothesis some more testable hypotheses may be deduced:

1.1. A political party will try to demonstrate that it is aware of the problems of society.

1.2. A political party will demonstrate that it has confidence in its own ability to take care of these problems.

1.3. A political party will try to convince voters that it has planned to do something to solve the problems—perhaps already has started to solve the problems.

The last part of the hypothesis is expected to be especially relevant to government parties, in that they want to continue as government parties.

1.4. A political party will demonstrate that it does not believe in the ability of other parties to solve the problems. This last hypothesis is directly related to the competition in the situation.

These hypotheses can be tested in the following way.

1.1.: references to issues versus general political statements,

1.2.: positive references to one's own party combined with references to own work,

1.3.: references to ongoing and planned activities,

1.4.: negative references to other political parties.

Within a given political system every political party will have a perception of the composition of actual and potential voters, generally a composition in socioeconomic terms. Differences between the political parties found in a given political system regarding their reference groups must be expected. Some parties have special social classes as reference groups. Generally a hypothesis like the following may be put forward:

2. Every party will have its own reference group to which it tries to appeal more than to other groups.

Based on the competition between the parties,

3. Every party will try to keep its earlier voters and at the same time try to win votes from the neighboring parties.

These hypotheses can be tested in the form of degree of references to various socioeconomic categories of the population. Hypothesis 3 includes a ranking of the parties according to which party is neighbor to which party.

Within the framework of a multiparty system we expect to find more parties having the same reference groups compared with two-party systems.

Relevant for hypothesis 2 is a hypothesis put forward as a result of an analysis of the Swedish 1970 election.

4. "When a party directs its propaganda to a non-selected mass audience the propensity to refer to groups in the electorate is lower than it is when the audience is in some sense more selected" (Kronvall, 1975: 237).

According to the Swedish results, we do not expect to find the same amount of references to specific groups of voters in the broadcast material as we expect in other types of political mass communication. However, references to specific groups were found in the Swedish campaign, and as a result, the following hypotheses were put forward.

5. "The positive references from the parties to groups in the electorate are preferentially directed to such groups which can be found in the clusters of wage earners/employees and enterprisers/employers." Besides the cluster mentioned, people with low incomes, workers, pensioners, families with children, old people, minor enterprisers, women, and farmers were mentioned in the Swedish campaign" (Kronvall, 1975: 237).
6. "On an average, the parties' propensity to refer negatively to groups in the electorate is low."
7. "This propensity is relatively lower among Bourgeois parties than among Socialist parties" (Kronvall, 1975: 235). The negative references in the Swedish election were primarily directed to groups in the cluster of enterprisers.

Hypothesis 4 is the only hypothesis which is media-specific. Hypotheses 1-3, 5 and 6 apply to election campaigns in general. Hypothesis 7 is the only one specifying different behavior from different political parties. However, all seven hypotheses allow us to conclude differently for the different parties.

To these hypotheses another could be added (put forward by Kronvall):

8. "The subject areas of taxation politics, economic politics, labour market issues, party descriptions, the government formation issue, and ideological messages, maybe also foreign politics, play a central role in every "normal" election campaign in a political and economical environment like the Swedish" (Kronvall, 1975: 236).

The last hypothesis can be criticized because it is very broad; but since it is stated as an expectation of system determination, it is included here.

JOURNALISTS AS AGENTS

Media organizations can themselves be looked upon as parapolitical systems (Chaffee, 1975) working within a general political system.

Depending on the specific kind of political system, as well as the media ideology that characterizes the organization, a number of hypotheses about journalistic behavior can be put forward:

> 9. Journalists generally follow news criteria when they are working with political mass communication.

This general hypothesis can be specified according to different news criteria[1]:

> 9.1. Journalists will focus on the highly politicized and conflict-loaded issues on the political agenda.
> 9.2. Journalists will try to focus on person-oriented issues.
> 9.3. Journalists will try to focus on the power elite in the political system.
> 9.4. Compared with politicians, journalists are more interested in future activities than in earlier activities, because the future, with its unknown results, makes better news stories than the past with its facts.
> 10. Journalists are critical toward the political system and attack the political representatives rather than defend them.

The last hypothesis stems from the perception of journalists as "watch-dogs."

> 11. Journalists attached to media such as television and radio with nonselected mass audiences will generally tend to take care of the interests of the masses rather than those of specific groups of the population.

In a monopoly situation the stress on this expected behavior will often be greater than if several television and radio networks were to compete.

About journalistic behavior in a campaign context it has been said that, generally, journalists will seek to avoid a quiet and eventually boring campaign (Seymour-Ure, 1974). "They tend to dramatize" (Lang and Lang, 1968); "avoid boring the audience while carrying out the burden of the preservation of the political culture" (Smith, 1976: 214). These British and American citations show some of the goals that political journalists are striving for, and they also give a frame of reference for the hypotheses above.

The hypotheses about journalists as agents can be tested as follows:

> 9.1.: The subjects raised as issues through questions put by journalists can be characterized as conflict-loaded or not according to extra-media data as well as intramedia data. Highly politicized issues are issues which receive attention from the politicians in the political debate in the parliamentary arena as well as in the public arena.
> 9.2.: The propensity to refer to politicians instead of political parties.
> 9.3.: The propensity to refer to the government party/parties and/or the largest parties compared with references to minor and/or less powerful political parties.

9.4.: The time dimension used by the journalists; future activities contrary to earlier activities.

10: The style used by the journalists will have a greater probability of being distrust than confidence.

11: The number of references to specific categories of the population is expected to be low.

DENMARK AS A TEST CASE

The project in relation to which the model and the hypotheses have been tested covers national election campaigns broadcast before the 1971, 1973, and 1975 general elections to the Danish parliament, the Folketing. The operationalizations given above for the nominal variables included in the hypotheses were used in a systematic quantitative content analysis of the total output from the broadcast part of the campaign.

The argument for selecting the broadcast part of the political campaigns is that it is a publicly financed campaign transmitted by mass media in a monopoly situation, and as such we can expect special qualities.

PLATFORMS AND WINDOWS

If a given mass medium can be used by a political party in a way which is only determined by the party itself, we can talk about a pure platform for this party. This is not to say that mass media or programs on such media exclusively in this way can act as platforms. Mass media and broadcast programs can serve as platforms for a political party even though they are not totally or at all directed by the given party.

Journalists representing state-supported monopoly mass media as Danish radio and television organized in the Danish broadcasting company (DR), which is run by licenses paid by listeners and viewers, are formally bound to have intentions according to the general rules for Danish broadcasting. These rules can be said to follow the ideas of social responsibility. The DR has also specified rules for political broadcasts, which state that political programs should help listeners and viewers in their performance of their democratic duties—that is, primarily their voting behavior.

Blumler and McQuail (1968) and Katz (1972) brought the concept of "window" into campaign research. Broadcasting should be less of a platform for election rhetoric and more of a window through which the voter can get a clear view of the political arena. The function of journalists working in a media organization like DR is to provide such a window through which the people can see what is actually going on in politics (Siune, 1975).

Diffusion of information about the political system and the political situation can be said to be the formally accepted goal for political broadcasts from a media organization like DR. A program structure intending to secure this goal can be said to search for the window function.

But the diffusion must have a further characteristic—it must be relevant to the electorate to make it possible for the voters to identify with the democratic political system. The question, then, is whether the journalists are willing and/or able to bring this kind of information to the mass audience. Are they aware of what is going on among the ordinary citizens? Or do they belong more to the parapolitical system made up by the media organization, identifying themselves with special political or professional interests? An analysis of journalistic behavior compared with information about problem perception among the voters is one way to search for an answer to these questions. The results of an analysis based on the 1971 election (Siune and Borre, 1975) showed that the journalists were not unaware of the mass perceptions but that they generally had their own ideas which made up an agenda different from that of the electorate.

In research limited to an analysis of the transmitted programs, the program structure in itself gives an opportunity to evaluate the possibility for windows versus platforms.

As a result of its formal position in the political and economic system, Danish broadcasting has general rules for programming requesting balanced and nonfavored programming. Based on this principle, the time on the air has been given equally to all Danish political parties running for the election, regardless of whether they are new or old, big or small, represented or not represented in parliament. The program structure for the 1971 election is described in detail by Siune (1975), and the later structure has been very much the same, though with some changes.[2]

The broadcasts included in the analysis consisted of

(1) presentations made by each of the parties (television and radio);
(2) questions put by journalists to politicians (television and radio at the same time);
(3) debates between representatives of all parties participating in the election (television and radio at the same time);
(4) meeting the press, which involves representatives of different mass media putting questions to the parties, one by one (only radio); and
(5) questions put by voters mediated via telephone (only radio).

The last program was not included in the 1973 and 1975 election analysis.

The majority of the time on the air for these programmes (1-4) was spent on questioning party standpoints. Only 20-25 percent of the total time was given to pure party platforms, defined as party presentations made by the parties themselves (Siune, 1979).

THE DANISH POLITICAL SYSTEM AND
THE SITUATION IN THREE ELECTIONS

From 1968 to 1971 the Danish government consisted of a coalition between three old parties—the Agrarian Liberals, the Conservatives, and the Radical Liberals.

In the 1971 election nine parties participated. Only five of them won seats in the parliament. The government was formed by the Social Democrats, as so often before.

In 1972 there was a referendum about Danish membership of the European Economic Community. Parties like the Social Democrats and the Radical Liberals were internally split on this issue and did not want to discuss it in the 1971 campaign.

In the 1973 election 11 parties were in the arena; two of these were new. Both these parties had very few themes on their agenda, but used them time and again: taxes and especially ideas about deductions and reductions. As a result of the election, 10 parties were represented in parliament, including the two new ones.

From 1973 to 1975 the Agrarian Liberals formed a minority government. The party called the 1975 election without being forced to it, wanting to strengthen the party before the upcoming general negotiations about collective wage agreements. Shortly before the election was called the government had proposed a "totality" plan for the solution of Denmark's economic problems.

As described briefly in this summary of Danish politics in the beginning of the seventies, the situations differed politically. Economically, the situation did grow worse from 1971 to 1975, starting especially with the oil crisis and the following general crises in 1973.

Contrary to the situation, the system has not changed during the period. Politically, it was already a multiparty system in 1971, though it has grown more diversified over time. The economic system can be characterized briefly as a system with great public spending, high taxes, inflation, and problems with balance of payment due to more importing than exporting.

As indicated in hypothesis 8, the condition for adding the "Swedish" hypotheses to those being tested is that Denmark has a political and economic system very similar to those in Sweden. The media structure with respect to radio and television is almost the same. The Swedish broadcasting is also a monopoly organization, and, following this, both organizations are guided and restricted by some of the same norms. According to the model, this similarity in system, together with similarity in the situation, should result in an output very much the same.[3]

RESULTS FROM THE CONTENT ANALYSIS

Results from the 1971 and the 1973 campaigns have been published separately (Siune, 1975, 1976; Siune and Borre, 1975). Comparisons of all three elections have been made regarding the structure and form of the broadcast campaigns, discussing the dominance of politicians in these programs (Siune, 1978, 1979). The conclusion is that representatives of the political parties spoke approximately 80 percent of the total time spent on these programs. The time perspective indicates that the platform function was basically possible for all parties.

The proportion of single statements goes from 30 percent in 1971 and 1973 down to 19 percent in 1975. The majority of the units of analysis[4] are questions and answers. In principle this structure of communication should favor the window function rather than the platform function.

The proposed model has proved its relevance with respect to issues. The top issues on the agenda for the three elections differed from situation to situation (Figure 8.2). Some of the top issues in the elections were the result of the economic system, with one of the highest tax burdens in the world. Other top issues were situation-specific; for instance, discussions about advantages and disadvantages of possible Danish membership of the European Economic Community, which was finally decided upon in a referendum in 1972. In 1971 the issue was put on the agenda by the journalists according to news criteria (hypotheses 9.1. and 9.4; see Figure 8.3). In 1973 this top issue from 1971 was low on the agenda from all but the parties opposing the Danish membership of the EEC, at that time already effectuated. In addition, the journalists lost their concern for the EEC issue sooner than did most of the political parties.

The 1973 election was characterized by the introduction of two new political parties, the Progress Party and the Center Democrats. The Progress Party particularly was expected to win many votes. This party based its campaign heavily on the tax issue, which already had high priority in the political and economic system, especially reductions in taxes in connection with cuts in public spending. The other new party, the Center Democrats, also had tax reductions on its agenda, especially tax reductions for houseowners (these being the top reference group for this party). The 1973 situation made taxes and housing top issues on the agenda (Figure 8.2).

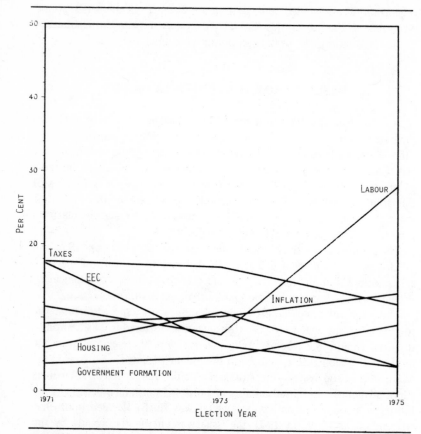

Figure 8.2   Issue Frequencies in the 1971, 1973, and 1975 Elections (all communicators)

NOTE: Issue references are multiply coded; several issues are possible in one unit of analysis.

The 1975 election campaign was still high on taxes, but it was extremely high for almost all parties on the labor market theme (Figure 8.4). Two factors in the situation helped this: a high level of unemployment and an upcoming bargaining session for collective agreements in wages. Generally high on the party agenda were inflation and the problems in the economic system (see Figure 8.5). Journalists showed increasing concern for this issue.

Always higher on the journalists' agenda than on the politicians' is the question about who will form the government after the election. Several issues were low on the agenda for all the elections, due to the political and economic system with nothing in the situation to change their priority.

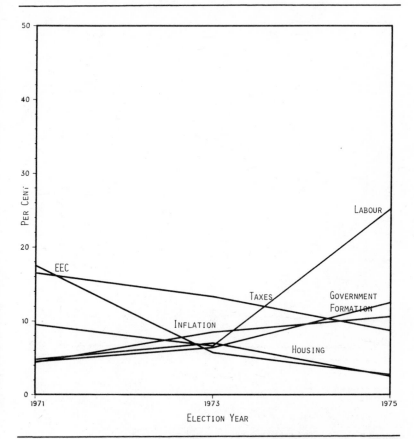

Figure 8.3   Issue Frequencies in Questions from Journalists Put to the Political Parties in the 1971, 1973, and 1975 Elections

NOTE: Journalists usually deal with only one issue per question.

The politicians preferred to speak of their own party activities and spoke less of the activities of other parties (Table 8.1). This is in accordance with the general platform tendencies and hypothesis 1.2.

The time dimension used by the politicians for all three elections was primarily the present. Future plans were not mentioned as often as expected in relation to hypothesis 1.3. The concentration on the ongoing work expanded in the period from 1971 to 1975, but the plans did not become fewer.

The reason behind this development is that the parties referred to plans already proposed. This was treated as ongoing work. They did not make up new plans, especially for the campaign. Hypothesis 1.3. shall as a result

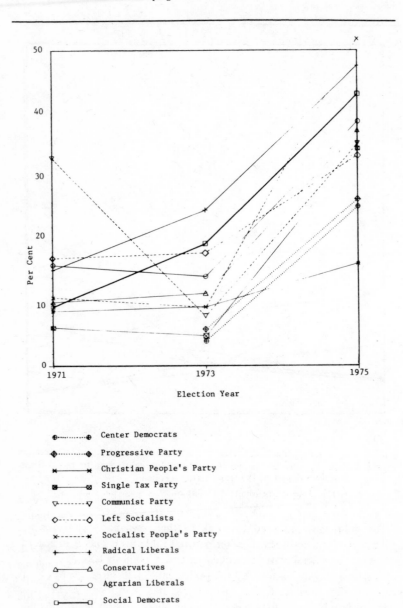

Figure 8.4   Party Preferences toward the Labor Market Issue in the 1971, 1973, and
          1975 Elections

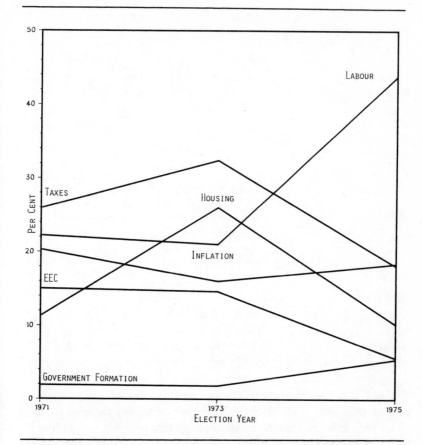

Figure 8.5   Issue Frequencies on the Party Presentation Programs in the 1975 Elections

of this finding be reformulated as 1.3.*ii*. A political party will try to convince the electorate that the party is already working on the problems.

Compared with the politicians, the journalists in 1971 and 1973 were relatively more oriented toward the future, as indicated in hypothesis 9.4. In 1975, the journalists were primarily concerned about the ongoing activities, the proposed solutions. How would the different plans handle the problems of the society? (This involves the future as well as the present.)

Attitudes between the parties expressed in the broadcast campaign show that hypotheses 1.2., regarding confidence in one's own party, and 1.4., regarding negative references to other parties, are verified (Table 8.2).

TABLE 8.1   References Expressed by Politicians (percentages)

References to:	1971	1973	1975
Own party work	76.5	60.0	61.5
Work of other parties	23.5	40.0	38.5
Total	100.0	100.0	100.0
No. of references to work	540	719	1338

TABLE 8.2   Positive and Negative References Directed Toward
Different Political Parties (percentages)

	1971		1973		1975	
	Pos.	*Neg.*	*Pos.*	*Neg.*	*Pos.*	*Neg.*
Own party	70.4	0.1	77.3	1.2	75.6	0.9
Other parties	29.6	99.9	22.7	98.8	24.4	99.1
Total	100.0	100.0	100.0	100.0	100.0	100.0
Number of attitudes expressed	81	193	203	325	168	217

The fact that the amount of negative references exceeds the amount of positive references is due to the competition among the parties, a competition built into the system—a multiparty system with free competition—and at the same time a result of the closeness to election. The largest number of negative references was at every election allocated to the governing party or parties.

All political parties at every election referred more to some groups in the population than to others; but not all had equally strong reference profiles. Hypothesis 2 about each party having its own reference group cannot be said to be verified in the three elections, perhaps due to the mass character of the media (hypothesis 4). Hypothesis 3 about the competition among the parties about reference groups comes closer to the picture found in the data. It was seldom the case that a party was left alone with a reference group of its own. As stated in hypothesis 5, workers and wage earners were very often referred to. But contrary to the Swedish results, relatively few references were given to employers and businessmen. In 1975 the unemployed were referred to frequently due to the labor market situation, which also made the labor market the top issue.

The two new parties had as their special reference groups homeowners (for the Center Democrats in 1973 as well as in 1975), who constitute more than half of the Danish population, and public servants (negative for the Progress Party in 1975 as well as in 1973).

Negative reference groups are rare, and when they consist of approximately one-fifth of the population, it sounds like a risky strategy. But when the group is presented as very expensive for the rest of the population (with relatively high wages, and thus causing high taxes), then it can be a good strategy—at least it was for the Progress Party.

Due to this strategy followed by the Progress Party, hypotheses 6 and 7 cannot be verified on these Danish elections. The amount of negative references was considerable and higher for this nonsocialist party than it was for any of the socialist parties.

So far the window function of the broadcast campaign has not been explicitly in focus, while the platform function has been the central point. Insofar as the journalists are aware of and interested in questioning the parties about their activities or plans with respect to such issues, the structure of the programs—in most cases not made by the political parties, although centered on them—gives the possibility for information about such issues, which are not salient for the parties but eventually salient for the population. However, the realization of this possibility depends heavily on the activities of the journalists.

The journalists did follow most of the proposed hypotheses, though not all were verified. Generally, journalists worked in accord with accepted news criteria.

Were the main issues dictated directly by political leaders, or did they stem from media professionals (Blumler and Gurevitch, 1975)?[5] The main issues in the Danish elections do not seem to be dictated by the political leaders, if we define political leaders as politicians representing the government party or the largest party. The issues are brought to the political agenda by politicians, as for instance the tax issue was brought into the 1973 campaign by the new Progress Party. However, it was *made* the main overall issue by the journalists. So it happened in 1971 as well, and it is expected to be a general situation in accordance with the above-mentioned hypothesis about journalists concentrating on the conflict-loaded issues on the political agenda.

Journalists had no special reference group, which is in accordance with hypothesis 11. But, contrary to another hypothesis 10, they made few evaluative comments on the different political parties. That they had almost no explicit evaluating references to the political parties, as well as no special reference group, must be considered in agreement with the ideas of journalists working in a public monopoly. A journalist in the 1975 election broadcasts stated it this way: "It is not for me to have an opinion."

Compared with this, the activities according to news criteria are debatable. News criteria have two faces—one which is sensationally oriented and one which is receiver-oriented. The term "receiver-orientation" is defined to mean it is an orientation in the direction of the mass and the mass identification with the issues. The sensation-oriented part of the journalistic work can be dangerous for the working democracy, while the mass orientation can be considered positively related to ideas about giving information to the participating electorate,[6] and in this way to the idea of serving a window function.

The analysis of the activities of journalists participating in broadcast election campaigns needs further elaboration, and it is hoped that this will be done in the future. The activities of political journalists and the impact of their activities is already an ongoing issue with the Danish elections, but it needs comparative research as well.

SUMMARY

A model for factors influencing the content of political communication has been introduced. Within the framework of the model a number of hypotheses have been presented.

The majority of the hypotheses have been tested on Danish election campaigns in the seventies. In spite of this special background in Danish politics, the model has wide applications. Neither in principle nor in reality is it bound to Danish, nor to Scandinavian, political systems.

The components in the model are general—too general, some will argue. But the hypotheses and the operationalizations used for testing the model demonstrate how the general model can be applied in a research context using data from quantitative content analysis to measure the nominal dependent variable.

The model as well as the hypotheses call for comparative research. One special opportunity for testing the relevance of the model cross-nationally is a European project comparing the nine European countries which are members of the European Commonmarket. All nine countries participated in a comparative project concerning the first direct election in 1979 to the European Parliament. This project offers opportunity to compare campaigns in different political systems occurring in different political as well as economic situations. Though it seems a perfect research setting, the ideal setting is more than one election. In future there will be more direct elections to the European Parliament and more data to test the proposed model.

The value of the proposed model is that it clarifies the need to look separately for effects from system characteristics and situational characteristics on mass-media-transmitted political content.

The hypotheses generally work within the interplay between system and situation. They are primarily based on general conditions and ideologies, including goals penetrating the political system and the communication system. Therefore, they are relatively stable over time. Modifications in the hypotheses can be found, determined by specific situational characteristics.

The predictive value of the model is that, given knowledge of the political and economic situation within a given political and economic system, it is possible to a certain degree to predict what will be the content of a coming election campaign.

NOTES

1. Ostgaard (1968) and Galtung and Ruge (1968) have written about news criteria. See also Rosengren (1974).
2. Fibiger in this volume refers to a wider category of programs, in that he includes regional broadcast as well as the third channel on radio.
3. There are differences between Denmark and Sweden with respect to access for political parties insofar as Sweden does not give totally equal time to all political parties participating in an election, only to those represented in parliament.
4. The unit of analysis is uninterrupted communication from one person from start to stop.
5. Blumler and Gurevitch (1975: 183) raise this question.
6. Milbrath (1965) has written about the needs of the participating electorate.

REFERENCES

BAKKE, M. and SIUNE, K. (1974). Radio and TV News in Denmark and Norway. Aarhus: Institute of Political Science.
BECKER, L. B., McCOMBS, M. C., and McLEOD, M. (1975). "The development of political cognitions." In S. H. Chaffee (ed.), Political Communication: Issues and Strategies for Research. Beverly Hills, CA: Sage.
BLUMLER, J. G. and GUREVITCH, M. (1975). "Towards a comparative framework for political communication research." In S. H. Chaffee (ed.), Political Communication: Issues and Strategies for Research. Beverly Hills, CA: Sage.
BLUMLER, J. G. and KATZ, E. [eds.] (1974). The Uses of Mass Communications. Beverly Hills, CA: Sage.
BLUMLER, J. G. and McQUAIL, D. (1968). Television and Politics, Its Uses and Influence. London: Faber and Faber.
CHAFFEE, S. H. (1975). "The diffusion of political information." In Political Communication: Issues and Strategies for Research. Beverly Hills, CA: Sage.
GALTUNG, J. and RUGE, M. H. (1968). "The structure of foreign news." Journal of Peace Research 5.

HØYER, S., HADENIUS, S. and WEIBULL, L. (1975). The Politics and Economics of the Press: A Developmental Perspective. London: Sage.
KATZ, E. (1972). "Platforms and windows. Broadcasting's role in election campaigns." In D. McQuail (ed.), Sociology of Mass Communication. London: Penguin.
KRAUS, S. (1962). The Great Debates–Background, Perspective, Effects. Bloomington: Indiana University Press.
––– and DAVIS, D. (1976). The Effects of Mass Communication on Political Behavior. University Park: Pennsylvania State University Press.
––– LANG, E. and LANG, K. (1975). "Critical events analysis." In S. H. Chaffee (ed.), Political Communication: Issues and Strategies for Research. Beverly Hills, CA: Sage.
KRONVALL, K. (1975). Politisk masskommunikation i ett flerpartisystem. Sverige– en fallstudie. Lund: Studentlitteratur.
––– (1972). Partipressen i dag. Lund: Studentlitteratur.
LANG, K. and LANG, G. E. (1968). Politics and Television. Chicago: University of Chicago Press.
MAISEL, L. (1976). Changing Campaign Techniques: Elections and Values in Contemporary Democracies. Beverly Hills, CA: Sage.
MILBRATH, L. W. (1965) Political Participation. How and Why do People Get Involved in Politics? Chicago: Rand McNally.
O'KEEFE, G. J. (1975) "Political campaigns and mass communication research." In S. H. Chaffee (ed.) Political Communication: Issues and Strategies for Research. Beverly Hills, CA: Sage.
OSTGAARD, E. (1965) "Factors influencing the flow of the news." Journal of Peace Research 2(1).
ROSENGREN, K. E. (1974) "International news: Methods, data and theory." Journal of Peace Research 11: 145-156.
ROSENGREN, K. E. (1979) "Bias in news: Methods and concepts." Studies of Broadcasting 15: 31-45.
SEYMOUR-URE, C. (1974) The Political Impact of Mass Media. London: Constable.
SIUNE, K. (1979) "Kan valgprogrammerne klaede de politiske partier af? Kommunikationspolitik, programpolitik og konsekvenserne for politisk kommunikation." In Pressens Årbog. Copenhagen.
––– (1976) "Broadcasted election campaigns in a multiparty system: A comparison between Danish elections in 1971 and 1973." Presented at IPSA, Edinburgh, 1976.
––– (1975) "Structure and content of an election campaign on Danish radio and television." Scandinavian Political Studies 10: 139-155.
––– and BORRE, O. (1975) "Setting the agenda for a Danish election." Journal of Communication 25: 65-73.
SJÖBLOM, G. (1968) Party Strategies in a Multiparty System. Lund: Studentlitteratur.
SMITH, A. (1976) "A maturing telocracy: Observations on the television coverage of the British general elections of 1974." In L. Maisel (ed.), Changing Campaign Techniques: Elections and Values in Contemporary Democracies. Beverly Hills, CA: Sage.
THOMSEN, N. (1965) Partipressen. En undersøgelse of danske dagblades politiske bindinger. Aarhus: Institut for Presseforskning og Samtidshistorie.
VALLINDER (1974) Political Parties and Newspapers in Sweden 1900-1970. Lund. (mimeo)
WESTERSTÅHL, J. (1972) Objektiv Nyhetsförmedling. Stockholm: Akademi Förlaget.

Chapter 9

INTERNATIONAL INFORMATION IN
DAILY NEWSPAPERS

Lowe Hedman

THE MASS MEDIA have often been criticized for choosing single events
with a supposedly high news value at the expense of background articles
and other articles which give explanations and analyses of events in more
structural terms, especially where international issues are concerned. The
result of this tendency has been that the public does not get the information about, understanding of, and interest in international issues which
would otherwise be the case. As early as 1930 Woodward said about the
American Press:

> A public uninformed and uninterested led by a few interested but
> uninformed appears the inevitable results where the press neglects
> foreign news for sports, comic, and the highly colored "human
> interest" novelties that are to-day so common a feature of the news
> columns.

Hedman (1978) shows that there is a positive correlation between the
degree of exposure to national morning papers and knowledge about,
interest in, and activities concerning developing countries and favorable
attitudes toward development aid. On the other hand, people who often
read morning newspapers do not have a more structural view than others
of the reasons for poverty in the developing countries or of how the
problems are to be solved. People give the same reasons for poverty in the
developing countries irrespective of how often they read a morning paper.
The reason for the absence of correlation may be that the newspapers do

AUTHOR'S NOTE: This study is part of a project called "Information Strategies—
Analysis and Evaluation of Attempts to Spread Information about Developing
countries through Multimedia." This project was financed by the Bank of Sweden
Tercentenary Foundation and is described in Hedman (1978). The author is indebted
to Henryka Schabowska and Karin Wengelin, who rendered invaluable assistance in
the preparation of the study and in its execution.

not emphasize structural reasons any more than other reasons when analyzing the situation in the developing countries. Well-informed people in general seem to look at the problems in different ways from less well-informed people.

There is a positive correlation between exposure to national morning papers and different indices of Third World orientation. However, there are no such correlations with exposure to the mass media in general. For instance, there is no positive correlation between exposure to television programs and knowledge about, interest in, attitude to, and activities concerning developing countries.

Himmelstrand (1970: 15) is of the opinion that to create a permanent active interest in the developing countries the mass media must *"communicate structures"* and not just report single events or episodes in these countries. Lindholm (1970: 221) points out that the symbols communicated by the mass media have not been clear and unambiguous enough and the symbol patterns not meaningful enough to integrate spot news.

This chapter discusses ways of measuring to what extent the press provides information which might increase readers' understanding of what goes on in the world and which might give them a structural picture of the relationship between different groups in society and between different nations. This kind of information is usually referred to as "background" or "explanations." Some variables to measure this are suggested.

FOUR CATEGORIES OF ARTICLES

There have always been criteria to differentiate between different types of articles in the daily press. A rough categorization can be made between "news" and "features." Vilanilam (1972), who is interested only in the international contents of the American and Indian presses, uses this categorization without defining the latter concept. By "news" he means "that part which 'signalizes an event.' " In a similar way Annersten and Martin (1975: 11) distinguish between "news"—that is, "pure news reports in the form of telegrams or statements and interviews"—and "commentaries"—"analyses in the form of comments, debates or features which may, of course, also contain interviews. There is room for a personal opinion." This distinction corresponds most closely to the one made in Britain between "news" and "current affairs." Since this distinction is usually limited to certain parts of the mass media, it is of less interest here.

The distinction sometimes made in Anglo-Saxon literature between "interpretative news" and "spot news" seems more relevant for our purpose. DeMott (1973: 102) defines "interpretative news" as "reporting that *explains* the *meaning* of the news." This definition is too general to be used operationally. In practice, it has been easier to define "spot news";

the articles which one has not been able to classify as "spot news" one may define as "interpretative news."

Himmelstrand (1970: 15) gives a definition which is most relevant for this study. He defines *"spot information"* as information which reports an episode or a single event of a dramatic, engaging nature without putting the episode or event into any perspective, and *"information which gives background and perspective"* as information which describes chains of events or structures where episodes or single events are clarifying examples.

In all these cases it is difficult to operationalize the concepts. A number of different criteria have been used, often with no system. Certain characteristics, such as contents giving background information, a certain length, or many statements, have been seen as signs of an article having an explanatory approach. The most commonly used criteria in this connection are described below.

Length. It has been considered that the longer an article is, the more likely it is to contain background information. At first sight this seems reasonable; however, in practice generally this is not true. There are many examples in which the length of the article bears no relation to its richness of information. If one studies a newspaper as a whole, one may find an interesting correlation; but if one studies each type of article separately— news, features, and so on—one is not likely to find the same high correlation.

Statements. Many statements—that is, statements from many different sources—have also been seen as signs of richness of background information. However, even if the statements come from a large number of people, they may reflect the same thing in the same way. Hence, the number of statements is not a good criterion in this connection. Also, a statement need give no explanation of an event or information to increase the understanding of the event. Looking at the number of statements and considering their contents increases the possibility of judging the richness of information. If the articles contain statements about the effects of a certain event and statements about expectations, this can affect the reader's opinion about the importance of the event considerably.

Explanations. The best criterion of richness of information is the extent to which an event is shown to be related to other events, because this can directly increase the understanding of the event.

Backgrounds. In some cases it is difficult for newspapers to give explicit explanations of events. Instead, they give general background information which can help the reader to understand the event.

DeMott (1973: 108) shows that "interpretative news" articles are longer, contain more stated opinions, and give more background information than other articles.[1] They are also more closely related to "soft news" than other articles. Of these variables, we have chosen not to consider the length of the article. It is especially interesting to know whether the information contains background, chains of explanations, or statements about effects and expectations. The first two factors should explain why different events occur; the latter two should give an understanding of future events and development processes. One can talk about two types of information—explanatory and predictive.

General background information ⎫
                              ⎬ Articles giving explanations
Chains of explanations   ⎭

Statements about effects   ⎫
                              ⎬ Articles giving predictions
Statements about expectations ⎭

To the extent an article contains explanatory and predictive information the following typology can be made:

Articles		giving explanations Yes	No
giving predictions	Yes	COMMENTS	PREDICTIONS
	No	EXPLANATIONS	REPORTS

Comments is used to mean articles which both explain a certain event by referring to earlier events or processes in the minds of individuals or groups or which contain general information which may affect the readers' understanding of the information. In addition, they contain statements about future effects of the explained event or about different expectations.

Predictions contain information about effects and expectations of the future, but do not contain background information and explanations. This type of article is probably relatively rare.

Explanations contain one or several chains of explanations and/or general background information.

Reports are merely reports of facts and do not give explanations, background, or statements about effects and explanations. This type of article is often referred to as "spot news" or "spot information."

A difficult question is, of course, where to draw the lines between the different groups; that is, which values on the variables are to be considered "high" and which are to be considered "low." This can be decided for each study using the empirical figures as a basis. However, this limits the possibilities of making comparisons between different studies, and a choice based on explicit logical reasoning is therefore to be preferred.

We have assumed that up to three background descriptions and three chains of explanations can be found in one article. It is probable that even the "simplest" report contains some form of causal reasoning. Therefore, the mere existence of a chain of explanations or just one kind of background description is not sufficient for the article to be classified as giving explanations. It must contain both kinds of information to be so classified.

In a similar way we have assumed that up to three statements about effects and five about expectations can be found in the same article. One statement about the future is not sufficient ground on which to classify the article as one giving predictions. At least two statements about effects or expectations are needed for this.

SOME DEFINITIONS

When we refer to *general background information* we mean information which in one way or another will help the reader to understand the event or the problem in question. Background information is often written at the newspaper office to explain a telegram from a news agency. When a catastrophe occurs, for example, the office can add background descriptions—the geological situation, the economic situation of the individuals involved, food supplies, and so on—to the description of the event. Background information is found both in separate articles and together with descriptions of single events, countries, or persons.

There are different kinds of background descriptions. We have chosen to distinguish between the following:

- social perspective,
- economic perspective,
- political perspective,
- cultural perspective,
- historical perspective,
- personal perspective,

- national perspective, and
- international perspective.

Social perspective refers to explanations in terms of social relations between individuals, groups, organizations, states, and so on. *Economic perspective* refers to explanations in economic terms, such as economic inequality between different groups in society. *Political perspective* refers to explanations based on, for example, discrepancies regarding the possibilities of different individuals or groups participating in or affecting the political decision-making process. *Cultural perspective* is coded when reference has been made to old cultural patterns, "handed-down" values and opinions, as explanations of events or of certain developments. *Historical perspective* is coded when information has been presented about events which took place a relatively long time ago but which are thought to influence the present situation. An event can also be described at different levels—individual, national, or international. By *personal perspective* we mean descriptions in terms of individuals; for example, if reference is made to changes in attitude or resources of individuals. If the situation within a nation is described, we have coded *national perspective,* and if the relations between different countries have been described, we have coded *international perspective.*

Chains of explanations can be given in two different ways. First, the event can be said to be related to certain events which occurred earlier. For example, "Event C occurred because event B had occurred, which, in turn, occurred because event A had occurred, etc." This we have called a *chain of events.* Every event before C we have called a link. Second, an event can be said to be related to thoughts, hopes, knowledge, attitudes, and the like—that is, some form of process in the minds of individuals. "The Egyptian President's journey can be seen as an attempt to break the increasing political isolation." If the links are "processes in the mind," the chain has been called *chain of mind.*

In some logical chains of explanations some links are events and some are processes of mind. In some cases the links are clearly stated (it says that C occurred because of B). This we have called an *explicit chain.* In other cases one can find the links from an interpretation of the article. A chain which needs interpretation we have called an *implicit chain.*

When explaining a certain event some doubt is sometimes expressed ("it is probable that they have acted in this way because of . . ." or "one likely reason for this is . . ."). In these cases the chain has been called a *speculative chain.* When no doubt has been expressed a *nonspeculative chain* has been coded.

We have coded different types of *statements about effects*—effects in the form of a new event or a change of mind. The effect can be explicit or implicit, speculative or nonspeculative; and the sources can be different.

We have also coded the terms in which the effects of an event have been described—social, economic, political, and cultural (for a definition of these terms, see above)—and "unspecified" when the terms are not clear.

Who is said to be *affected* by the event in the article? Does the event affect

- individuals?
- groups of people, such as political or ethnic minorities, or different classes in society?
- a nation/organization (that is, does the event affect the development of the nation/organization)?
- other nations/organization (that is, other nations or organizations than those where the event occurs)?

Statements about expectations or the future are sometimes difficult to find if they do not appear with words like "expect," "will," and the like. They may be implicit in phrases such as ". . . for fear of further bombings" (explicitly: further bombings are expected). The expectations may be by the source or by persons cited in the article. If the source has expressed opinions about the future, we have coded "own," and if someone else has, we have coded "cited."

Negative, positive, and unspecified expectations refer to the person's (own or cited) opinion about the future—that is, in what terms he or she expressed the expectations. An expression like "the Government saw this as a first step towards peace" has been coded "cited, positive expectation." Every party expressing expectations about the future has been coded separately and only once.

As seen from above, the description of the variables and their categories shows that classifying the information is often left to the judgment of the person responsible for the coding. One of the classical problems in content analysis is determining what is to be analyzed—the manifest or the latent content, or both? To what extent, if any, is the coder to be allowed to "read between the lines"? When operationalizing the above-mentioned variables, it has been difficult to find operational definitions which leave nothing to the coder's own judgment, especially when coding the amount of background information in an article.

How has this affected reliability? We studied the difference in judgment between two independent coders and also the same coder (who has done all the coding) on two different occasions. In the latter case the reliability was surprisingly high, whereas the former was somewhat lower. The intrareliability was 0.93 for "background information," 0.89 for "chains of explanations," 0.93 for "effects," and 0.93 for "expectations." The interreliability was 0.85, 0.83, 0.76, and 0.70 for the same variables, respectively. The reason the interreliability was relatively low for "expectations" was probably that statements about the future are often indirect and difficult to discover. Some coders may also find it easier than others to find some kinds of statements. The intrareliability may be, but need not be, an effect of this.

For chains of explanations and chains of effects, the coder's judgment is more important the less explicit and the more speculative the wording is. This may, of course, affect the frequency of observed phenomena. This could explain why the most common chain of explanation is one which refers to nonspeculative events explicitly expressed by the source. The same is true of the chains of effects.

FINDINGS

In a study of the international coverage in Swedish daily newspapers we have paid special attention to the question to what extent the readers are given the above-mentioned types of information. The study was made in 1974 of a random sample of newspapers, and all the issues from a two-week period were analyzed. Here we present the results from three of the newspapers: one large, one middle-sized, and one small paper. They also differ in other ways.

Dagens Nyheter (DN), the largest morning paper in Sweden, had a distribution of 444,000 in 1974 when the study was made. *DN* used to call itself a "liberal" paper, but now presents itself as an "unpolitical" or a "politically independent" newspaper. It has for a long time had a liberal accent, and is close to the Liberal Party in Parliament. The newspaper is published in Stockholm, and is most common in the middle of Sweden. This is the only one of the three papers studied which may be said to have a national distribution.

Kvällsposten (KvP) had a distribution of 117,000 in 1974 and is an "independent liberal" paper. *KvP* is published in Malmö; its main distribution area is in the southern part of Sweden.

Västernorrlands Allehanda (VA), with a distribution of 19,000 in 1974, calls itself a Conservative newspaper. It is published in Härnösand, and its distribution is limited to two northern regions.

Most articles which dealt with international affairs[2] did not contain any general background information (see Table 9.1). We have limited the analysis to articles which described an event. Of the articles we classified as international, 86 percent described an event.[3] As seen from the table, only 12 percent of the event-oriented articles in *VA* contained background information. The percentage was larger for the two larger newspapers (25 percent for *KvP* and 35 percent for *DN*). The table also shows that it was most common to give only one type of background description. Also commonly given was political information—that is, information based on,

TABLE 9.1 Percentages of Articles Containing Various
Amounts of General Background Information

		DN		KvP		VA		Total	
Background information {	1 type	24		18		10		21	
	2 types	9		6		2		7	
	3 types	2	35	1	25	0	12	2	30
No background information			65		75		88		70
Total			100		100		100		100
n =			(611)		(249)		(115)		(975)

TABLE 9.2 Percentages of Different Types of Chains of Explanations in
the Articles Containing One "Simple" Chain

			EXPLICIT		IMPLICIT	
		Source	Non-speculative	Speculative	Non-speculative	Speculative
DN	Event	A.Own	62	12	1	1
		B.Cited	12	6	1	1
		C. A+B	0	0	0	0
	Mind	A.Own	1	0	0	0
		B.Cited	4	1	0	0
		C. A+B	0	0	0	0
KvP	Event	A.Own	54	10	0	4
		B.Cited	10	7	0	2
		C. A+B	0	1	1	0
	Mind	A.Own	4	1	0	0
		B.Cited	3	4	0	0
		C. A+B	0	0	0	0
VA	Event	A.Own	84	3	0	0
		B.Cited	14	0	0	0
		C. A+B	0	0	0	0
	Mind	A.Own	0	0	0	0
		B.Cited	0	0	0	0
		C. A+B	0	0	0	0

for example, discrepancies with regard to the possibilities of different
individuals or groups participating in or affecting the political decision-
making process. This was true of all three papers. For the two largest
papers, *DN* and *KvP*, the second most common terms to use for background information were economic; for example, references to inequality
between different groups in society. We found no cases of information of
that kind in *VA* during the two-week period we studied.

TABLE 9.3   Percentages of Articles Giving Chains of Explanations and General Background Information in the Three Newspapers

Chains of Explanations								
	DN		*KvP*		*VA*		*Total*	
Back-ground Information	*Yes*	*No*	*Yes*	*No*	*Yes*	*No*	*Yes*	*No*
Yes	50	18	46	10	19	9	47	15
No	50	82	54	90	81	91	54	86
Total	100	100	100	100	100	100	101	101
n =	(329)	(282)	(105)	(144)	(37)	(78)	(471)	(504)

On average, 47 percent of the articles contained some form of chain of explanations[4] —that is, *one* earlier event or process of mind was given as a reason for the event in question. Fifty-four percent of *DN*'s, 42 percent of *KvP*'s, and 32 percent of *VA*'s articles which dealt with events contained chains of events. Most of these chains had only one link. Chains with more than one link were very rare.

DN and *KvP* used more types of explanations than *VA*. All in all, *KvP* used 12 and *DN* 11 of the 24 possible variations of explanations, while *VA* used only 3 (see Table 9.2). The most common type of explanation was a nonspeculative event expressed explicitly by the source. Eighty-four percent of *VA*'s, 62 percent of *DN*'s, and 54 percent of *KvP*'s articles which contained single chains of explanations were of this type. Although this kind of explanation is undoubtedly the easiest to identify, the number of articles in this category was too large for this to be important. Also the reliability of the coder was high (see above).

One hundred percent of the explanations in *VA*, 94 percent of those in *DN*, and 88 percent of those in *KvP* were explanations in terms of events. The rest were explanations in terms of "processes of mind"—that is, the event was referred to thoughts, hopes, changes in level of information, attitudes, and so on of individuals or groups of individuals.

Hence, we conclude that it was more common for event-oriented articles to contain explanations than general background information. The question is, then, was the latter found in the same articles as the former? It was not, but there was a strong correlation (see Table 9.3). In *DN* 50 percent of the articles with chains of explanations also contained general

TABLE 9.4   Percentages of Articles Containing Statements about
Future Effects of the Event in Question

		DN		KvP		VA		Total	
Number	1	40		31		22		36	
of	2	1		1		4		1	
effects	3	0	41	0	32	1	27	0	37
No effects mentioned			58		68		74		63
Total			99		100		101		100
n =			(611)		(249)		(115)		(975)

TABLE 9.5   Percentages of Articles Containing
Statements about the Future

		DN		KvP		VA		Total	
Number	1	19		15		4		16	
of	2	1		0		0		1	
expectations	3	0	20	0	15	0	4	0	17
No expectations mentioned			79		85		96		83
Total			99		100		100		100
n =			(611)		(249)		(115)		(975)

background information. The percentage decreased for the smaller newspapers. We can therefore conclude that the percentage of articles which
contained chains of explanations or general background information was
larger than we originally expected. As much as 62 percent of the event-
oriented articles in *DN* contained at least one of these ingredients. The
corresponding figures for *KvP* and *VA* were 48 percent and 38 percent,
respectively. Also, the percentage of articles which contained both chains
of explanations *and* general background information was high—at least in
the largest newspaper: 27 percent of the articles in *DN* contained both
these types of information. The corresponding figures for *KvP* and *VA*
were 19 percent and 6 percent, respectively.

Table 9.4 shows that 41 percent of the articles dealing with international affairs in *DN* gave predictions of effects—usually one effect—of
the event in question. The corresponding figures for *KvP* and *VA* were 32

TABLE 9.6   Percentages of Statements about Effects and
Expectations in the Three Newspapers

	Effects DN		KvP		VA		Total	
Expectations	*Yes*	*No*	*Yes*	*No*	*Yes*	*No*	*Yes*	*No*
Yes	33	12	30	8	13	1	30	10
No	68	88	70	92	87	99	70	91
Total	101	100	100	100	100	100	100	101
n =	(255)	(356)	(80)	(169)	(30)	(85)	(365)	(610)

percent and 27 percent, respectively. For all three newspapers it was most common for the source to make the statement, and this was usually a nonspeculative, explicit statement about an event.

Of the articles in *DN*, 20 percent contained statements about the future. The corresponding figure for *KvP* was 15 percent and for *VA* only 4 percent (see Table 9.5). For both *DN* and *KvP* it was most common for the statements about effects to be made by the source; these were neither positive nor negative. The next most common statements were not the same for the two newspapers: For *KvP* they were "negative statements by the source (= the newspaper)," "positive statements by the source," "negative statements by cited party," in that order. For *DN* the order was "positive statements by the source," "positive statements by cited party," and "negative statements by the source."

Tables 9.3 and 9.6 show that it was less common for articles which contained statements about effects to also contain statements about expectations than for articles which contained chains of explanations to also contain general background information. As before, the largest paper, *DN*, gave the most information. Of the articles which contained statements about effects, 33 percent also contained statements about expectations. The corresponding figures for *KvP* and *VA* were 30 percent and 13 percent, respectively. In all, 49 percent of *DN*'s articles, 37 percent of *KvP*'s, and 27 percent of *VA*'s contained *either* statements about effects *or* statements about expectations. A relatively small part of the articles contained *both* statements about effects *and* statements about expectations (14 percent in *DN*, 10 percent in *KvP*, and 4 percent in *VA*).

If we return to the original typology, Table 9.7 shows how the international articles in the paper analyzed fell into these different categories.

TABLE 9.7 Percentages of Event-Oriented International Articles in Different Categories

	ARTICLES		giving explanations Yes	No	Total
DN		Yes	COMMENTS 7	PREDICTIONS 7	14
	giving predictions	No	EXPLANATIONS 20	REPORTS 66	86
	Total		27	73	100 (n = 611)
	ARTICLES		giving explanations Yes	No	Total
KvP		Yes	COMMENTS 4	PREDICTIONS 6	10
	giving predictions	No	EXPLANATIONS 16	REPORTS 75	91
	Total		20	81	101 (n = 249)
	ARTICLES		giving explanations Yes	No	Total
		Yes	COMMENTS 1	PREDICTIONS 3	4
	giving predictions	No	EXPLANATIONS 5	REPORTS 91	96
VA	Total		6	94	100 (n = 115)

As expected, the distribution was uneven. In all three newspapers the reports constituted the largest percentage of articles. Articles giving comments constituted a small percentage of the total number of articles—in VA less than one percent, which was one article. The results in Table 9.7 are, of course, completely dependent on the definitions made above of the concepts "articles giving explanations" and "articles giving predictions." Other definitions would have given other results.[5]

Throughout, the differences between the newspapers were great. In all respects *DN* gave more information than the two smaller newspapers. This

TABLE 9.8   Degree of Richness of Information (percentage)

Degree of richness of information	DN	KvP	VA	Total
0	29	47	53	36
1	21	13	24	19
2	26	23	18	25
3	17	13	4	15
4	7	4	1	5
Total	100	100	100	100
n =	(611)	(249)	(115)	(975)

is perhaps most obvious from Table 9.8. The table shows the percentage of articles of different degrees of richness of information—from value "0," which means that the article did not contain any chain of information, general background, statements about effects, or expectations, to value "4," meaning that the article contained all these kinds of information.

DISCUSSION OF THE FINDINGS

The empirical results shown above on the whole confirm our hypotheses. A large percentage of the newspaper articles about other countries are event-oriented and give no general background information to enable the reader to put the information into perspective. The articles often lack even the simplest form of explanation of why some events occur. Many articles also lack statements about the future. This also limits the reader's possibilities to follow the course of events. These things mainly affect people who read only a local or regional newspaper and not so much those who read several newspapers with a larger distribution. To those who receive all their information about other countries from a limited number of local newspapers, the world must seem chaotic. Schabowska and Himmelstrand (1978) compare the situation with the phenomenon called the "autokinetic effect." It has been observed that people in a completely dark room perceive small movements of a point of light which is, in fact, completely immobile. This is due to the absence of any contextual stimuli that would enable the subjects to relate the shining point to some other points of information and also to the constant eye movements characteristic of humans.

> The average reader finds himself in a somewhat similar situation when he confronts a point of information regarding some dramatic event in a distant and foreign continent. In the absence of any contextual information, he can easily be led to believe that the spot of information on some critical event which he has received signifies a major change of a political or social nature in one or the other direction. The information received may indeed signify such a change, but the direction of that change can easily be misapprehended through processes of social communication and influence in the absence of relevant contextual information [Schabowska and Himmelstrand, 1978: 17].

From the presentation of the findings we saw that the differences between the newspapers were great. One of the reasons the richness of information varied was, of course, that the size of the circulation varied. The newspapers having large circulations have enough financial resources to employ permanent correspondents abroad, to send temporary correspondents when something special is happening, and to generally report on what is happening in the world and on the situations in other countries.

Two additional reasons for the different results among the three newspapers may be that they publish different kinds of information and information in different forms. These factors are also related to the financial situation of each newspaper. Most of the international articles in *DN* and *VA* dealt with the national politics of some other country—22 percent and 15 percent of all the articles, respectively. Of the international articles in *KvP*, 15 percent also dealt with national politics, but it was even more common for *KvP*'s international articles to deal with sports (28 percent).

About half the international articles in *DN* were political (25 percent in *KvP* and 38 percent in *VA*), while 58 percent of *KvP*'s and 46 percent of *VA*'s international articles were about accidents, sports, and other general information usually classified as "human interest." The latter type of article does not need background information or explanations to the same extent and is therefore cheaper for the newspaper.

As much as 90 percent of the international articles in *VA* were general news reports—that is, descriptions of events, often in the form of a telegram from a transnational news agency. If we look only at the extended foreign information or the pure foreign information, the percentages of general news reports were even higher (93 percent and 96 percent, respectively). A small newspaper like *VA* is, consequently, to a great extent dependent on news agencies for international news. In the two larger newspapers general news reports were a smaller percentage of the international information: in *DN* on average 67 percent and in *KvP* 51 percent. Both newspapers gave more international information in other forms, such as features which gave more information than general news reports.

The two larger newspapers may appear to be similar if one looks at the figures above; however, looking at the absolute number of articles and the length of the articles reveals obvious differences between them. *DN* gives its readers much more international information and also more explanations and predictions than *VA*. Above, we also saw that the differences between the kinds of information transmitted by these two papers were great.

It has generally been thought that the aspects of news coverage mentioned above have improved during the last decade. We have no results to confirm this, but it seems a reasonable assumption. Some newspapers have increased their circulation and thus also their financial resources; this, together with the fact that the representatives of the mass media have raised their level of information about international affairs, could explain an improvement in the international news coverage. Bailey (1976) says, for instance, that the fact that American newsmen have accumulated the necessary knowledge about the war in Vietnam is the reason why the percentage of background descriptions and explanations in the news reports on television gradually increased during the five-year period he studied.

NOTES

1. The "interpretative" articles were selected by the daily newspapers themselves. They were instructed to select "the four most outstanding examples of interpretative reporting done by newsmen on its staff during the previous 12 months." The articles with which to compare these were selected by the researchers, who chose the article taking up the largest space on the front page of each edition from which the "interpretative" articles were selected.

2. We used four categories to describe the editorial matter in the newspapers:

—pure foreign articles with no reference to Sweden or Swedish matters (these articles constituted 19 percent of the total number of articles);

—foreign articles with some references to Sweden or Swedish matters (4 percent);

—Swedish articles in which other countries or people were mentioned (6 percent); and

—pure Swedish articles.

One could refer to these categories as pure foreign information, extended foreign information, extended Swedish information, and pure Swedish information (see Olsen, 1969). We have combined the first three categories and call them international articles (29 percent of the total number of articles). This is probably not the most common way of identifying the international information in the mass media. It is probably more common to use definitions based on thematic content or story datelines (see, for example, Furhoff and Nilsson, 1968). In this respect the results from our study cannot be compared with the results of other studies. In practice, our definition is close to the one used by Larson (1979).

3. 'At an earlier stage of the analysis the articles were divided into those mainly describing (a) events, (b) countries/organizations, and (c) persons.

4. The event for which we tried to find chains of explanations and statements of effects was the one we thought was the subject of the article.

5. The results look quite different if by articles giving information we mean articles which contain one general background description or one or more chains of explanations, and if by articles giving predictions we mean articles which contain one statement about effects or expectations. Then we get the following result:

	DN	KvP	VA
Comments	40	32	18
Predictions	9	6	9
Explanations	22	16	20
Reports	29	47	53
	100	101	100
n =	(611)	(249)	(115)

If we use these definitions, the biggest category in *DN* is composed of the articles which give comments. In the other two newspapers reports still constitute the largest category.

REFERENCES

ANNERSTEN, B. and MARTIN, A. (1975). "En jämförande studie av etermedias utbud av nyheter och nyhetskommentarer i Sverige och Storbritannien, våren 1974." (mimeo)

BAILEY, G. (1976). "Interpretative reporting of the Vietnam war by anchormen." Journalism Quarterly 53, 2: 319-324.

DeMOTT, J. (1973). " 'Interpretative' news stories compared with 'spot' news." Journalism Quarterly 50, 1: 102-108.

FURHOFF, L. and NILSSON, L. (1968). "Utländskt nyhetsmaterial i svenska och utländska prestigetidningar." Statsvetenskaplig tidskrift 1968: 83-108.

HEDMAN, L. (1978). Svenskarna och u-hjälpen. En studie av den svenska allmänheten, lokala opinionsbildare och journalister. Studia Sociologica Upsaliensia 14. Almqvist & Wiksell International.

——— (forthcoming). "Mass media, opinion-makers and public opinion on development issues." Communication, 5.

HIMMELSTRAND, U. (1970). "Kommunicera strukturer." Klaraborgaren 15/1970: 15-17.

LARSON, J. F. (1979). "International affairs coverage of U.S. network television." Journal of Communication 29, 2: 136-147.

LINDHOLM, S. (1970). U-landsbilden. Stockholm: Almqvist & Wiksell.

OLSEN, O. J. (1969). "Den internationale nyhedsformidling: En undersøgelse af udenrigsmeddelerser i nogle europeiske og nordamerikanske aviser." Copenhagen: Institute for Peace and Conflict Research. (mimeo)

SCHABOWSKA, H. and HIMMELSTRAND, U. (1978). Africa Reports on the Nigerian Crisis. News, Attitudes and Background Information. Uppsala: Scandinavian Institute of African Studies/Almqvist & Wiksell International.

VILANILAM, J. V. (1972). "Foreign news in two U.S. newspapers and Indian newspapers during selected periods." Gazette 28, 2: 96-108.

WOODWARD, J. L. (1930). Foreign News in American Morning Newspapers. Colombia.

Chapter 10

NEWSPAPER OPINION AND
PUBLIC OPINION
The Middle East Issue

Gunnel Rikardsson

FOR A LONG TIME the questions if and how the mass media influence public opinion have been much debated. The optimism which gained ground during the first half of the century, especially, perhaps, after the discovery of the two-step flow of communication (Lazarsfeld et al., 1948), was gradually replaced in the 1950s by a more pessimistic view concerning the possibilities of ascertaining the effects of the mass media. By degrees, the more differentiated viewpoints that we hold today developed: in some circumstances the effects of mass media are considerable while in other circumstances they are much smaller. Still, however, a great many questions remain to be answered before we know how and when the mass media actually influence the recipients and the surrounding society.

The purpose of this chapter is to compare on a macro level the development of two aspects of public opinion: the press opinion as expressed in editorials and the public opinion as expressed in polls. (Hereafter the latter will be called public opinion.) The subject matter of public opinion concerns an issue which has been in the foreground for some thirty years: the relationship between the Arab states and Israel.

Some questions come to mind in this connection; for example:

- Are there any discernible trends in the public opinion and the opinion expressed by the newspapers? If so, how similar or dissimilar are the two trends?
- Which opinion—press opinion or public opinion—is the most extreme toward the two parties involved? Does it shift over the years?
- Which opinion leads the development? If we presume that it is the newspaper opinion, there arises the question:
- How long ahead of the public opinion is the press opinion?

These questions cannot be analyzed in detail here, as in general we do not possess comparable data on both the press opinion and the public opinion within the same country. We do possess, however, a fairly large number of polls undertaken in eight countries.[1] Therefore, we will try to survey some common features in the development of a "world opinion" as mirrored in these polls and relate them to a content analysis of leading Swedish newspapers. The questions we want to answer, then, are these:

- Are there any conspicuous differences or similarities between attitudes in the Swedish newspapers as regard the Middle East conflict and a general "world opinion"?
- If so, what do these differences or similarities tell us about the relationship between press opinion and public opinion?

THE MATERIAL

In Sweden public opinion polls concerning attitudes toward the parties of the Middle East conflict have been carried out on two occasions, in 1969 and 1973, both by Törnqvist (1970, 1974). The results pertaining to the seven other countries have been compiled from various sources.[2] The eight countries from which I found public opinion measurements are the following: Sweden, Denmark, Norway, West Germany, the Netherlands, Great Britain, France, and the United States. The results are shown in Appendix 1. In the following, the mean value of these measurements will be called the "general world opinion."

The material upon which the assessment of the opinion in Swedish newspapers is based was originally presented in Rikardsson (1978). It comprises editorials in the *Dagens Nyheter* (*DN*), the *Svenska Dagbladet* (*SvD*), and the *Arbetet* (*Arb*)—three newspapers whose total circulation accounts for 60 percent (1977) of all Swedish morning papers. Most Swedish newspapers have a more or less clear political profile. *DN* is liberal, *SvD* conservative, while *Arb* is Social Democrat. The sample used consists of every second editorial out of the 1247 editorials in the three newspapers which dealt with the Middle East during the years 1948-1973. The editorials have been analyzed by means of several different methods—both traditional and ad hoc—in order to trace attitudes toward and evaluations of the parties in the Middle East conflict.

As examples of traditional methods we may mention an overall assessment of evaluations in the editorials and an analysis of explicit—manifestly expressed—evaluations. Among the ad hoc methods a "background event analysis" is among those which agree best with the two traditional methods. In short, the latter method provides an opportunity to reveal concealed evaluations in seemingly objective reports of events by means of studying trends in types of background events used as compared with trends in types of contemporary events reported upon (Rikardsson, 1978: 35ff).

In this study we will use some data relating to explicit evaluations. Appendix 2 shows the number of explicit positive and negative evaluations in the sample of editorials from the three newspapers under study.

A note of warning in this connection: In order to compare the two types of opinion—Swedish press opinion and world opinion—it is necessary to view them as homogeneous units. In this process the variations and differences between the papers (and between the countries) will be smoothed out in a way which is not always desirable. Statements claiming, for example, that the Swedish press has "for a quarter of a century been positive towards Israel" or "at times mainly pro-Arab" may be true of the newspapers regarded as a whole but not individually. More differentiated results will not be dealt with in this study, but Appendices 1 and 2 offer some possibilities to the interested reader. For a full account, including more differentiated analyses, the reader is referred to Rikardsson (1978).

RESULTS

How has the Swedish press opinion developed over the years compared with the "world opinion"? Figures 10.1 and 10.2 show a compilation of results relating to the two trends concerning Israel and the Arab states, respectively. The press opinion comprises the number of explicit evaluations in the three newspapers in total (see Appendix 2). To obtain comparable values for the general "world opinion" we have summed the percentage shares of sympathizers relating to all countries and divided this by the number of countries in which an opinion poll has been found for the year in question (see Appendix 1).

Regarding press opinion, data indicate a clearly positive attitude toward Israel from at least 1956, with marked peaks during the three war years (1956, 1967, 1973) and gradual decreases in the interwar periods. The attitude toward the Arab side shows a clearly upward trend during the last few years.

The "world opinion" results for those years when opinion polls have been found show a similar development: a strongly increasing number of Israeli sympathizers from 1956 with peaks during war years, and an increased number of Arab sympathizers during the last few years. In 1955-1956, however, there are some public opinion poll results from Germany which disturb the picture. It is hardly surprising if, for historical

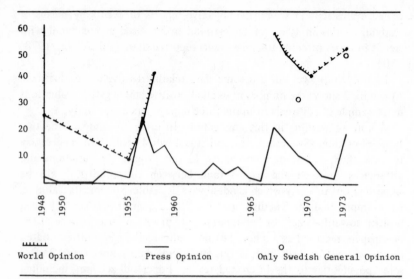

Figure 10.1   Pro-Israel Sympathies in the General "World Opinion" 1948-1973

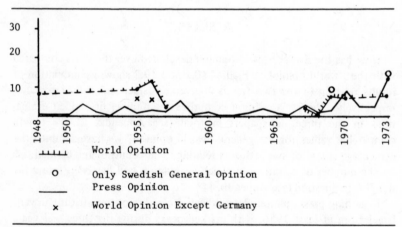

Figure 10.2   Pro-Arab Sympathies in the General "World Opinion" and in the
Swedish Press Opinion 1948-1973

reasons, the Federal Republic should have a different climate of opinion
with respect to the parties of the Middle East conflict.[3] An omission of
the figures relating to the German public opinion makes the "world
opinion" result tally more with the press opinion—especially with respect
to the Arabs. It has been indicated by "x" in Figure 10.2 how this would
affect the "world opinion" with respect to the Arab states.

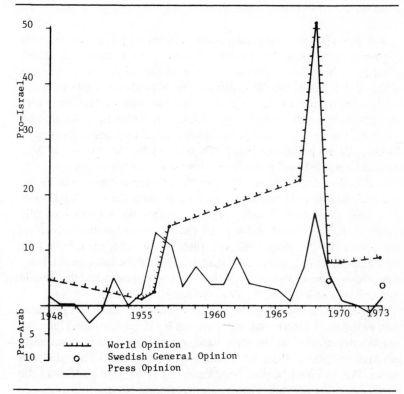

Figure 10.3   Comparison Between General "World Opinion" and Press Opinion Concerning Sympathies for Israel and the Arab States

The most marked difference between the two opinions which can be traced in Figures 10.1 and 10.2 above is the comparatively high level of sympathies for Israel in the "world opinion" from 1967 onward as compared with the years prior to 1957. The sympathy level of the Swedish newspapers is much lower during these years. This difference may have started as early as 1957.

The Swedish public opinion has been indicated by circles. If we compare it with the "world opinion," we can see that the Swedish attitude is somewhat more positive toward the Arab states and less positive toward Israel. If a comparison is made between the press opinion and the public opinion in Sweden, we note that the increased Arab sympathies of the newspapers correspond well to the Swedish public opinion. This is also the case with the attitudes toward Israel. The Swedish public opinion shows a very strong increase to Israel's advantage in 1973 as compared with 1969, which is also the case with the newspapers, although the public opinion seems to be considerably more positive than the opinion of the news-papers.

In Figure 10.3 an overall comparison between public opinion and press opinion is undertaken. The number of positive evaluations in newspaper editorials of Israel has been related to the number of positive evaluations of the Arab side, dividing the largest number of positive evaluations by the smaller one, so that a value larger than one was obtained. (In case of zero evaluations, the value of one was inserted in order to make division possible.) The corresponding public opinion values have been produced by dividing the proportion of Israeli sympathizers by the number of Arab sympathizers (the Israeli proportion being always the largest one).

It is evident from Figure 10.3 that the two trends have taken similar courses.[4] Before 1957 the two trends are at much the same level, while after 1967 the general "world opinion" stands forth with an essentially greater share of sympathies for Israel than is found within the Swedish newspapers. In the years 1967 and 1968 the Swedish newspapers have been assessed as very pro-Israel (Gahrton, 1967; Rikardsson 1978). How-ever, we see from Figure 10.3 that in comparison with the "world opinion" they find themselves on a considerably lower level.

Between 1970 and 1973 the "world opinion" is much less pro-Israel than in the years before that, but there still is a clearly pro-Israel line. The Swedish newspapers, on the other hand, sometimes take a predominantly pro-Arab attitude in these years—albeit only in relation to the pro-Israel shares. For, as could be seen from Figure 10.1, the total position of the three newspapers together is clearly positive toward Israel.

There is another matter to complicate the picture which will only be dealt with briefly; namely, the fact that negative attitudes toward the parties are not studied here. This is due to the fact that most opinion polls do not provide such data. This is a pity, since, at least with the news-papers, this would differentiate and would undoubtedly give a "truer" picture. For example, during most years the papers show predominantly positive attitudes toward Israel and negative attitudes toward the Arabs. This way of presenting attitudes toward the parties has been applied in Rikardsson (1978) and can also be seen in Appendix 2.

In reply to the question concerning which opinion changes first and leads the development, one might be tempted to state that it is the press opinion in the years 1954-1957. However, due to the uncertainty with respect to the German opinion polls it would not be safe to draw that conclusion. For if we look at the "world opinion" without including the German values, the results no longer indicate that newspapers are at the head of the change.

How, then, do the Swedish newspapers stand in relation to Swedish public opinion? According to Figure 10.3, both opinions take up positions fairly close to one another on both occasions. The differences between them do not appear from Figure 10.3, but they mean that although the public opinion is both more pro-Israel and more pro-Arab than the newspapers, the difference between the opinions is considerably greater as concerns Israel: The public opinion on both occasions is much more positive toward Israel than are the newspapers (see Figure 10.1).

Figure 10.3 also indicates that the total Swedish opinion—both press and public opinion—on both occasions in 1969 and 1973 was less pro-Israel and more pro-Arab than the "world opinion."

CONCLUSIONS

The comparison made between the attitudes of Swedish newspapers and the general "world opinion" toward the parties in the Middle East conflict suggests that very similar developments have occurred in the two types of opinion.

Nothing has been found to substantiate any time lag in the attitude change in the public opinion as compared with the change in newspaper opinion. Changes seem to have taken place in the same year or else it would seem that, contrary to our presumptions, the newspapers follow up a change that has already taken place in the public opinion.

Newspapers are continuously collecting and publishing results from public opinion polls made in various countries. It is highly probable that in that process they are influenced, in part directly by the changes in the opinion reported upon and in part indirectly by other papers changing their opinion as a result of some opinion poll.

It seems warranted to conclude, then, based on this study, that newspaper opinion under certain circumstances may be affected by public opinion as reflected in the polls. Under what circumstances, in which issues, and when does this happen? These questions will be left open to future study.

APPENDIX 1. Public Opinion Polls

Sympathies (%)	1948	1955	1956	1957	1967	1968	1969	1970	1973
USA:									
Israel	35				44		49		48
Arabs	16				3		5		6
Both/Neither/									
No opinion	49				50		46		46
Great Britain:									
Israel		13	31		57		43		36
Arabs		7	5		3		6		8
Both/Neither/									
no opinion		80	64		41		52		57
France:									
Israel		11	40	43	61		35		
Arabs		3	4	3	3		7		
Both/Neither/									
No opinion		86	56	54	34		58		
Norway:									
Israel	26				74		76		
Arabs	2				5		7		
Both/Neither/									
No opinion	72				21		17		

222

APPENDIX 1. (continued)

Sympathies (%)	1948	1955	1956	1957	1967	1968	1969	1970	1973
Denmark:									
Israel	19				56			43	61
Arabas	2				2			6	3
Both/Neither/									
No opinion	79				42			51	36
West Germany:									
Israel		4	5						57
Arabs		14	24						8
Both/Neither/		35	54						
No opinion		47	17						35
Holland:									
Israel					66	52			73
Arabs					0	0			5
Both/Neither/									
No opinion					35	48			23
Sweden:									
Israel							33		49
Arabs							7		14
Both/Neither/									
No opinion							60		37

APPENDIX 2 Number of Explicit Evaluations Toward the Parties in *DN*, *SvD*, and *ARB*

		1948	1951	1952	1953	1954	1955	1956	1957	1958	1959	1960	1961	1962	1963	1964	1965	1966	1967	1968	1969	1970	1971	1972	1973	Total
DN: Israel	Pos	1			2	3	2	11	9	14	7	2	2	5	1	7	2	1	13	7	4	3	1	1	11	108
DN: Israel	Neg				2		2	4			2		1		2				5	2	1	3		4	3	32
DN: Arabs	Pos		1	1		1		1	2	2					1	1			2	1	1	6	1	3	4	28
DN: Arabs	Neg	2	9	5	8	7	9	12	36	18	24	1	1	3	26	23	3	8	26	7	4	9	9	13	5	268
DN: Guerillas	Pos																			4	1			4	3	12
DN: Guerillas	Neg																									
DN: Refugees	Pos																					1				1
DN: Refugees	Neg																								1	2
SvD: Israel	Pos	2											2									3			2	11
SvD: Israel	Neg	1					1											1				2			2	15
SvD: Arabs	Pos					1																				3
SvD: Arabs	Neg		4			3	1	5	8	2	1	4			2		1	1	2	3				3	3	49
SvD: Guerillas	Pos	1	2															1	4	1	1	2	6	1	1	6
SvD: Guerillas	Neg																									
SvD: Refugees	Pos																				3			1		
SvD: Refugees	Neg																									
Arb: Israel	Pos	3			3			15	3	1		2	2	3	3				8	9	7	3	2	1	6	68
Arb: Israel	Neg																1				3				17	24
Arb: Arabs	Pos					1	1	1		3		1			2	1	1		2		1	2	2		9	25
Arb: Arabs	Neg					1	1	11	4	3	2	4				1	1		6	4	3	5	2		9	58
Arb: Guerillas	Pos																								4	4
Arb: Guerillas	Neg																									
Arb: Refugees	Pos																									
Arb: Refugees	Neg																									

*For 1949 no explicit evaluations are registered.
For 1950 one explicit positive evaluation toward the Arabs is registered in *Arb*.

NOTES

1. Most public opinion polls have been found from the USA (Gallup Opinion Index, 1974).

2. In order to produce comparable figures on as many points as possible, different sources have been used. For Norway in 1969 the figures are the author's own construction, based on the answers to the question concerning "who carries the main responsibility for the unrest between Israel and the Arab countries." In cases when more than one survey relates to the same year, the mean value of these has been calculated. The figures relating to Great Britain in 1973 are based on January 1974, but as the figures of most other countries are based on measurements in November-December 1973, the 1974 figures of Great Britain have also been transferred to 1973.

The following sources have been used: From Erskine, POQ 33/1969-70, No. 4, pp. 627-640, the following information has been taken: USA 1947, 1948, 1967, 1969. Great Britain 1955, 1956, 1967, 1969. France 1955, 1956, 1967, 1969. Norway 1955. Denmark 1955. West Germany 1955, 1956. The Netherlands 1967, 1968. The rest of the information relating to Denmark, 1967, 1969, 1970, 1973 has been taken from, in the corresponding order: *Ugens Gallup, Gallup Markedsanalyse AS, Scan Gallup AS,* Hellerup 1967 Artikel 27, 1969 Artikel 11, 1970 Artikel 22, and from the *Observa,* Vedbaek/ the *Jyllandsposten,* Nov 1, 1973. The information concerning Norway is taken from: *Norsk Gallup Institutt A/S,* Oslo, Aug. 19, 1967 (on the year 1967) and May 1969 (on the year 1969). The figures relating to France 1957 are taken from Lapierre 1968, p. 219. The rest of the information is from Törnqvist 1974. All figures refer to the national total except for those for United States in 1969, which refer to the informed opinion.

3. There is such a great difference between the figures relating to public opinion in Germany and those relating to the other countries that it nearly suggests reverted figures as regards the parties in the years 1955-1956. If this were the case—that is, if the values given for the Arabs in these years were instead to relate to Israel, and *vice versa*—the results would correspond entirely with the general trend for both parties. On the other hand, it is, of course, possible that the West German public opinion trend deviates from that of other countries. The information concerning Germany has been provided by the USIA (United States Information Agency). The author has written several letters to different quarters in order to verify this information, but no answers have as yet been received.

4. If the correlation between the two opinion trends is calculated by means of Spearman rank correlation, the result is a significant correlation (r_s = .70. N = 9; p < 2.5%), on the condition that the West German values are omitted. If the latter are included, we get no statistically significant correlation.

REFERENCES

ERSKINE, H. (1969). "The polls: Western partisanship in the Middle East." Public Opinion Quarterly 33: 627-640.
GAHRTON, P. (1967). "Palestinakonflikten och Pressen." Liberal Debatt 5: 2-9.

LAPIERRE, L. (1968). L'information sur l'état d'Israel dans les grand qotidiens francais en 1958. Paris: Editions du Centre National de la Recherche Scientifique.

LAZARSFELD, P., BERELSON, B., and GAUDET, H. (1948). The People's Choice. New York: Free Press.

"Public sides with Israel" (1974). Gallup Opinion Index 103: 11-15.

RIKARDSSON, G. (1978). The Middle East Conflict in the Swedish Press. A Content Analysis of Three Daily Newspapers 1948-73. Lund: Scandinavian University Books.

TÖRNQVIST, K. (1974). "Svenskarna och Konflikten i Mellersta Östern." Psykologiskt Försvar 64.

——— (1970). "Attityder till Några Internationella Problem och Massmedier." Psykologiskt Försvar 47.

Chapter 11

MASS MEDIA CONTENT, POLITICAL OPINIONS, AND SOCIAL CHANGE
Sweden, 1967-1974

**Gösta Carlsson, Alf Dahlberg, and
Karl Erik Rosengren**

THE ROLE OF THE MASS MEDIA in connection with social change—a classic problem in the sociology of communication—has recently received increased attention among sociologists (for example, Katz and Szecskö, forthcoming). This chapter presents data on the interplay among changes in economic conditions, media content, and political opinion in Sweden during the years 1967-1974. The first section gives a theoretical background. The second section presents the data and methods used and relates them to the theoretical background. In the third section the main results are presented. The fourth and last section of the study offers a discussion of the results and some suggestions for future research in the area.

THEORETICAL BACKGROUND

For a long time mass communication research has been preoccupied with either the effects or the determinants and the more precise nature of individual mass media consumption (Liebert and Schwartzberg, 1977; Blumler and Katz, 1974). In both cases the perspective has been individualistic and the approach mainly cross-sectional. Use of the mass media has been related to hypothesized causes or consequences of that use, in or for the individuals under study. Perhaps the most important result of this type of research can be summarized as suggesting that the media act mainly as mediators and reinforcers of tendencies in society and within individuals.

Parallel to these broad research traditions, more or less sporadic attempts have been made to relate various aspects of media content, conceived as a macro phenomenon, directly with other macro phenomena, such as (changes in) crime rates, occupational trends, fertility, and so on (for instance, see Inglis, 1938; Davis, 1952; Middleton, 1960; Shaw, 1967; Funkhouser, 1973; Towers, 1977; Beniger, 1978). The variation necessary to establish a relationship has been obtained by means of time series data, rather than cross-sectional data. (The third possibility, regional or cross-national comparative research, seems to have been much less used; see, however, Brandner and Sistrunk, 1966). That is, instead of an individualistic perspective and a cross-sectional approach, research of this type has worked with a macro perspective and a longitudinal approach. We feel that more research of this type is needed if the problem of mass media and social change is to be better understood. (Innovative combinations of attitudinal data on a micro level with macro measurements of media content have been made by George Gerbner and Elisabeth Noelle-Neumann; see Gerbner et al., 1979, and Noelle-Neumann, 1977.)

A traditional formulation of the "mass media and social change" problem is the catchword "Molders or Mirrors?" (Brandner and Sistrunk, 1966), which suggests an either-or-approach: either media molds the social structure or the social structure determines the content of the media, so that media mirror society. Peterson (1976), treating the related but broader problem of culture and social structure, points to three rather than two possibilities: culture determines social structure (idealism); social structure determines culture (materialism); and culture and social structure are independent (autonomy). Rosengren (1978) presented four alternatives, ordered in a fourfold typology, which is applicable also to the relationship mass media content-social structure (Figure 11.1).

The typology of Figure 11.1, as can be seen, is highly abstract. It may call to mind various Marxian approaches, based upon the relationship between "base" and "superstructure." Within the Marxian tradition(s) few empirical investigations have actually been carried out in this area (see Williams, 1973). When it comes to empirical work, Figure 11.1 must be specified, conceptually and with respect to the time perspective.

The time perspective is very important in this connection. Social change may take place within days, weeks, months, years, decades, or centuries. The time scale, then, may vary with a factor of up to, for example, 100,000. It would be strange indeed if the relations between culture and social structure would be the same under those very different circumstances. It may well be that a relationship found to operate on a given time scale is not at all valid on another time scale, and vice versa (see Smith,

		Social structure influences culture	
		Yes	No
Culture influences social structure	Yes	Interdependence	Idealism
	No	Materialism	Autonomy

Figure 11.1   Four Types of Relationships Between Culture and Social Structure
SOURCE: Rosengren (1978).

1971). And in some cases of interdependence, the causal influence in one direction may be operating on a time scale completely different from the influence in the opposite direction. For instance, changes in social structure may affect almost immediately opinions in the population—or at least opinions among certain strata in the population—while opinion changes may affect social structure—at least some aspects of social structure—only with considerable delay.

On the whole, grand theory on social change has tended to use a long time perspective, while empirical research has tended to use a short time perspective, sometimes very short indeed. The specific models demanded by the various time perspectives are all subsumable, in principle at least, under Figure 11.1. However, they may have to be rather differently structured—a difficulty which has not always been given sufficient attention.

The time perspective has other theoretical consequences as well. In a short time perspective it will seem questionable to think about relationships between base and superstructure as relationships between social structure and culture. As the time perspective narrows down to years or less, concepts like "changes in social structure" tend to be replaced by cyclical or random changes in the parameters of a social structure remaining basically the same. "Cultural change" tends to be replaced by more or less short-term fluctuations in beliefs and opinions.

METHODS AND DATA SOURCES

Our time perspective encompasses eight years. We focus on political opinions (as expressed by the population and in the press), influenced by economic changes of cyclical or quasi-cyclical character. Our main concern, then, is factors behind changes in political opinion, a problem which calls for a combination of intra- and extramedia data (Rosengren, 1979).

A natural starting point when studying the interplay among political opinion, mass media, and social structure is the political polls. In Sweden, political polls have been regularly undertaken since 1967. They are carried out by the leading Swedish polling institute, the SIFO, and sponsored by three leading newspapers. For each of the eight years under study, 1967-1974, they offer about 10 polls with a representative sample (random, weighted for missing data) of the Swedish electorate (approximately 1000 respondents).

During this period, Sweden had a one-party, social-democratic government. The opposition consisted of three bourgeois parties and one (small) communist party. The SIFO samples are asked to state their party preferences at the time of the interview; we will concentrate on the proportion favoring the government party (the Social Democrats), measured as a percentage of those expressing an opinion. The values are presented as straight averages of the polls falling within each quarter of the year. (The number of polls within each quarter varies somewhat because of the uneven time schedule of the SIFO.) These values represent our dependent variable: governmental support in the population. We have two groups of independent or intervening variables: social structure and media content.

Social structure could be measured in an infinite number of ways. We are interested mainly in economic variables which may be supposed to affect political opinion, and our final choice is managements' estimates of their need for labor in the immediate future. This need is tapped in regular surveys published quarterly as an integral part of the official system of economic analyses and forecasts. The larger the proportion who say they have a need for more people, the more favorable economic conditions are supposed to be. We will use the percentage of all firms questioned expressing a need for more unskilled labor. There is also another series not used here, on need for skilled labor. The two run parallel, and nothing seems to be gained by using both. Still other indicators could have been used, of course, but they present certain technical problems, such as breaks in the series.

It will be realized that our operational translation of "social structure" means locating the concept in the economic sphere. Furthermore, it has been stretched to cover cyclical or quasi-cyclical aspects of the economic machinery of the Swedish society rather than more or less basic changes of that machinery (see above).

Media content was measured by means of quantitative content analysis of "first-page news" and "first editorials" in a random sample of the

Swedish daily press, drawn for the purpose and weighted for circulation (ranging between some 1000 and some 600,000) and periodicity (from one to seven issues a week). The sample consists of some 1200 first-page news stories and 1200 first editorials drawn from about 1200 issues of the roughly 150 Swedish newspapers of the period—that is, about 40 news stories and 40 editorials for each of the 32 quarters studied. The newspapers were represented in the sample in proportion to their circulation (as semiofficially measured by the auditing company jointly owned by the organizations of the publishers and advertizers), and then randomly distributed over the calendar. Newspaper issues which did not appear on a day assigned to them were not included in the sample, a procedure which equals weighting for periodicity. Because of this procedure, not all Swedish newspapers are necessarily represented in the sample.

The coding was done by a graduate student of sociology specializing in content analysis. The newspaper issues sampled were coded in random order. Repeated tests of the reliability of the coding procedure were undertaken. The overall average intercoder reliability was 0.77.

The coding sheet was the same for editorials and first-page news. The leading ("first") editorial and the leading (biggest headline and similar signs of prominence) first-page news story in the sample issues were coded along some 30 variables, out of which half a dozen were elected for inspection. Our final choices were proportion of editorials with comments negative to the (Social-Democratic) government, and proportion of editorials expressing negative evaluations of the subject editorialized. (The intercoder reliability of the former variable was 0.95; of the latter, 0.70.) Substantively, the former variable is rather self-evident in this connection; the latter is less straightforward. Editorial evaluations of this type, of course, are not always partisan or political by nature. However, the point is that a high incidence of negative evaluations in the editorials of the daily press points to a general mood of pessimism, to a general feeling that conditions are getting worse, perhaps even running out of control.

These, then, are our four main variables: the state of the economy, governmental criticism in the press, general pessimism in the press, and governmental support in the population. The relationships hypothesized among the four variables are outlined in Figure 11.2. It will be seen that the relationships have been conceptualized as reciprocal. The reciprocity is subject to the restrictions imposed by the time scale used (see Section I above). Causal relationships symbolized by broken arrows are regarded as "slower" than those symbolized by full arrows.

The quarterly values of the four variables are given in Table 11.1. They will be analyzed in the next section of the paper.

TABLE 11.1   Main Variables: Quarterly Data

		% of firms needing more labor	% in favor of Soc. Dem. in polls	% of editorials critical of government	% of editorials pessimistic
1967	1	5	41.5	26	50
	2	6	42.5	18	39
	3	11	42.0	26	50
	4	9	42.3	26	56
1968	1	6	42.8	26	28
	2	9	44.5	22	32
	3	16	48.0	24	56
	4	16	51.2	18	56
1969	1	30	51.5	13	46
	2	39	51.5	17	39
	3	45	52.8	16	32
	4	43	52.3	16	42
1970	1	41	50.7	21	58
	2	42	50.0	30	64
	3	38	46.5	36	56
	4	22	44.0	19	49
1971	1	13	44.0	38	67
	2	12	43.0	17	67
	3	8	43.0	27	61
	4	5	42.5	37	58
1972	1	5	40.2	43	60
	2	11	39.0	26	51
	3	9	42.0	29	44
	4	9	41.7	32	37
1973	1	9	41.8	36	51
	2	14	40.5	22	47
	3	18	43.0	30	67
	4	16	41.5	27	49
1974	1	25	42.0	41	53
	2	28	43.5	17	43
	3	30	44.2	20	59
	4	21	44.8	15	42

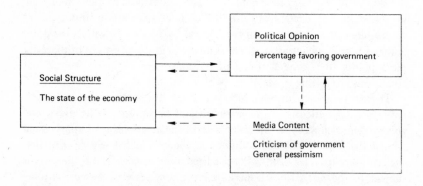

Figure 11.2   Hypothesized Relationships Between Variables under Study

RESULTS

The distribution of party sympathies according to opinion polls will here be regarded as response to events either directly felt by the public or transmitted through the media. We concentrate on the percentage favoring the Social Democratic government (see above). Figure 11.3 gives the time course of political opinion thus defined.

It is immediately striking that support for the Social Democrats oscillates in a smooth pattern, the celebrated "tides" of political life, or at least one manifestation of them. This is not an artifact due to the formation of quarterly averages, for the original series looks much the same. A convenient measure of the smoothness is the serial (auto-) correlations obtaining within the series. That is, pairs of observations are formed by taking the first and the second, the second and the third, and so forth for the serial correlation with lag 1. Similarly, the first and the third, the second and the fourth, the third and the fifth, and so on give the serial correlation for lag 2. With higher lags we proceed in an analogous manner. For 32 quarterly values the serial correlations with lags 1, 2, and 3 are 0.92, 0.79, and 0.62, respectively. A quasi-cyclical pattern, as shown by the opinion data in Figure 11.3, at the same time contains clues to the underlying forces and could obscure the true state of affairs. The series does not yield much information through direct inspection. It contains one marked peak, around 1969-1970, and a rise toward the end. This is more variability, and in that sense more information, than is contained in a series which is all trend, rising or declining. However, what we have is a far cry from 32 independent observations; rather, we have one or two swings.

There are principally two explanations of aggregate response of this type (Carlsson, 1965):

(1) Stimulus conditions likewise move smoothly with more or less identical oscillations.
(2) Response occurs with a nonnegligible degree of inertia to change in stimulus conditions.

With slow response—case 2 above—even a highly erratic, unordered series of stimulus changes could result in smooth response variations. The average length of the "cycles" will depend more on the speed of response than on the presence of any similar cycles in stimulus conditions. In that sense the response series might be quite misleading if we jump to a conclusion about underlying causes.

Let us begin, however, by looking at an explanation coming under case 1. Apart from the series of opinion data, Figure 11.3 also shows the ups

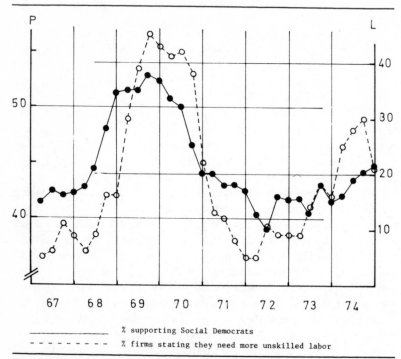

Figure 11.3 Party Preferences and Business Cycles 1967-1974

and downs of business conditions according to the indicator chosen, management's estimation of the need for unskilled labor in the immediate future (see above). One gets a strong impression of a close relationship between political opinion and business conditions. A period with ample job opportunities, according to the index, is also one of strong support for the governing party, the Social Democrats. Slump years, as 1971-1972, were also lean years for that party. In fact, the correlation between the two series for the 32 quarterly pairs of values 1967-1974 is + 0.79. One aspect of this is that opinion and election results (for the two generally agree closely) in the fall are predictable to some extent on the basis of business conditions in the late spring and early summer. Of course, a better predictor of later opinion is an earlier measurement of the same opinion, as witnessed by the high level of serial correlation within the series of poll data.

Seemingly, we are in the rare predicament of having succeeded all too well; not much remains to be explained about the tides of political sentiment. And it is not difficult to understand the relationship: the public holds the government (and the party it represents) responsible for bad times and gives it credit for prosperity. However, on second thought, the issue becomes a little less clear-cut.

As both response (governmental support in the population) and the alleged stimulus (economic conditions) are equally marked by a strong quasi-cyclical pattern of variation, there is much less evidence than first appears on which conclusions can be based. This fact has already been noted and need not be elaborated. Two wavelike phenomena presumably could be approximately in phase for a short period of time without any deeper significance.

Also, one would rather expect the economic series to be the leading one and the political series to lag. Of this there is little sign if the two curves are inspected; nor do correlations with lags introduced give much guidance. With the economic series leading by one-quarter, the correlation becomes + 0.68; with political data leading and the economic lagging, it is + 0.83, actually higher than before and suggesting a different kind of relationship between the two. Not much importance should be attached to these minor differences in correlation, based on rather few observations, but the possibility of alternative explanations needs to be kept in mind.

There is supporting evidence from other sources for the causal bond between economic conditions and political climate. Apart from the strong presumption from common sense and everyday experience, a study of British politics (Butler and Stokes, 1969: 417) presents a similar picture of high correlation between Labour's lead over the Conservatives and unemployment data (the Conservatives were in power at the time). In the present case it may be that we are one step removed from the economic forces affecting the voters, in that the indicator used is somewhat psychological and indirect in nature. The figures refer to an expressed need for more labor, not to a precise and direct measurement of actual employment or unemployment. Such judgments could be influenced by a general mood of optimism or pessimism. In fact, voter's reactions and employer's evaluations could be parallel responses to the stream of events (partly mediated by the mass media). This would explain a high correlation without assuming a clear-cut, unidirectional causal nexus. It is not necessary for the two responses to occur with identical lags or degrees of inertia; correlations could well be high even with moderately different speed characteristics.

To sum up, the argument for an economic explanation of shifts in party preferences is strong—strong enough to make it a rather meaningless exercise to test the hypothesis that the true correlation is zero. However, there is a difference between something being one or even one of several major determinants and that something being the only determinant. On the technical side, it should be noted that the correlation obtained from the sample (+ 0.79) could easily arise as a fluctuation in a universe with a true correlation around + 0.40 or + 0.50. A simple simulation experiment

(which will not be described in detail here) shows that sample values of
+ 0.70 and + 0.80—as well as values close to zero—are quite common with
a true value of + 0.40, if there is a marked serial correlation in the data.

In any case, there is still the question of how much of the economic
realities are perceived immediately, as part and parcel of everyday experience, and how much is transmitted through media. It is here that evidence
on media content is needed.

In Section II the manner of sampling media was set forth and the
coding system outlined. Here only a few of many potential indicators of
media content will be used. The first, and seemingly the most relevant, is
the incidence of comment negative to the (Social Democratic) Government in editorials. It is an obvious choice in the context of party sympathies. The difficulties inherent in this type of analysis soon will become
equally obvious. The outcome, however, is not devoid of interest.

Figure 11.4 shows the incidence of negative comment in the shape of
two series, one on a quarterly and the other on a semiannual basis. Both
represent the fraction of all editorials within the period coded as negative.
The quarterly curve, as might be expected, is too much influenced by
sampling errors to give a clear visual impression. As a rule, the total
number of editorials on which the percentage of critical editorials has been
computed is a little less than 40. The semiannual series is somewhat less
marked by this weakness. As can be seen by comparing Figures 11.3 and
11.4, there is indeed a negative correlation between critical comment and
support for the Social Democrats according to the polls. In terms of
correlations the results are as follows:

Quarterly series: $r = -0.50$ (n=32);
Semiannual series: $r = -0.75$ (n=16).

Another variable tested in the analysis is the explicit evaluation of the
person, institution, or event presented in the text—here again, editorials
(see Section II). This indicator, however, proved less closely related to
partisan attitudes or economic conditions as here measured. There is a
correlation with criticism of the government, though not a strong one.
(The coding reliability of this variable, it should be remembered, was fairly
low.) All correlations are shown in Table 11.2.

If one bears in mind the small number of observations—for half-year
data only 16—and the high level of serial correlation in the data, it is clear
that any elaborate schemes of multivariate analysis of the data of Table
11.2 are out of the question. The outcome would be much too dependent
on chance fluctuations. The most that can reasonably be tried is a couple
of partial correlations.

The partial correlation between opinion data and editorial criticism of
the government, holding constant the business-cycle indicator (demand for
labor), comes out as -0.62, to be compared with the corresponding

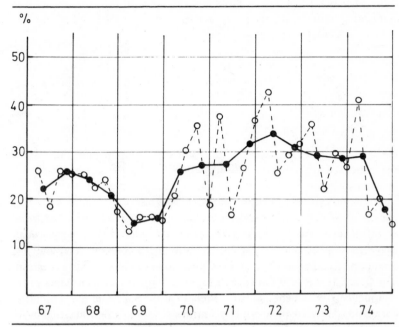

Figure 11.4 Proportion of Editorials with Negative Comment on Government: Quarterly and Semiannual Data

TABLE 11.2 Intercorrelations of the Four Main Variables

	L	P	G	E
L	–	+ .81	– .55	– .07
P		–	– .75	– .15
G			–	+ .40
E				–

L Demand for labor

P Poll data: Support for Social Democrats

G Editorial criticism of government

E Negative evaluations in editorials

zero-order correlation of − 0.75 (see Table 11.2). On the other hand, the partial correlation between business conditions and political opinions, partialing out media criticism of the government, is 0.71, to be compared with a zero-order correlation of 0.81. As far as the evidence goes, the two partial correlations provide at least tentative empirical support for the intuitively appealing notion that political opinions in the population are molded partly by economic realities in their own right (this is probably the dominating influence), partly by media content itself, and partly by economic realities as relayed by the media.

Still other indicators of media content have been considered. Where computations were carried out the results were inconclusive. In some of these series, there is hardly enough variability over time to give promise of an outcome worth the trouble. This, of course, raises the question of in what manner the press conveys, or fails to convey, real changes in the sociopolitical situation, a point which will be discussed in a moment.

DISCUSSION

The results so far presented can be called suggestive rather than definitive in their implications. There is the expected relationship between objective economic conditions and partisan attitudes. It *may* be somewhat exaggerated in strength by sampling errors in the present case, and the tides of politics may thus be more open to other influences than appears in our data. There is also the expected correlation between newspaper criticism of the government and party strength in the polls, and also a negative correlation between prosperity and criticism of the government (though somewhat weaker). None of this is sensational, but at the very least it supports the idea that newspaper content can be sampled and meaningfully measured, with the possibility of applications less restricted by common-sense assumptions.

If one reflects on the background of the data, the outcome becomes rather less predictable. It should be kept in mind that with editorial content there is seldom a question of newspapers changing from a generally critical to a generally friendly view of the government. With few exceptions, Swedish newspapers have a standing commitment, for or against, and are not likely to deviate far from the set course. Presumably what happens is that they tend to give expression to their basic and relatively fixed attitude and, hence, variations in the balance between critical and noncritical material. Editorial content, then, may convey a mood, changing only gradually and manifested often enough to be both clear to the reading public and accessible afterwards through sampling and content analysis. The data give support to such a view. (It would be quite possible to have a counterstream of positive comment in newspapers supporting the government, as opposition newspapers become more frequently and openly critical. However, there is little sign of this if one looks at the respective time series, though no detailed analysis was undertaken.)

With news items (noneditorial material) the situation is different. We may encounter difficulties with isolated but important events and with short-term fluctuations. It may well be that readers of newspapers are strongly influenced when they read about a big industrial firm closing down and many employees being laid off, or about the energy situation getting out of control. But such messages are relatively few and far between, though they have a marked impact. As too much material cannot be analyzed, *some* kind of sampling must be utilized. And with this arises the possibility of missing the rare but critical event.

Obviously, much depends on how rare such events are relative to the size of the sample and on the sensitivity of the coding system. With 40 items sampled for each quarter, one may perhaps say that content variations through time will be discovered if the true (universe) frequencies vary between 1-2 percent and 10 percent. With half-year periods and around 80 articles sampled for each half-year, one may be successful with even lower frequencies. Clearly, insufficient numbers can be compensated to some extent by changing the period of observation, but only at the price of missing information on the time pattern.

The trouble with ordinary news is the great amount of irrelevant material, chiefly crime and accidents (if by "relevant" we mean likely to influence political opinions in the population). It is reasonable to expect a rather high amount of short-run fluctuations in such material—fluctuations which may or may not result in corresponding fluctuations in the opinions of the population. To complicate matters further, these "real" fluctuations are then combined with sampling fluctuations in both the media material used and the survey sample of the population.

Since there are few realistic possibilities of ever measuring such short-term, almost day-to-day changes in population opinions for a sufficient period of time, this would point to the necessity of moving up one step in the time scale when looking for the importance of news: not monthly, quarterly, or semiannual measurements of media content, but yearly ones. This, in turn, leads to the demand for longer time series: decades or more. Since there are few opinion data available for such long periods of time, one would then have to turn to other indices of opinions in the population: debate material, letters to the editor, aggregated data on discretionary behavior, and the like. Such measurements could be more profitably undertaken if based on specific theoretical considerations.

On the methodological side, then, our attempts to combine data about social structure, population opinions, and media content have resulted in a couple of insights. To be fruitfully used in this context, news material must probably be sampled for relatively long periods of time and along dimensions suggested by a rather specific theory. Editorial material, on the other hand, may be less demanding in this respect.

Substantively, our results suggest that political opinions in the population are molded both by economic conditions and by media content, probably somewhat more by economic conditions than by media content. (The media, of course, also relay information about economic conditions.) The traditional notion of the mass media is that they mainly rely on and reinforce influences from other forces in society. Recent research, however, suggests that the mass media may be more powerful than conventional wisdom among social scientists reflects (Gerbner et al., 1978; Noelle-Neumann, 1977). With all their limitations, our data support the latter standpoint rather than the former.

REFERENCES

BENIGER, J. R. (1978). "Media content as social indicators." Communication Research 5: 437-454.

BLUMLER, J. G. and KATZ, E. [eds.] (1974). The Uses of Mass Communications. Beverly Hills, CA: Sage.

BRANDNER, L. and SISTRUNK, J. (1966). "The newspaper: Molder or mirror of community values?" Journalism Quarterly 43: 497-504.

BUTLER, D. E. and STOKES, D. (1971). Political Change in Britain. Harmondsworth: Penguin.

CARLSSON, G. (1965). "Time and continuity in mass attitude change." Public Opinion Quarterly 29: 1-15.

DAVIS, F. J. (1952). "Crime news in Colorado newspapers." American Journal of Sociology 57: 325-330.

FUNKHOUSER, G. R. (1973). "The issues of the sixties: An exploratory study in the dynamics of public opinion." Public Opinion Quarterly 37: 62-75.

GERBNER, G., GROSS, L., SIGNORIELLI, N., MORGAN, M., and JACKSON-BEECK, M. (1979). "The demonstration of power: Violence Profile No. 10." Journal of Communication, 29: 177-196.

INGLIS, R. A. (1938). "An objective approach to the relationship between fiction and society." American Sociological Review 3: 526-533.

KATZ, E. and SZECSKÖ, T. [eds.] (forthcoming). Mass Media and Social Change. A Symposium. London: Sage.

LIEBERT, R. M. and SCHWARTZBERG, N. S. (1977). "Effects of mass media." Annual Review of Psychology 28: 141-173.

MIDDLETON, R. (1960). "Fertility values in American magazine fiction." Public Opinion Quarterly 24: 139-142.

NOELLE-NEUMANN, E. (1977). "Turbulences in the climate of opinion: Methodological applications of the spiral of silence theory." Public Opinion Quarterly 41: 143-158.

PETERSON, R. A. (1976). "The production of culture." American Behavioral Scientist 19: 669-684.

ROSENGREN, K. E. (1979). "Bias in news: Methods and concepts." Studies in Broadcasting 15.

――― (1978). "Mass media and social change: Some current approaches." Lund: Dept. of Sociology. (mimeo)

SHAW, D. L. (1967). "News bias and the telegraph: A study of historical change." Journalism Quarterly 44: 3-12, 31.

SMITH, R. F. (1971). "U.S. news and Sino-Indian relations: An extra media study. Journalism Quarterly 48: 447-458, 501.

TOWERS, W. M. (1977). Reality, Pseudo-Reality and Fantasy: The Crystallization and Reinforcement of Crime as an Issue 1964-1973. University of Oklahoma. (mimeo)

WILLIAMS, R. (1973). "Base and superstructure in Marxist cultural theory." New Left Review 82: 3-16.

Chapter 12

FREEDOM AND EQUALITY
Indicators of Political Change in Sweden, 1945-1975

Eva Block

THIS CHAPTER deals with one of the central issues in the study of domestic political debate in Sweden: freedom and equality. It analyzes the contents of newspaper editorials. It has been carried out as part of a project entitled "Values and Evaluations in Swedish Domestic Political Debate 1945-1975," which in turn is part of the research program "Cultural Indicators: The Swedish Symbol System 1945-1975" sponsored by the Bank of Sweden Tercentenary Foundation 1976-1980. The main task of this research program is to construct and test instruments for measuring the cultural climate in Sweden and its changes. The program consists of five different projects dealing, respectively, with domestic and foreign political debate, literary debate, secularization, and advertising. All five treat the same period of time and use the press, mainly in the form of daily newspapers, as their source of material. They will all document their results in time-series, each showing developments in some sector of the cultural life (Cultural Indicators, 1976). Each will be printed in separate reports, although an overall report for the whole research program is being prepared in which the results of the five projects will be considered as a whole.

DETERMINING IDEOLOGICAL POSITION IN PUBLIC DEBATE

For at least two hundred years "freedom" and "equality" have been honorable words in political debate. In very simplified form it could be said that these two concepts were presented together within the so-called radical ideology during the French Revolution in 1789; however, during the course of history certain alterations have occurred. Different political groups have adopted these terms, often maintaining them as a pair—as a slogan to represent an important part of the political heritage in the western countries. Nevertheless, they have been emphasized differently in different political camps: liberals have worshipped freedom; socialists, equality. Different meanings have been attributed to them. As a result of the extended use of the two values since World War II, their meanings have become so expanded and thereby so imprecise that today they can hardly be said to function well as an indicator of political positions in current debates. Everyone accepts both "freedom" and "equality," though with different emphases and meanings. As a consequence, perhaps, the common labels "liberal," "conservative," and "socialist" no longer contain any precise definitions of ideological positions either.

But in the same way we assume that the ideological battles must have reflected real antagonism in the past, so must we take for granted that the political values in today's debates also have significance. In *The Nature of Human Values* Milton Rokeach (1973) found that among a large variety of values, "freedom" and "equality" were the two most indicative of different political positions, in spite of the fact that the individuals meant different things or stressed different aspects of these values. Rokeach differentiated four ideologically separate groups according to the way they evaluated "freedom" and "equality," respectively, as either positive or negative. He found these groupings more indicative of today's opinions than the traditional labels:

(1) freedom high, equality high;
(2) freedom high, equality low;
(3) freedom low, equality high;
(4) freedom low, equality low.

Rokeach's results confirm an old observation: The denotation one puts on the words "freedom"—national independence, private economic freedom, and so on—and "equality"—equal pay, equal chances for education, and so on—indicates different opinions about the relation between the two values. For many years socialists thought that "freedom" and "equality" should be achieved together; one is fulfilled only if the other is also realized. Liberals and conservatives, even if they have furthered both concepts in practical politics, have viewed governing in this respect as a balancing act, because they believe in a basic opposition between them: "equality" presupposes a governmental reduction of individual freedom. Therefore, they are of the opinion that a choice must be made between them, and they seem to have chosen "freedom."

One of the arenas for political debate is in the mass media. In Sweden, by tradition the daily newspapers have taken political stands, in contrast to weeklies, radio, and TV. This means that the newspapers have published the various views of the political parties and recommended that their readers vote in certain ways. This situation has given the newspapers a unique position as being both a reflection of and a participant in political life. Looking at the period 1945-1975 as a whole, we find that this entire group—and therefore, perhaps, also other mass media with political interests—has changed political positions. Small wonder: society has changed. The whole range of opinions has altered. This is obvious if we look at archived newspapers from 1945 and compare them with today's. What was considered radical left-wing in 1945 in Sweden is no longer particularly remarkable, and what was then conservatism is today scarcely to be found even in the most right-wing "letters to the editor." If we wish to study that overall change, we must not only determine whether the newspapers print positive or negative statements about the political parties—the parties have also changed. Instead, we can measure the newspapers' use of the traditional values, freedom and equality.

Behind the idea in quantitative content analysis of measuring the content of a text lies the idea that "what the mouth speaks is in the heart": a large amount of some content shows that the author of the text—in mass communication, the sender—wants to stress that content and that it is an important part of his message. Whether it has in addition a positive value is an open question in many cases. (In the above-mentioned project, this will be one of the questions for study.) In this chapter, it will be presumed to be the case in the editorials studied, mainly because these values have been formulated positively in the coding instructions: freedom instead of self-indulgence or anarchy, equality instead of unidirection or conformity. All such negative concepts can be registered separately.

CONDITIONS FOR OPINION-MAKING
IN POLITICAL SITUATIONS

For many reasons, newspapers have been chosen as the source of material for the study of the political cultural climate, and the editorials have been given preference over other types of subjective texts. I will not discuss here newspapers, economic conditions, nor the importance of any historic persons.

Among the conditions for newspapers, in their role as opinion makers, is that normally no one polemicizes against values which are generally accepted—for instance, democracy or human value. If a detailed text study reveals derogatory expressions or large quantitative differences between interests for such values, this is probably a sign that the political situation is polarized. In Sweden, both "freedom" and "equality" can be said to belong to a group of such generally accepted values.

Concerning the relation between freedom and equality described above, one would think it a rather easy task to determine what stand a newspaper takes. It seems probable that no serious political debater would change such a basic opinion overnight; but it has proven difficult to find expression for them, as will be shown below. Therefore, one basic presumption regarding the content analysis has been made: if a newspaper considers "freedom" and "equality" to be mutually connected, it need not print that in so many words. It suffices to write equally as much about each of them. Based on the argument above about traditional ideological differences, we can expect this to be the case for socialist newspapers. If, on the other hand, a newspaper believes "freedom" and "equality" to be basically unassociated, it will have to chose one of the values as the higher. If this has been the case for liberal and conservative newspapers, we can, accordingly, expect them to have chosen freedom as the higher value. Furthermore, if a change in the whole spectrum of opinion has taken place, this should be evidenced by a similar pattern shift in newspapers adhering to different political parties.

In Sweden, the Social Democratic Party governed since the early thirties to the middle of the seventies. Its opposition consisted of three bourgeois parties—one conservative, one liberal, and one farmers' (from the middle of the fifties, a center) party—and one small communist party. The left-wing parties combined received slightly more than half of the votes, while the three big opposition parties received slightly less than half. Many felt that if the three opposition parties to the right of the Social Democrats could have united their resources, they would have been able to take control. But this did not happen until 1976. For three decades after World War II, the three opposition parties were more concerned about their special political profiles than about what could unite them, and they also tried to attract each others' voters. This political situation is constant for the whole period under study. It has been said that Sweden in this respect has maintained remarkable stability. The political situation has also had importance for the press. If we examine the political role of the Social Democratic newspapers, it seems to have been a fairly simple one—namely, to put forward the policy of the government being in the interest of the people. But for the newspapers connected with the opposition parties, the political situation has been more complicated.

The newspapers were expected to attack not only the Social Democratic Party press but also each other. When one of them (*Sydsvenska Dagbladet*; more on this below) tried to campaign for a unified bourgeois opposition during the sixties, other opposition newspapers adopted an

attitude toward it that could be personified as an astonished but con-
temptuous smile. However, their opposition must have placed them under
considerable stress. It is highly probable that all the opposition papers had
to pay greater attention to Social Democratic writings, opinions, and
values and to seriously consider them to a far greater extent than if the
Social Democrats had not always been in power. This was not because (or
not only because) the Social Democratic Party, through holding power or
through personal resources, was "agenda-setting." This is also a result of
the fact that since the Social Democratic Party has constantly made
decisions about social reforms and other changes in almost every part of
Swedish society, the bourgeois press of 1975 has had to comment upon
quite another society than that of Sweden in 1945. Ever since the origin of
the political press, part of its raison d'être has been to follow the news;
and in reality all presses would write themselves out of existence politically if they did not accept changes of society that are enacted by the
government. We can therefore expect that this general political condition
for making opinion has created a bourgeois press with inconsistent and
confused contents from an ideological point of view. The Social Democratic press has not had these difficulties, and we can expect it to carry on
ideologically consistent and clear message.

THE STUDY

The operationalization of the above discussion has resulted in a registration of the occurrences of the values "freedom" and "equality" in newspapers' editorials, both literally and thematically, and of the relations
between them according to the texts.

The content analysis within the project contains considerably more.
Nine groups of ideological content have been coded: freedom, democracy,
equality, socialism, security, economically defined groups of citizens,
economic growth, environment, and oppression. For the group "freedom"
seven subconcepts were registered: freedom, national independence, freedom of religion and of opinion, freedom of speech and of the press, free
economy, personal freedom of choice, and liberal ideology. The group
"equality" has as many: equality, fairness, equity, compensation, solidarity, distribution, and social equality. The registration of literal and thematic occurrence was intended to show what words serve a special function as slogans, but this will not be described here; the figures for each
value each year are the sum of literal and thematic occurrences of all
subconcepts within each group. Registrations of positive and negative
contexts are not yet analyzed and are thus not included here.

A content analysis was made of editorials in five of the widest circu-
lated morning papers in Sweden: *Arbetet (The Labour)*–Social Demo-

cratic and second biggest in Malmö, *Dagens Nyheter (Today's News)*—liberal from Stockholm and the largest morning paper in Stockholm and the country, *Göteborgs-Posten*—liberal and the largest in Göthenburg, *Sydsvenska Dagbladet (South Swedish Daily)*—conservative and later liberal, the biggest in Malmö, and *Svenska Dagbladet (Swedish Daily)*—conservative and the second biggest in Stockholm. Editorials taken from all five were coded on the same days in a sample taken every eighth day for seven months for every year 1945-1975, which yielded 11,717 texts with a total of 36,000 registrations for the 60 subconcepts in the nine groups of ideological content. The second part of the project uses material from a sample taken from all the newspapers in the country during the same period.

For every subconcept, the occurrence was registered only once per editorial. The figures in the result were later controlled for the amount of editorials per day, so that changes would not reflect the fact that through the years, the number of editorial texts has increased although the amount of space allowed has been kept about the same. The intention is to show the amount of ideological content a newspaper gives its readers through editorials in a way that can be compared from year to year.

The reliability of the five coders was measured systematically and indicates 75-85 percent identical coding for all 60 subconcepts. The groups "freedom" and "equality" lie in the upper part of this range.

RESULTS

The emphasis on the values "freedom" and "equality" in each newspaper is shown in Figure 12.1. In all five papers there is a tendency to decrease the emphasis on "freedom" and to increase it for "equality." This tendency is strongest in *Arbetet* and *Dagens Nyheter*. In 1945 there was a gap between these values in all the papers. This is highly understandable, since World War II was still going on, and an overwhelming part of the political interest was then concentrated on the process of winning back national freedom from German oppression in Europe. The gap disappeared in *Arbetet* the following year, and in the bourgeois papers interest for "equality" increased in the early fifties. After a period of difference between the values in *Arbetet* during the fifties, they reunite from 1959; and in the opposition papers, there is an obvious rapproachement between them during the second half of the sixties.

All the newspapers moved to the left in 1975 compared with their positions in 1945. The difference in emphasis on the two values—between 30 and 50 percent of those editorials which mentioned them—has diminished to almost nothing. The newspapers changed their content so that they all currently write approximately as much about these values—occur-

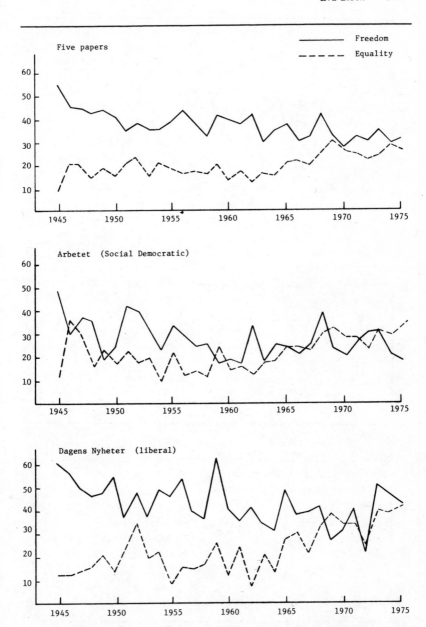

Figure 12.1 Development of the Values of Freedom and Equality in Five Leading
Swedish Newspapers

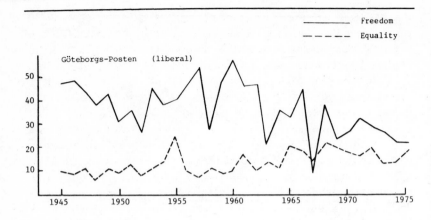

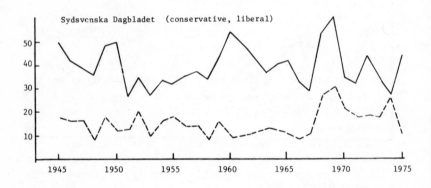

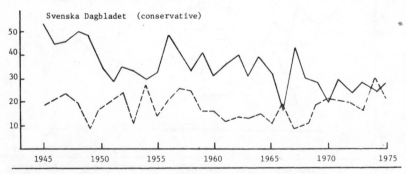

Figure 12.1   Continued

ring in 20-30 percent of all editorials, in *Dagens Nyheter* in about 40 percent—and they have had about the same level of interest, without regard to which political party they were connected to. The political position does, however, have importance for the ideological content insofar as the bourgeois papers changed later than did the Social Democratic paper. One more difference to be noted is that the swings between different years were wider in the opposition papers than in the one that supported the government.

Since the values "freedom" and "equality" have tended to be equally emphasized, it is also probable that they are thought of as being associated together—that is, that the relation between them is positive for the writers, in addition to the fact that as a rule both values have been put in positive contexts in the editorials. Even if the exact figures are not yet computed, it is the decided opinion of the coders that the value "freedom" has been used negatively very seldom (one case, for example, was the dubious freedom to import stilettos). The evaluation of "equality" was not as obviously positive for the conservative newspapers in an early part of the investigation period. But it is obvious that all newspaper editors have realized that it is an "in" thing to value "equality" highly. Even if some editor in a conservative paper should want to attack some aspect of "equality," he would have to begin by praising it—even at the expense of "freedom." Also, in this respect we can see that all papers swung to the left during the postwar period, and that especially the second half of the sixties was a period of change.

As has been mentioned, it should be easy to read in the texts what stand a newspaper takes on the question of the relation between freedom and equality. The coders sought explicit expressions of this nature, but the result is hardly uplifting. Of the 11,717 coded editorials, only 27 can be said to have in any way dealt with the relation. Of these, *Arbetet* had 10 texts, the bourgeois papers about 5 texts each except *Göteborgs-Posten*, which had only one. In most cases, the papers did not take a definite stand on the question of whether freedom and equality were basically related.

	Arb	DN	GP	SDS	SvD
Freedom and equality are connected:					
—mentioned together	6			2	
—explicit statement	4			1	
—citation without denial		3		1	2
Discussion without taking a stand:		2			
Freedom and equality opposing:					
—mentioned				1	
—explicit statement			1		4
Total	10	5	1	5	6

Of these newspapers, *Arbetet* has taken the stand that the relation is a positive one. The others show mixed feelings. *Göteborgs-Posten* has yielded very little material concerning the question, and *Sydsvenska Dagbladet* is not consistent: most of the registration in *SDS* were printed during the first half of the period except the explicit statement of a positive relation, which was published in 1969. Therefore, perhaps *SDS* can be said to have changed opinion in this respect. Compared with them, *Dagens Nyheter* and *Svenska Dagbladet* have so far shown a little more interest and somewhat more consistent behavior, so that their writings in this matter cannot be said to show any change to the left.

But the ideological message in the bourgeois press has been complicated, as was stated above. If we compare the quantitative findings concerning the emphasis on each value with the qualitative investigation of their statements about the relation between them, we find that only the Social Democratic newspaper has been ideologically consistent during the years after World War II. Of the bourgeois papers, *Göteborgs-Posten* has avoided explicitness, *Sydsvenska Dagbladet* has written about both positive and negative relations in a way that may indicate a change of opinion, and *Dagens Nyheter* and *Svenska Dagbladet* have expressed opinions opposite to the tendencies indicated in the value registrations. None of the bourgeois newspapers show a consistent and clear opinion according to this indicator of political position. It is obvious that the position of the daily press connected to the political opposition has been complicated in the three decades since World War II.

All the same, the results of the content analysis undertaken are clear enough to warrant continued study of the values of freedom and equality, and the relationship between the two, as important components of the political climate and its development over time. The data indicate that in the five leading Swedish newspapers under study, freedom was the dominant value during the forties and fifties. But toward the end of the sixties, the gap between the two values closed. It does not take much imagination to attribute this to other events and processes in Sweden during the late sixties and early seventies—events and processes with parallels in many other countries. This will be done in the final report of the project.

REFERENCES

Cultural Indicators: The Swedish Symbol System 1945-1975. (1976). Lund: Department of Sociology, University of Lund. (mimeo)

ROKEACH, M. (1973). The Nature of Human Values. New York: Free Press.

Chapter 13

COMPETITION AND NEWSPAPER CONTENT
Sweden, 1912-1972

Folke Johansson and Dan Wiklund

SURVIVAL IS A PRIMARY GOAL for all kinds of organizations, newspapers included. If economic strength is not maintained no other kinds of success will help in the long run. Not even heavy economic support from the government will solve the problems.

For newspapers survival is assured by keeping and preferably enlarging their circulation. This is directly linked with the struggle for obtaining advertisements, the most important source of income. Most newspapers can for only a short period put the task of molding public opinion before that of maximizing their circulation (see Jonsson, 1977).

In this chapter changes in different Swedish newspaper material will be examined, using as a starting point the idea that adjusting the content with the purpose of keeping or enlarging the number of readers is one means of competition. The basic distinction made here is between controversial and noncontroversial material. Possible strategies concerning such different types of material will be discussed.

A few words are in order about the situation for Swedish newspapers during the twentieth century. Up to 1919 the number of recently started Swedish newspapers was greater than the number of discontinued newspapers. Since that time development has moved in the opposite direction. Apart from the fact that the newspaper market, as well as other markets, tends to reach a saturation point, it is fairly safe to assume that higher manpower costs have been important in this development. Newspapers are high users of manpower, for both production and distribution.

At the same time, newspapers have had to meet a more direct competition. New kinds of daily newspapers emerged, the so-called tabloids, normally published as evening papers. Although these tabloids are read in addition to the larger dailies, they still represent a threat to newspaper circulation.

Radio, and later television, also presented a serious threat to all kinds of newspapers. They were no longer the fastest media when it came to supplying news. During recent years, as an effect of the new local radio stations and television broadcasts, not even local news is reserved for the newspapers.

This long-lasting competitive situation has led to the closure of a large number of newspapers,[1] although this process of elimination has terminated during the last few years. Now those newspapers nearest to the brink of ruin are saved by a large governmental support system. That system is primarily aimed at newspapers facing a bigger local competitor. These so-called "second papers" have been most severely hit by the competition. Governmental support has meant a break in the development toward monopoly on more and more local markets. It also means that even if it is still more or less impossible to establish new newspapers, the competition is somewhat less today (see Tollin, 1965; Gustafsson and Hadenius, 1976; Høyer et al., 1975).

CONCEPTUAL FRAMEWORK

Controversial material is material that can attract or be of special interest to certain groups of readers, but at the same time may push back other potential readers. Political material and other kinds of opinion material on issues where there are already well-established and conflicting interests are examples of controversial material.

Material which does not risk losing readers will be denoted as *noncontroversial*. Examples of this kind of material are news, entertainment, sports, and material with a local touch as its most relevant characteristic.

For these two kinds of material it is possible to distinguish between two basic strategies for the newspaper editor or publisher concerning changes in the newspaper content for competitive reasons. An editor will want to include in his paper attractive material included in competing papers. With controversial material, of course, he is restrained by the opinions expressed in the material.

The difference between the two strategies is, however, the handling of exclusive material. Concerning noncontroversial material editors' interests are to find new kinds of material that can differentiate them from their competitors. No risks are run of losing readers by introducing this new material.

Regarding the controversial material, however, the strategy will have to be different. Now the editor's primary interest, from a competitive point of view, will be to choose a position as close to his competitors as possible.

As mentioned above, basic opinions cannot be excluded, not even if they make the material less attractive to some readers. However, controversial material can be decreased in relative and possibly also in absolute terms. The editor can also try to present it in the same way as do his competitors. (About the relationship among competition, concentration, and media content, see Willoughby, 1955; Nixon, 1961; Nussberger, 1971.)

Political material will be used here to illustrate this development. It is quite evident that political material has "news value." When it is used here as controversial material this is because about 75 percent of this material either emanates directly from or concerns directly the party with which the newspaper is affiliated. To a substantial degree, this material was written to satisfy the interests of the readers who have the same political opinion as the one the newspaper supports. If there is a reduction in this material it is therefore reasonable to view it as a reduction of material which not all potential readers would prefer if they could choose.

One distinction that has been made of the Swedish press is between *wide-coverage* and *narrow-coverage* press. Wide coverage means that the readers hold different political opinions from those of the newspaper. Narrow coverage refers to that greater part of the readership having the same political views as the newspaper. There are some exceptions, but mainly the bourgeois press is of the wide coverage type, while socialist press has narrow coverage (Westerståhl and Jansson, 1958). This distinction gives rise to another, more specific hypothesis. Since the socialist newspapers have relatively few readers with other than socialist attitudes, they will have to change more than bourgeois newspapers in order to gain new groups of readers. The bourgeois newspapers have earlier (often from their inception) chosen a strategy that would win them readers from outside their own political domain by making some of the necessary adaptions.

CONTENT ANALYSIS DESIGN

In this article, results from two different studies will be presented. The two studies are based on the same material, a quantitative content analysis of a sample of Swedish newspapers from the years 1912, 1924, 1936, 1948, 1960, and 1972. Both these studies are secondary analyses. The material can answer the principal questions, but there is no basis for the more detailed studies that would have been desirable on some points.

The sampling technique in this study, *"Världsbildsundersökningen"* (Man's view of the world mirrored in the press), makes the material representative for the Swedish daily newspapers (morning newspapers and afternoon newspapers of a subscription type) with the following exceptions:

(a) newspapers published less than three days a week, and
(b) newspapers with a circulation less than 1/125 of the total newspaper circulation in the country.

The newspapers have been weighted for circulation. For the socialist press, which would otherwise have been so weakly represented that any analysis would have been impossible, a special, supplementary sample has been drawn.

It is not possible at this point to say anything in detail about the precision of the measurements. A special report on details in the sample design with the information needed for more strict statistical estimates will be presented later by Claes-Olof Olsson, who has had the responsibility for the design and the data collection within the *"Världsbildsundersökning."* Westerståhl has been in charge of the entire project (Westerståhl, 1968).

For the analysis presented here the precision has been judged satisfactory. Of course, it is necessary to be careful with trend interpretations when 12 years separate between each sampling point. A discrepancy from an observed trend will be discussed only when it can be expected on the basis of factors that can be linked to the model of the analysis undertaken. Relevant parts of the primary data collection are illustrated in Figure 13.1. The extent of the material collected, measured in number of articles and space on newspaper pages, can be seen in Table 13.1.

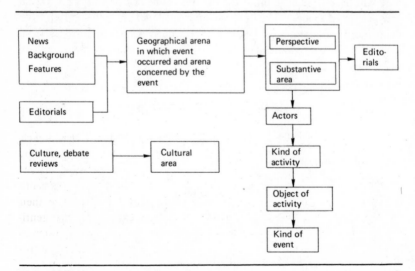

Figure 13.1

TABLE 13.1 Total Newspaper Material, Special Sample
of Socialist Press Excluded

	1912	1924	1936	1948	1960	1972
Number of articles	2873	3633	3858	5145	6283	7040
Space in newspapers (square metres)	41	56	67	63	90	125

The two studies in this article are based on the idea discussed above. In the first study all the material in the newspapers concerning Sweden will be used. The purpose is to find possible changes as discussed above. Noncontroversial material is expected to increase in relative terms and to become more differentiated. Controversial material is expected to decrease and to become more homogeneous.

The first part of this study of a possible differentiation cannot be made on the material now described, however. For this a study of three regionally based newspapers in a part of Sweden called "Värmland" will be used.[2] This study covers the same period of time as the *"Världsbildsundersökning."*

The second study presented here concerns the treatment in the press of different kinds of voluntary organizations. The starting point is principally the same. Organizations considered somewhat controversial and for some reason ideological or traditional, initially favored by one part of the press, will gradually be treated more or less in the same way by all parts of the press. Organizations considered noncontroversial will be treated in the same way.

STUDY 1: DIFFERENTIATION AND HOMOGENIZATION IN THE TOTAL PRESS CONTENT

The ever-increasing number of specialized magazines is a clear indication that there are potential newspaper consumers who can be attracted by new kinds of material. Naturally, dailies will not give up those readers without a fight. The newspapers either try to keep them or, if this is not possible, try to encourage readers to include daily newspapers in their consumption. Consequently, the newspapers can be expected to differentiate their content in order to make it possible for as many groups as possible to find something of interest. This differentiation of noncontroversial material can be observed in our material.

TABLE 13.2 Material in the "Värmland Press" — Different Types of Articles (percentages)

	1906	1911	1916	1921	1926	1931	1936	1941	1946	1951	1956	1961	1966
News	35	33	30	37	40	44	46	43	36	38	32	32	34
Commentaries	8	6	11	8	8	3	4	3	3	8	5	2	2
Culture/entertainment/sports	15	14	13	15	23	27	28	30	29	28	34	27	25
Other material	1	4	6	4	2	3	5	6	5	8	11	11	10
Advertisements	41	41	40	37	27	24	17	18	26	17	18	29	29
Total	100	100	100	100	100	100	100	100	100	100	100	100	100
Column metres	578	611	593	950	204	229	311	317	341	1594	1961	4177	4918

A change in content from news and opinion material to entertainment, sports, and culture can be seen in Table 13.2. There is an irregular increase of news up to 1936. After that year this kind of material diminishes to the end of the period.

Editorials, commentary articles, and letters to the editor have been grouped under the heading "commentary material." As expected, this type of material tends to fill an ever smaller part of the total space. Culture, entertainment, and sports items increase. It can also be noted that the entertainment material changes character. Novels, with or without continuation, make up a smaller part, while material about radio and television increases.

The remaining material, which includes everything except advertisements, also increases its part of the total space. It should be observed that all pictorial material is included in this category. The pictures represent the main part of the increase for this kind of material.

The remaining analysis is built on material from the *"Världsbildsundersökning."* The material will first be used to illustrate a differentiating tendency. In this case we will also introduce a classification of the press with regard to the place of publication.

A general trend is that regional material—that is, material concerning the primary circulation area—increases its share. In Table 13.3 this seems to happen at the expense of local material (material concerning the place of publication). This is, however, partly an effect of the arena categorization which is based on the place of publication. What has really taken place is a differentiation of the material, so that all kinds of newspapers (but especially provincial newspapers) concentrate on covering their nearest regions. The task of covering foreign countries and foreign politics as well as great national issues is partly handed over to the metropolitan

TABLE 13.3   Arena on which Events Occur—Total
Press Material (percentages)

	1912	1924	1936	1948	1960	1972
Foreign countries	34	32	40	35	29	22
National material	31	31	24	29	26	27
Regional material	8	12	11	15	26	30
Local material	27	25	25	21	20	21
Total material	100	100	100	100	100	100

NOTE: In this table all material is included, not only material where Sweden is the arena concerned, as is the matter in the other parts of the analysis.

press. One could interpret this as concentration, on the part of all news-papers, on the task and region where it has relatively or absolutely better resources to make a competitive product.

Events treated in news, background, and feature material were categor-ized as (1) events which can be presumed to appear negative or unpleasant to readers and (2) such events which appear to win readers' sympathy. Examples of the former, negative, types are wars, crises, strikes, disasters, unemployment, and bad social conditions. Examples of the latter, positive, type are peace treaties, economic progress, social reforms, and different kinds of festivities, such as the launching of a new vessel or an inaugura-tion of some kind.

The events classified as negative became fewer in the provincial press. This is probably partly an effect of the increase in local and regional material. Obtaining enough of this type of material means going beyond the big, dramatic, and very often "negative" events. In the metropolitan press there is no change in proportion of events of the two different types.

Concerning the material of a controversial character, a partly different development was expected. Of course, one way to diminish the possibly negative effects of this type of material would be to use relatively less. This is equivalent to using more material of another and preferably less controversial kind. Another way of handling this problem would be to change the character of the material: It could keep its relative volume but become less controversial. The press would become more homogeneous in this respect either way.

The controversial material studied here is the political material. One simple indication of a development in the direction hypothesized is that the percentage of newspapers without precise and explicit political affilia-tion increases over time: four percent in 1912 and more than three times that at the end of the period (Tollin, 1965). This is a clear indication of an intention to lessen the controversiality in the political material. In some cases such a change is probably combined with a reduction in space for this kind of material. Such a reduction, however, is not necessary in order to reach the first goal.

Actors

Behind most news events there is some kind of activity. For news, background, and feature material the actor (if any) in that activity has been registered. A few changes have taken place during the period, con-cerning which actors or group of actors that have appeared. In all kinds of newspapers, less space is given to political institutions (among which are parliament, government, and local political assemblies). In the metropoli-

TABLE 13.4 Material with Different Actors—Political
Press Groups

Bourgeois press	*1912*	*1924*	*1936*	*1948*	*1960*	*1972*
Countries/int. org.	11	8	14	16	16	10
Political institutions	22	20	16	14	9	12
Authorities	25	26	25	23	24	24
Political parties	4	9	5	5	4	7
Trade unions	3	4	2	2	2	3
Business/B. organizations	7	6	6	8	9	11
Popular movements	8	12	11	10	15	12
Others	8	5	10	7	7	8
Individuals	12	9	12	14	14	13
Total	100	100	100	100	100	100
Socialist press						
Countries/int. org.	7	6	15	15	15	5
Political institutions	20	21	14	13	11	13
Authorities	21	25	25	21	22	27
Political parties	12	12	8	9	5	6
Trade unions	13	14	8	7	5	5
Business/B. organizations	8	4	4	7	9	10
Popular movements	5	7	9	11	12	14
Others	2	3	6	6	4	6
Individuals	11	10	12	12	16	14
Total	100	100	100	100	100	100

tan press authorities also gradually become less frequent as actors, but that group maintains its position in the provincial press. This means that public bodies and authorities get less space in the press.

The fact that authorities retain their place in the provincial press can be one effect of an increased stress on local material. The authorities are available as objects for news coverage on this level, and the material they can provide normally has a direct local connection.

The increase noted in the provincial press for material from popular movements can also be attributed to a concentration on local material. These actors are to a great extent available on a local or regional level (see also Study 2 in this chapter).

The changes now mentioned, however, are also of a differentiating kind. New material is introduced, or the existing material is changed so that new groups will find it interesting. Such changes, however, do not necessarily change the paper's controversiality, even if changes in the relative frequency of actors can change the controversiality as well.

In the socialist press decreasing amounts of space are given to political parties and labor organizations alike. That reduction is marked, even if over the whole period the bourgeois press has even less space for these actors. The change is significant enough to almost completely eliminate the difference between the two press groups in this respect.

Perspectives

The last mentioned change, of course, means a homogenization of the press from a political point of view. But if one looks instead at the kinds of perspectives that are put on different kinds of material, another change becomes evident.

It is clearly possible for the newspapers to treat one and the same substantive area in different ways. The environmental question is a good example. For example, a decision may be described in parliament concerning the use of poisonous liquids, providing a political perspective. Discussing increased costs for the business corporations as a result of new laws concerning the improvement of environmental conditions indicate an economic perspective. A social perspective would be to discuss an individual's problems as a result of bad working conditions.

In Table 13.5 the perspectives are distributed on five different groups. The press is divided according to political affiliation, and in metropolitan and provincial press. Up to the year 1960 there is a reduction in the percentage of political perspectives in the news. This reduction is especially great in the provincial press. In addition, legal perspectives are relatively heavily reduced. The perspectives used instead of these are economic-technical and other of a more mixed character.

The political perspectives reduced are those concerning discussions within political bodies about alternative solutions and those with information about decisions made. Those two kinds of perspectives are the most common in this group. Furthermore, perspectives with theoretical-ideological content are reduced in the socialist press.

The legal perspectives reduced in the material are primarily descriptions and discussions of legal conditions *before* a decision is made. The decision can be a piece of law-making or a judgment from a court.

The economic-technical perspectives becoming more frequent concern partly growth in business and partly discussions about groups or individuals in the production process. The increase in social perspectives also means that more discussion occurs regarding what happens to a certain group in society, or relations between groups.

TABLE 13.5 Different Perspectives (percentages)

	1912	1924	1936	1948	1960	1972
Bourgeois press						
Political	46	45	38	37	26	32
Legal	14	16	15	10	8	6
Economic-techn.	21	17	22	28	32	33
Social	6	4	6	5	7	12
Others	13	18	20	21	26	18
Socialist press						
Political	44	44	41	39	27	31
Legal	15	15	17	10	7	6
Economic-techn.	27	26	24	31	37	30
Social	9	8	5	6	10	12
Others	5	7	13	14	20	21
Metropolitan press						
Political	42	42	37	35	29	32
Legal	13	16	14	13	8	5
Economic-techn.	24	20	21	28	35	35
Social	7	5	7	6	6	17
Others	14	17	22	18	21	11
Provincial press						
Political	58	48	41	42	24	29
Legal	16	17	17	7	7	6
Economic-techn.	14	17	25	29	32	31
Social	3	4	5	4	8	8
Others	9	15	12	19	29	26

NOTE: This table is based on domestic news, background, and feature material and editorials.

The reduction in political perspectives is completely limited to the news material. The editorials naturally have a much higher percentage of political perspectives during the whole period studied. This means that the reduction may be regarded as a way of lowering the level of controversiality in the news. This could be expressed as making them more objective, at least from a political point of view. Since there is no reduction of political perspectives in the editorials, there is no base for interpreting the change as a sign of some general "depoliticization." Political perspectives are approximately 75 percent of the perspectives in the editorials. There are no systematic changes between the years, nor are there changes between different kinds of perspectives.

Linking different kinds of perspectives to the above-mentioned division between "positive" and "negative" events reveals that the reduction in political perspectives stems entirely from the group of negative events. There are, however, very few political perspectives on the positive events, which also reduces the theoretical basis for such a reduction.

Activity

There are no systematic changes in the types of activities registered. The newspapers do not devote more space in the beginning than in the end of the period to, for example, criticism or support.

Object

The greater part of the activities reported aim at some specific object. The types of objects registered are the same as the actors (discussed above). There are certain changes between the objects concerned by the activities. Only one change is totally systematic; this is a reduction in the focus on political institutions as objects for criticism or support.

Both authorities and businesses are more important as objects during the first and the last of the years studied. For political parties the situation is the opposite. A relatively greater part of the activities aiming at an object concerns political parties in the mid-years compared with the first and last year.

TABLE 13.6   Activities by Objects (percentages)

	1912	1924	1936	1948	1960	1972
Countries/int. org.	2	8	8	19	15	7
Political institutaions	24	18	16	18	10	16
Authorities	16	11	8	11	11	15
Political parties	1	8	5	6	2	3
Trade unions	3	3	2	1	1	2
Business/B. organizations	11	6	3	4	5	9
Popular movements	4	2	4	3	3	4
Others	5	9	5	3	5	4
Individuals	34	34	49	36	49	39
Total	100	100	100	100	100	100

Criticism

A certain object can be aimed at in different kinds of activities. Here follows first a specification of how much of these activities are criticism. The starting point is the object concerned. In the next step, the total amount of criticism will be the basis, and the purpose will be to find out to which objects this criticism is directed.

There are very few systematic changes. The reduction in criticism directed toward individuals, however, is one. There is no continuous decrease, but rather two different levels: up to 1924 a high level and after that a lower level. This pattern is the same in different groupings of the press.

For political parties in the bourgeois press and authorities in the provincial press, there is a tendency toward a U-shaped curve for the percentage criticism. There was a high percentage for criticism in the beginning and the end of the period, while it was smaller (for authorities much smaller) during the mid-years.

"Net-criticism" (percentage support subtracted from criticism) results show that political parties are the only area in which systematic changes have occurred. In the bourgeois press and in the metropolitan press the net criticism diminishes over time.

There are also diminishing differences between the bourgeois and social-ist press in the percentage of criticism directed toward businesses and employers. This percentage is greater for the socialist press during all six years of measurement, but it gradually increases in the bourgeois press,

TABLE 13.7   Percentage Criticism of Material
              Concerning Each Object

	1912	1924	1936	1948	1960	1972
Countries/int. org.	5	18	13	20	9	23
Political institutions	13	28	6	19	15	44
Authorities	30	46	15	22	19	37
Political parties	67	64	45	52	45	61
Trade unions	8	64	31	15	24	15
Business/B. organizations	4	33	10	7	13	17
Popular movements	3	31	8	9	10	10
Others	21	35	8	28	6	26
Individuals	16	15	2	7	3	3

with homogenization in this respect as a consequence. Less criticism directed against the parties and more criticism directed against business means that the differences in opinions between the newspaper groups become smaller. The techniques are different, but in this respect the results are the same.

It is now time to change the analysis and look at the objects for the criticism found instead of the treatment of certain objects.

Distribution of Criticism on Different Objects

Seventeen percent of the activities directed against any object were critical. As it is here that attitudes toward different groups in society can be traced, a division will be made of this material on different objects. Certain changes in the distribution of criticism of different groups appears in such a division. There are no groups whose shares rise or decline over the whole period, though the criticism of individuals tends to decrease more or less continually.

Changes of another kind can be found, however. For political parties, political institutions, and authorities these changes are interesting. In Figure 13.2 authorities and political institutions have been grouped with "public bodies." The criticism against them is most widespread in the beginning and in the end of the period and smaller in between, with the lowest percentage in 1936. The criticism of political parties shows a totally opposite pattern with smaller percentages the first and last year and greater in the mid-years.

One may regard these two curves for criticism of authorities and political institutions on one hand and political parties on the other as essential when it comes to understanding the picture of society offered in the daily press. In the beginning and in the end of the period the relatively anonymous administrative bodies are the main objects of criticism, while there is a more party-politicized situation in between.

When the greater part of the activities are directed against political parties, it is not just a question of criticism. Though a great share of the total criticism is directed against political parties in the middle of the period studied, the percentage of criticism in the total material directed against parties does not increase. Other kinds of material are also increasing.

The starting point for this study, the competition as a basis for strategies involving changes in the content, does not help in interpreting these kinds of changes. Without a doubt, however, there has been a change in the public discussion and in the political climate. Political parties are seen as more central than before by different kinds of actors. Their

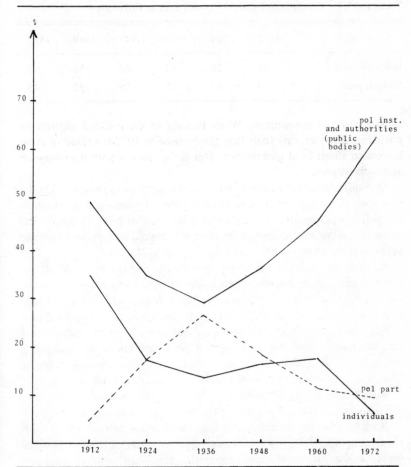

Figure 13.2   Criticism Aimed at Different Objects

position is, however, not more central than the public bodies (parliament, government, local government and authorities) taken together.

One could regard the curve over the political parties as a description of their rise and fall in the public discussion. Their breakthrough in the *political debate* takes place a decade before the first year studied here, and their breakthrough in *public debate* seems to take place during the period 1920-1950 (Johansson, 1977). It should be mentioned, however, that during this period public bodies are three times more common as objects than are political parties.

Since government is one among the public bodies, one possible explanation could be that criticism of the party could be substituted for criticism

TABLE 13.8   Percentage Political Perspectives in Criticism

	1912	1924	1936	1948	1960	1972
Bourgeois press	46	50	61	62	50	63
Socialist press	24	47	37	59	35	45

of the party in government. When looking at the political institutions criticized, however, one finds that the increase in 1972 is a result of more discussion about local government. This is the same in both the bourgeois and socialist press.

One difference that can be noted between party press groups is that the bourgeois press tends to criticize more in political terms—that is, it ends to use political perspectives more than does the socialist press. In this respect there are no systematic changes between the groups, though the difference between them varies over time.

Part of the basis for this study was the observation that most of the political material in the newspapers came from the party supported by the newspaper. One possible step in a process of homogenization could then be a less pronounced link to the own party. Such a change does not appear in this material. In both the bourgeois and socialist press, material from the own party constitutes approximately three-quarters of the total political material. That share is the same during the whole period. There is, however, a slight tendency in the socialist press in the expected direction. It should also be remembered that the bourgeois press can treat three different parties and still remain within its own group as defined here.

Societal material in culture, debate, and review articles tends to be reduced up to 1960. After that year there is a rise in the metropolitan press. In the provincial press, where the downward trend is most pronounced, it continues also through 1972.

STUDY 2: POPULAR MOVEMENTS IN THE PRESS

CHANGES IN COVERAGE

The popular movements in Sweden were established around the turn of the century, often after influences from abroad. They shared some common purpose. Economic security was the principal goal for the labor movement; the consumer cooperatives also had economic goals. The free churches and the temperance movement were working for a new way of life in two different parts of society. Of course, one common characteristic

TABLE 13.9   Material on Popular Movements

	1912	1924	1936	1948	1960	1972
Total number of articles	302	439	559	735	1087	1177
Percentage of domestic news	13	17	15	15	20	19

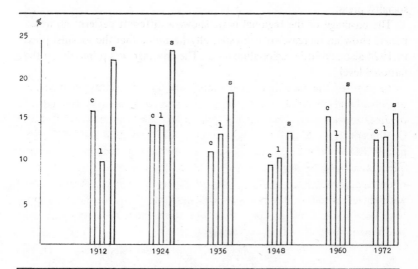

Figure 13.3   News about Popular Movements in the Presses
(as percentage of total domestic news)

c = conservative; l = liberal; s = social democratic.
News in the national arena.

of all popular movements is that they are based on a large number of
members and have a democratic organization.

The material to be used in the study of the treatment of these popular
movements is also from the *"Världsbildsundersökning."* As can be seen in
Table 13.9, there is a substantial increase in the relative space given to the
popular movements. The increase comes from the provincial newspapers.
In the metropolitan press the share remains unchanged. The material that
has increased is regionally connected. Material concerning the national
level constitutes the same share over the years.

Many of the older voluntary organizations had some connection with
the labor movement. It therefore seems reasonable that social democratic
newspapers should have relatively more material on organizations than the
conservative or liberal press. It can be seen from Figure 13.3 that the social
democratic press has the highest coverage of organizational news (national

events) expressed as a percentage of the total domestic news material. The percentage is highest for all the years studied, but the difference from the other press groups becomes smaller over time. It is no coincidence that the highest share for the socialist press can be seen in 1924. That was a year with many labor conflicts, and it is primarily trade unions that are treated. After that, all newspapers reduced their coverage of national material on popular movements up to 1960. This reduction is most noticeable in the socialist press.

The coverage of the regional news shows a different pattern: all newspapers show an increase. It can especially be noted that the socialist press in 1924 also had little regional material. The coverage was primarily on the national level.

In spite of the fact that trade unions are an important group in the organizational material, no party profilation concerning percentage of organizational material can be seen during the period after World War II. On the contrary, all differences are leveled out up to 1960 and 1972. This means that when it comes to the kind of coverage studied here, it is more important that the newspaper be published than what political color it represents. An analysis of the treatment of some organizations in presses with different political tendencies will illustrate this. The organizations have been chosen on the basis that they have either an ideological or a traditional linkage to a certain party group.

LO (National Labour Organization)

It has already been said that the socialist press (here equivalent to the Social Democratic press) has given relatively greater amount of space to the organizations than the other (bourgeois) newspapers. One very reasonable way of interpreting this would be to say that a great volume of material concerning LO is the basis for this difference. The ideological link is strong between LO and the Social Democratic party.

The clearest result revealed in Figure 13.4, however, is that the Social Democratic presses diminish their coverage (percentage material) of LO. This reduction can be one effect of competition on the newspaper market. The newspapers have to cover groups that have not previously been in their "domain." They have to increase their base of potential readers. One way of doing this is to adjust the material to these new readers. Liberal and conservative newspapers tend, even if slightly, to increase their coverage of LO. The explanation is probably the same. Bourgeois newspapers try to win socialist readers. The total effect is that with respect to this material there is homogenization of the press.

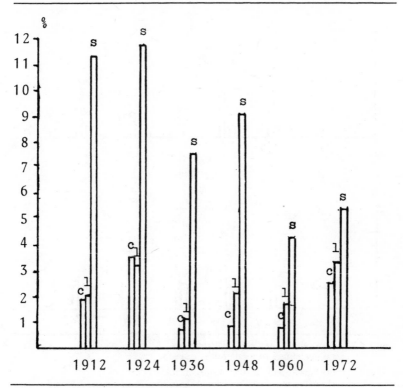

Figure 13.4 News about LO in the Presses
(as percentage of total domestic news)

c = conservative; l = liberal; s = social democratic.
Events of national character.

There are no corresponding changes in the regional material. The Social Democratic press has for every year slightly more material than the bourgeois press.

Consumer and Housing Cooperatives

The first consumer and housing cooperatives were formed in the late nineteenth century with a clear orientation toward the Social Democratic party. Only a few years later, however, they claimed political independence. All the same, the ideological link to the Social Democratic party can be seen in the differences between the newspapers during the first years, for both national and regional coverage. The Social Democratic press, however, diminishes its coverage, especially from 1936. From 1948 the bourgeois newspapers tend to increase their material.

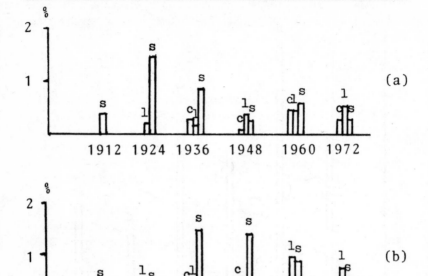

**Figure 13.5   News about Cooperative Movements
(as percentage of total domestic news)**

(a) based on events of national character.
(b) based on events of regional character.
c = conservative; l = liberal; s = social democratic.

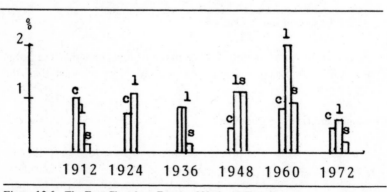

Figure 13.6   The Free Churches–Events of National Character

This figure shows another example of the diminishing differences between the different political press groups in coverage of organizations. The party profilation is reduced.

Free Churches

There is no special ideological linkage between the free churches and any political party. There is, however, a rather strong traditional link between the free churches (or, many of them) and the liberal party. It can be seen from Figure 13.6 that from 1924 on it is in the liberal press that the free churches get the most extensive coverage. The Social Democratic newspapers do not give them any noticeable coverage until 1948, at least not concerning national material.[3]

The Social Democratic newspapers, however, are more active in their regional coverage. In this material there is a continuous increase from 1936 and onward (see Figure 13.7). Although the liberal newspapers show a peak

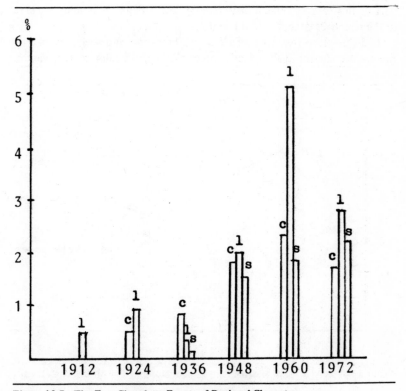

Figure 13.7 The Free Churches–Events of Regional Character

in their material in 1960, there is a clear tendency toward diminishing differences between the coverage that the different press groups give to the free churches.

Press Coverage of Labor Movements

All the organizations taken together that can be linked ideologically to the labor movement will be studied in bourgeois and social democratic presses to see if there are any changes in their way of covering them. The organizations linked to the labor movement are in this study LO (The worker's national trade union organization), ABF (The worker's study organization), Folkets-hus rörelsen (The movement for building houses for different kinds of worker-connected activities), Hyresgäströrelsen (The tenant's movement) and KF (The consumer cooperative movement). This study includes only regional material.

It has already been shown how the social Democratic Press has decreased the amount of space given to the LO. The LO material is a big part of this total organizational material, but it is not as dominating here in the regional material as in the national material.

In Figure 13.8 it can be seen that the bourgeois and social democratic presses become more alike with respect to the space allotted to organiza-

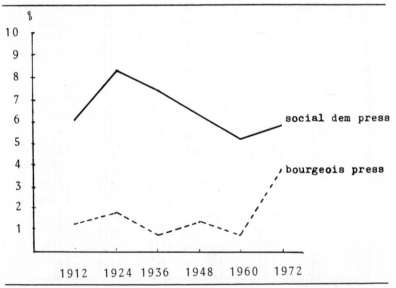

Figure 13.8   Percentage of Material on the Labor Movement of All Regional News

tions within the labor movement. The bourgeois press is the conservative and liberal presses combined.

One notices a decrease in the political profilation. Up to 1960 it is mainly diminishing material in the social democratic press and after that an increase in the bourgeois press that contributes to the equalization between the two groups. One reasonable explanation for this development is the desire of newspapers to reach new groups of potential readers. When the competition is hard, the newspapers are willing to give up some of their ideologically loaded material in order to gain new readers. It becomes more essential to get material that is of interest also to other groups than those with the same ideological commitment.

COMPETITION AND PRESS CONTENT

What results have been reached concerning the question of competition and its possible effects on newspaper content? First, it is evident that the differentiation expected in the noncontroversial material has been found. This holds true for "type of material" (for example, more entertainment material) as well as for material with differential regional/local connection. Both changes can be interpreted as effects of a competitive situation.

The controversial material, here represented by the political material, has also changed as expected. There are signs indicating a depoliticization of the press and of the news material. With respect to the press in its totality, it can be seen by the increase in the number of newspapers without a clear political label. In the news material it can be seen by the diminishing share of political perspectives. Politically conflict-oriented views of the problems become fewer, and other aspects are discussed instead. There is, however, no general depoliticization in the newspapers keeping their political label. The political perspectives remain in the editorials. Only in news items is material presented in a new way.

The changes now mentioned imply a depoliticization which is at the same time a kind of differentiation, also of the controversial political material. The change means that new kinds of material are put in, material with other perspectives than the political perspectives dominating in the early phases of the period under study.

There are, however, also changes showing a homogenization of the political material. There is a decrease in the linkage of the socialist press group to related organizations, brought about primarily by a diminishing number of parties and party-linked organizations in the socialist press. There is also a reduction of the criticism of political parties in the bourgeois press. The difference between bourgeois and socialist press becomes smaller with respect to criticism against employers and authorities, primarily criticism from individuals or groups of individuals. This can be seen as an effect of the bourgeois press giving space to newer kinds of interest groups or activist groups. At the same time as criticism against political parties is diminishing in bourgeois press, it can be observed that more of the criticism is put forward in political terms in this press group than in the socialist press.

The trend toward increasing homogenization observed in part one in this study is supported by the results in part two. In that part of our study it was shown that the bourgeois and Social Democratic presses have become more alike in their way of treating the popular movements. After having been greater in the Social Democratic press, the coverage given to these organizations became almost exactly the same in all presses (expressed as a percentage of the total space).

An analysis of the treatment of different organizations with different forms of ideological and/or traditional linkage to the different press groups gave still more support to the hypothesis, showing an increasing similarity between the press groups. There was an increasing tendency to give the same space to different organizations, regardless of more or less close linkage. This is most obvious in the coverage of the trade unions, but it is also evident with respect to consumer cooperatives and free churches.

Analysis of all organizations more or less closely linked to the labor movement, and consequently to the socialist press, pointed in the same direction. It seems quite reasonable to interpret these results within the conceptual framework used here—that is, as signs of a conscious intent by the newspapers to adjust the content to make it attractive to as large groups of potential readers as possible.

CONCLUSION

Different strategies for newspapers to meet competition were discussed, and possible effects on newspaper content as results of these strategies were hypothesized. A number of results have been presented which support these hypotheses. This is true for both noncontroversial material, where the signs of differentiation are clear, and for the controversial material studied. In the latter material the expected homogenization and a form of differentiation that means a lower percentage of controversial material have been shown. It is not possible to say with any certainty whether the latter kind of development is valid also for other kinds of controversial material than the political material studied here.

Under the assumption that the interpretation model used here is correct, one interesting conclusion can be drawn. Newspapers try to enlarge the number of potential readers among new groups of readers, rather than making more attempts to get new readers in the group to which they are already politically or otherwise attached. That the signs of a higher percentage of political perspectives shown for 1972 can be seen as effects of governmental support to the press cannot be determined from this material.

The results presented here concerning the strategy used by newspapers in seeking support from enlarged bases of potential readers do not quite agree with the results Svennik Høyer (1968, 1977) has presented concerning the Norwegian press. By means of an analysis of changes in newspaper structure related to party strength in the region, Høyer shows that the newspapers have primarily been looking for support in regions where they already have strong support. He has, however, also presented results which point in the same direction concerning the way of handling noncontroversial material (*"alment lesestoff"*).

Although the basic idea in Høyer's study is the same as the one used here, that the newspapers try to maximize their circulation in order to survive, the techniques used to study it are different. If one looks at the newspaper strategies in two steps, a long and a short perspective, the two results can be made to agree. An effective newspaper is one that is started in a district where the opinion it intends to represent is as strong as possible. (Of course, one must take into account the possibility that this base is already exploited.) However, once a paper is started in a certain place and it seeks to strengthen its position, this choice is no longer available. It is normally not possible to change the place of publication. The paper can try to enlarge its base by making its product acceptable also to groups other than the one that is the primary basis.

●

NOTES

1. The total circulation for the dailies has increased substantially. However, large parts of that increase fall on a limited number of newspapers, a fact that makes it even worse for the rest.

2. This study includes the following newspapers: Nya Wermlands-Tidningen, Karlstads-Tidningen, and Värmlands Folkblad. It was conducted at the Institute for Political Science in Göteborg by Lennart Weibull.

3. For comparison, the percentage of material on church and religion of all domestic news material is given below. It can be seen that the changes in this material correspond to the changes in the free church material discussed here. The state church is given the same coverage over the total period.

	1912	1924	1936	1948	1960	1972
Bourgeois press	2	3	3	3	5	3
Social Dem. press	0	0	1	2	2	4
All presses	2	3	3	3	5	4

REFERENCES

GUSTAFSSON, K-E. and HADENIUS, S. (1976). Swedish Press Policy. Stockholm: The Swedish Institute.

HØYER, S.   1977). Norsk Presse mellom 1865 og 1965 (Norwegian Press between 1865 and 1965). Oslo: Institute for Press Research.

— — — (1968). The Political Economy of the Norwegian Press. Scandinavian Political Studies.

— — — HADENIUS, S, and WEIBULL, L. (1975). The Politics and Economics of the Press: A developmental Perspective. Beverly Hills, CA: Sage.

JOHANSSON, F. (1977). Sverige partipolitiseras. Dagspressen som en spegel av politisk utveckling 1896-1908 (Party politization in Sweden. The Daily press as a mirror of political development 1896-1908). Lund: Gleerup.

JONSSON, S. (1977). Annonser och Tidningskonkurrens. Annonsernas roll i tidningsekonomin och betydelse för koncentrationsprocessen i Stockholm, Göteborg och Malmö (Advertisements and Newspaper competition. The role of the advertisements in newspaper economy and their significance for the concentration process in Stockholm, Gothenburg and Malmö). Dissertation, Department of Economic History, University of Gothenburg.

NIXON, R. B. (1961). "Trends in newspaper ownership and inter media competition." Journalism Quarterly 37.

NUSSBERGER, U. (1971). Die Mechanik der Pressekonzentration. Berlin: Walter de Gruyter & Co.

TOLLIN, S. (1965). Svenska dagstidningar 1900-1965. Antal och politisk gruppering (Swedish Newspapers 1900-1965. Number and Political Affiliation). Stockholm: Svenska Tidningsutgivarföreningen.

WESTERSTÅHL, J. (1968). Comparative Political Communication. Scandinavian Political Studies.

WESTERSTÅHL, J. and JANSSON, C-G. (1958). The Political Press. Studies Illustrating the Political Role of the Daily Press in Sweden, Department of Political Science, University of Gothenburg.

WILLOUGHBY, W. F. (1955). "Are two competing dailies necessarily better than one?" Journalism Quarterly 32.

NAME INDEX

ABOUT THE CONTRIBUTORS

DAG ANCKAR is Professor of Political Science at Abo Academy (Finland). He has published books and articles on party strategies, political communication, political institutions, and systems theory. He is presently engaged in research on agenda-building in policy formation.

GUNNAR ANDRÉN is a member of the Department of Philosophy, University of Stockholm. In the field of mass communication research he has published empirical, normative, and analytical works on the contents of Swedish and U.S. advertising, and on concepts of objectivity and their applications to the mass media. Within philosophy his main interests are moral epistemology and axiology.

EVA BLOCK received her Ph.D. in 1976 from the University of Lund based on a thesis dealing with the image of the United States in Swedish daily newspapers. She has been working with a project concerning values in Swedish domestic political debate during the postwar decades. She is interested in the role and the situation of the mass media in the opinion-making process in a changing society. At present she works at the Swedish Archive for Sound and Picture.

TOM BRYDER is Associate Professor of Social Science at the University of Luleå, Sweden. He received his Ph.D. from the University of Lund, and has taught political science, political psychology, and public administration at the universities of Ålborg, Århus, and Copenhagen, Denmark. Among his publications are *Power and Responsibility* (1975) and *Systems Theory and Political Behaviour* (1976).

GÖSTA CARLSSON is Professor of Macro-Sociology at the Humanities and Social Sciences Research Council and the University of Stockholm. His research activities cover social demography, behavioral epidemiology, and the analysis of behavioral trends.

ALF DAHLBERG is a graduate student and a research assistant in the Department of Sociology, University of Lund. He is interested in the sociology of culture and communication.

BO FIBIGER is senior lecturer in the Department of Scandinavian Language and Literature, University of Århus. He has contributed to the study of political communication and mass communication in several books and articles (in Danish).

OLLE FINDAHL is a researcher in the Audience and Programme Research Department of the Swedish Broadcasting Corporation in Stockholm, and a Ph.D. in psychology at the University of Uppsala. He is working on a long-term project dealing with comprehension of news.

LOWE HEDMAN received his Ph.D. in sociology from the University of Uppsala. He is currently leading a project on local communication in the Department of Sociology in Uppsala, and serves as a consultant to a governmental committee on neighborhood radio in Sweden.

BIRGITTA HÖIJER is a researcher in the Audience and Programme Research Department of the Swedish Broadcasting Corporation in Stockholm, and a Ph.D. in psychology at the University of Uppsala. She is working on a long-term project dealing with comprehension of news.

FOLKE JOHANSSON received his Ph.D. from the Department of Political Science, University of Gothenburg. He is presently working as research associate in the Department of Political Science, University of Gothenburg.

KENT LINDKVIST is a doctoral student at the Institute of Political Science, University of Lund, Sweden. His main interests are political language and ideology.

VIVECA RAMSTEDT-SILÉN is a doctoral student in the Institute of Political Science at the Åbo Akademi, Turku, Finland. She is also working as a junior lecturer at the Swedish School of Economics and Business Administration in Helsinki.

GUNNEL RIKARDSSON received her Ph.D. from the University of Lund in 1978 and is presently working as a consultant to a governmental committee investigating the economic influence of local gratis advertisement papers on the traditional daily press. Her research interests include communication theory and methodological development.

KARL ERIK ROSENGREN is Associate Professor of Sociology at the University of Lund and a Research Fellow of the Swedish Council for Research in the Humanities and the Social Sciences. He has published several books and articles on the sociology of culture and communication.

PREBEN SEPSTRUP is Associate Professor at the Århus School of Economics and Business Administration, Arhus, Denmark. He has a Ph.D. in consumer economics. His main interest is in consumption of information, especially advertising, consumer information, and public information.

KAREN SIUNE is Associate Professor at the Institute of Political Science at the University of Århus. She was a visiting fellow at the Institute for Social Research and the Department of Journalism at the University of Michigan in 1974-1975. She is a member of a European research committee working on a comparative project on the first direct election to the European Parliament.

DAN WIKLUND is a doctoral student in the Department of Political Science, University of Gothenburg. His primary research interests are information and formation of opinions.